HERE COMES EVERYBODY

Catholic Studies in
American Higher Education

**Edited and Introduced by
William C. Graham**

University Press of America,® Inc.
Lanham · Boulder · New York · Toronto · Plymouth, UK

Copyright © 2009 by
University Press of America,® Inc.
4501 Forbes Boulevard
Suite 200
Lanham, Maryland 20706
UPA Acquisitions Department (301) 459-3366

Estover Road
Plymouth PL6 7PY
United Kingdom

Library of Congress Control Number: 2008937873
ISBN-13: 978-0-7618-4431-0 (clothbound : alk. paper)
ISBN-10: 0-7618-4431-7 (clothbound : alk. paper)
ISBN-13: 978-0-7618-4432-7 (paperback : alk. paper)
ISBN-10: 0-7618-4432-5 (paperback : alk. paper)
eISBN-13: 978-0-7618-4433-4
eISBN-10: 0-7618-4433-3

Dedicated to the Benedictine Sisters

of Duluth's St. Scholastica Monastery

both living and dead

whose foresight and generosity

built the Church

in the Diocese of Duluth

and endowed

The Braegelman Program in Catholic Studies

What has been is what will be,
and what has been done is what will be done;
and there is nothing new under the sun.
• Ecclesiastes 1:9

And the One who sat upon the throne said,
'Behold, I make all things new.'
• Revelation 21:5

Acknowledgements

I am grateful to all who have had a hand in developing this book and bringing it to publication: the authors and the lecturers; mycolleagues both in ministry and in the academy who have been generous in their support not just of this project but of the emerging Braegelman Program in Catholic Studies at The College of St. Scholastica, named for three siblings in the College's founding Benedictine Community, Mother Athanasius Braegelman and Sisters Benedicta and Bernice Braegelman; the Sisters of The Monastery of St. Scholastica who endowed the program; the editors of *Listening: Journal of Religion and Culture* for permission to reprint the essays in Parts I and II of this book which were originally published in the Winter, 2007 and Winter, 2008 issues; the anonymous friend of The College of St. Scholastica whose generosity made possible the lecture series which gave shape to Parts II and III of this book; Sister Mary Richard Boo, O.S.B., Brother Mark McVann, F.S.C., and my colleague Dr. Randall A. Poole who were generous with their editorial and proofreading skills; and, the students who were the intrepid pioneers, the first graduates who generously and patiently helped shape the curriculum: Zachary D. Bennett, Amy Kaminski, David V. Berthiaume, Collin Berry, and Brandon Butler.

All of these have "filled the hungry with good things" (Luke 1:53); they have shaped this work, but any deficiencies here are my responsibility alone.

William C. Graham

for Dave,
with thanks!
wm graham
Dec. 2008

INTRODUCTION

All things work together for good for those who love God.
(Romans 8:28)

Perhaps James Joyce presaged the developing Catholic Studies programs in U.S. Catholic higher education with his famous description of the Roman Church, "Here Comes Everybody." These programs, it seems to me, are about more than Catholic institutions exploring and asserting their identity. Surely those involved seek rigorous engagement with the Catholic Intellectual Tradition. Those engaged in Catholic Studies examine religious ideas and ideals, and participate in the ongoing study of Catholic thought and culture. They seek dialogue with Catholics of all mind sets, with Christians from other denominations, believers from other faith traditions and all, including nonbelievers, who seek the truth with sincerity.

The various programs in Catholic Studies developing across the United States, I think, seek to introduce students to the Catholic Intellectual Tradition on which the very idea of a modern university is based. That Tradition sweeps across and includes all fields of study with the conviction that all seeking is search for truth and those who seek truth will find God.[1] Thus, these program seek to invite and facilitate dialogue between faith and modern culture. The interdisciplinary nature of the study highlights for students the complementary interaction of faith and reason. A curriculum, beginning with and grounded in theology and philosophy, must then be both broad and diverse as it seeks to engage students with the transformative realities of the arts and sciences. The curricula are often designed to appeal to the student of any faith tradition who seeks greater appreciation for the heritage on which the colleges and universities are built and which has shaped western culture.

A Catholic Studies major is designed to fit nicely with any number of other fields of study and will work well as a double, or second, major for many students. Therefore, these interdisciplinary programs of Catholic Studies usually invite the participation of faculty in the fields of theology, history, the arts, the social and natural sciences, philosophy, and English. A major in Catholic Studies is not a major in theology, though it often begins in the theology or religious studies department with a series of introductory courses, usually including some variety of Introduction to Catholicism or Introduction to Christian Theology, followed by Introduction to the Bible, or another Scripture course, Sacraments and Liturgy, a Christology course, and concluding with a Catholic Studies Seminar. In addition, with the help of the program director, students will choose other credits from theology, the arts, philosophy, social sciences and natural sciences. Students are encouraged to select courses that demonstrate the depth and breadth of the Catholic Intellectual Tradition.

The Braegelman Program of Catholic Studies at The College of St. Scholastica in Duluth, Minnesota, was inaugurated in September 2005. I asked our first two graduates, now gone on happily to further study, what prompted them to sign on:

GLORIFIED HUMANITIES

As a cradle Catholic, I recognized the academic blessing of the Catholic Studies major. I was attracted to the program and delighted to be accepted in order to learn how the faith elevates disciplines from the secular to glorify the Almighty. With a double major in biology and Catholic Studies, I enjoyed the opportunity to expand my liberal arts education in light of the Catholic intellectual tradition.

While the Catholic Studies major began with a variety of theology classes, the curriculum offered an extensive selection from across the many disciplines. Many of my Catholic Studies classes complemented one another, converging to a single focal point. This point, as St. Paul identifies it, is Christ: "For from him and through him and to him are all things . . ." (Rom 11:36). For instance, while studying Genesis in my Scripture class, I was also enrolled in "Religion and World History." The two classes meshed perfectly. At first, this surprised me; it should not have. The material presented in one area of studies correlated with another discipline. While I was reading about God's covenant with Abraham I was also studying the cultures of Abraham's Mesopotamian neighbors and their influence on him. I was obtaining a worldview of my faith that always existed; I just was never exposed to it.

At my Alma Mater, the College of St. Scholastica, the Catholic Studies Seminar is a required class for all earning the major. The attempt of the seminar is to form young minds of diverse backgrounds into intellectuals with the faculties capable of reading critically, writing and rewriting intensively, and participating in collegial discussion. The seminar, lightly referred to as "Catholic Book Club" by some enrolled in it, requires an eagerness to examine studiously a variety of topics from across the academic spectrum in light of the Catholic Intellectual Tradition. The syllabus grants flexibility. If a class attempts to scratch the surface of a two thousand year old intellectual tradition, I think it merits this flexibility. The core curriculum consists of daily reading assignments, weekly papers, occasional guest speakers, and a final project. Issues as old as creation and as hot as the daily news are discussed. The seminar helped me to set aside my biases, and develop a strategic methodology for critical evaluation. I learned that it does not first matter whether I agree with an author or not, but that I understand what the author is featuring in the text. If I am not able to cite, quote, and explain an argument from a given text or presentation, then any opinion I might have is premature. In short, the Catholic Studies Seminar is preparation for a life of learning for aspiring Catholic Intellectuals.

When people ask me what Catholic Studies is, I reply that it is a Glorified Humanities major. I believe that this is an accurate description of a liberal arts program that, like the saints of old, celebrates the same faith seeking understanding as: "[T]he monk Boso said to Anselm, 'It appears a neglect if, after we are established in the faith, we do not seek to understand what we believe.' " [2] *The search for deeper faith and understanding attracted me to the program. I was studying biology and aspired to be a dentist. Though my education in the sciences was excellent, I still felt a need to broaden my studies in the liberal arts. Catholic Studies was the bridge in my academic life between the natural sciences and the liberal arts, or between the liberal arts and the Catholic faith. My mode of learning transferred from the science labs to the library where I would engage in the literature of the tradition and write papers in response. My study skills sharpened and my writing improved. I continue to ponder the glory of Christ in his Church as I study. In my educational journey, I seek to imitate Mary who "kept all these things, pondering them in her heart" (Luke 2:19). My studies foster a deeper love for Christ, the Church, the Magisterium, and the gift of faith. Catholic Studies is not intended to transform aspiring doctors and lawyers into priests and religious; rather, it develops one's academic tools and methodology as beneficial to all occupations.*

Catholic Studies has prepared me well for further education, and growth in the faith. The interdisciplinary studies through the lens of faith fills the gap in my education with intellectual stimulation, and spiritually beatifying means, namely the Catholic Faith. When envisioned, this gap is the space between the fingers of God and Adam in Michelangelo's Sistine Chapel. Like Adam awaiting the awakening touch of the Creator, my education, though excellent, was given new life by a Glorified Humanities major called Catholic Studies.

Zachary D. Bennett

FROM MONASTICISM AND CHRISTOLOGY TO THE INTERPLAY OF SCIENCE AND RELIGION

I began my time at the College of St. Scholastica with the intention of majoring in biology/pre-medicine and religious studies for the purpose of making both medicine and lay ministry my career. I knew right from the start that my education would not be complete if I did not study the things of God along with the things of this world. Yet, while I followed this path for nearly three years, a time came when my religious studies major no longer seemed appropriate.

However, much to my delight, the inception of the Catholic Studies program at St. Scholastica gave me the opportunity to take that on as my new second major. This allowed me to make use of several religion classes I had already taken, looking at the knowledge I had gained in a new way. Adding this knowledge to that gained in a few additional classes gave my studies a new life and a new direction.

Catholic Studies at St. Scholastica is an interdisciplinary program. While some of the courses contained in it are directly about Catholicism, others are linked to the faith in more subtle ways. Class topics are quite numerous, so each student may select a course of study that best complements his/her other ambitions. I opted for variety in my selections. Each topic I studied gave me another piece of the whole. With more pieces, I could make greater sense of the whole and thus, have a better educational experience.

One of my courses, "Philosophy of Religion," exposed me to beliefs that conflicted both with each other and with my own views. While considering the origin of religion, we read both David Hume and Ludwig Feuerbach. Hume, in writing that, "the whole frame of nature bespeaks an intelligent author," testified that the existence of God is made obvious when one examines the natural world (21). However, Feuerbach thought instead that God was merely a creation of the human mind, a projection of human values and attributes, and wrote that, "Consciousness of God is self-consciousness . . . Whatever is God to a man, that is his heart and soul" (12).

As a religious person, I am a good deal more partial to a worldview in which God actually exists. However, it was still valuable for me to be exposed to other views. In the process, I learned to examine and understand such views before disagreeing with them.

Several of my other Catholic Studies classes gave me insight into such topics as Scripture, sacraments, and ethics. I learned to appreciate modern biblical scholarship, which examines the bible as literature, asking who wrote it, when, and why, while still knowing that it cannot replace prayerful reading of the Bible as the Word of God. I came to see ritual and symbolism as effective ways to communicate what words cannot. I learned to use a Christian ethical framework and to apply it to any situation.

The Catholic Studies Seminar was my final course in the program. I might call the class a crash course in the Catholic intellectual tradition. With 2000 years of history to choose from, it was quite impossible to study everything. Thus, our rather flexible syllabus included a sampling of topics from monasticism and Christology to the interplay of science and religion and vigorously debated issues such as the death penalty. It seemed the perfect way to finish my already varied course of study.

Majoring in Catholic Studies expanded my world to include the richness and depth that is present in the Catholic intellectual tradition and the academic study of religion. I am rendered speechless by the sheer size of what I have found. Before beginning this journey, my experience of Catholicism, and indeed of religion itself, was little more than attending Mass and my parish catechesis program. Mass and catechesis are very good things, but they are no longer enough for me. I will forever want to know more.

Catholic Studies also did much to complete my liberal arts education. It provided the perfect complement to my science classes. In said classes, I memorized useful facts from my professors' lectures and learned to perform procedures in the laboratory. Catholic Studies was a completely different experience. The primary avenues for learning were reading, writing, and discussion. With all of the practice that this afforded me, my skills in all three areas improved immensely. I also learned to evaluate the arguments of others and to properly form my own.

Finally, I believe that my experience in Catholic Studies will make me a better doctor. The communication skills I have gained will be invaluable, but the perspective I have acquired is also important. I now have a heightened appreciation of the things of God and of the spiritual life. These are integral parts of what it means to be human, so by considering them along with the physical aspects of the human body, I will be a more effective healer.[3]

Amy Kaminski

HUMAN RESPONSE TO GOD'S CREATIVE GENIUS

Praised are You, O Lord our God, King of the Universe.
You fix the cycles of light and darkness;
You ordain the order of all creation ... .
In Your goodness the work of creation
Is continually renewed day by day.[4]

Genesis inspires us to recognize the handiwork of God with awe and wonder: "God saw everything that he had made, and indeed, it was very good. And there was evening and there was morning, the sixth day" (Gn. 1:31). In imitation and praise of the Creator, we reflect on and rejoice in the gifts that are ours to share: "And on the seventh day God finished the work that he had done, and he rested on the seventh day from all the work that he had done. So God blessed the seventh day and hallowed it, because on it God rested from all the work that he had done in creation" (2: 2-3).

In Sabbath posture, we are granted both moments of grace and the occasional mystical moment. True mystics, it seems to me, are granted a brief and ecstatic encounter with God, and then spend the rest of their lives discerning the hidden meaning of that searing moment. Others of us, not mystics, but open to grace, sometimes feel the power of that grace in overwhelming ways. We, too, must spend the rest of our lives working out the meaning of those grace-filled moments. Our active minds and lives flow from that energy. Responding to such grace is, I believe, how the best college professors and true public servants are formed.

Perhaps St. Theresa of Avila, Doctor of the church, mystic and reformer, is a model for such people. Her mystical experience came when she was past forty years of age. God touched and seared her heart: "I saw an angel close by me, on my left side, in bodily form. He was not large, but small of stature and most beautiful-his face burning, as if he were one of the highest angels, who seem to be all of fire.... I saw in his hand a long spear of gold, and at the iron's point there seemed to be a little flame. He appeared to me to be thrusting it at times into my heart, and to pierce my very entrails; when he drew it out, he seemed to draw them out also, and to leave me all one fire with a great love of God." [5] Bernini's seventeenth-century statue in Rome portrays this encounter. And a physician's testimony, after Theresa's death, reported that her heart was marked by a long, deep scar.[6] The searing presence of God can be both comforting and terrifying. It demands first our undivided attention, and then our whole-hearted response.

Our response to God's creative genius is to be creative ourselves. In his book entitled *Creativity*, Matthew Fox writes, "Creativity, when all is said and done, may be the best thing our species has going for it.... Creativity constitutes the very meaning of our being human and our powers of creativity distinguish us from other species."[7] We are summoned to the use of our imagination in all of Christian life. Thomas Aquinas prepares us for the use of our imagination and creativity. Thomas was convinced that God encourages in us "an affirmative attitude toward nature" which, according to Ian G. Barbour, contributed to the rise of science. For Thomas, reason "is an important preamble to faith" because God is at least partially disclosed in the universe. In his *Proofs for the Existence of God*, Thomas uses reason to demonstrate that God must exist.[8]

So, why do we serve or study? Why do we confer and write? What is literature for? What are books for? Susan Warner's *The Wide, Wide World*, a sentimental and pious novel first published in 1850, provoked a reader in Philadelphia to write to Warner, who then used the pen name Elizabeth Wetherell, that her book gave him "exquisite pleasure." But his highest praise was that it had "done me good," making him "a wiser and better man-more strengthened to duty, more reconciled to suffering."[9] Both inquiry and education are about the business of salvation, so books and literature and all our efforts are directed to the pursuit of truth, and to moving and touching hearts. The French Saint John Baptist de LaSalle writes that "God wills not only that all come to the knowledge of truth, but also that all be saved."[10] According to de LaSalle, procuring salvation meant seeking the total well-being of each student, and this would begin with teachers seeking to touch the hearts of the students entrusted to them. He writes, "You carry out a work that requires you to touch hearts, but this you cannot do except by the Spirit of God."[11] That same Spirit prompts the diverse authors of this issue to address issues of enduring significance.

CONTRIBUTORS AND CONTRIBUTIONS

The essays in Part I, "American Catholic Studies: Theory and Practice," were first published in the Winter 2007 issue of *Listening: Journal of Religion and Culture*. I invited these authors to contribute articles based on their expertise and considerable experience in developing programs of Catholic Studies from New York to California. Programs of Catholic Studies are found in Catholic colleges and universities and in public and private institutions as well. Certainly one of the issues in which Catholic Studies will seek engagement is the question of what makes a college or university Catholic. I address that issue in "Seven Attitudes and Approaches that make a College Catholic." The idea is not simply to seek compliance with the aims of *Ex corde ecclesiae*, but to ensure that the Catholic intellectual tradition remains a living reality at our institutions as they seek to claim or reclaim both character and mission.

Paul J. Wojda directs the M.A. Program in one of the first and best regarded programs of Catholic Studies at the University of St. Thomas in St. Paul, Minnesota. He addresses the question, "What is Catholic Studies, anyway?" He considers three attempts to size-up the phenomenon, but sees such efforts at clarity bedeviled by the absence of any consensus about how best to go about the task.

Richard M. Liddy of Seton Hall University offers "Catholic Studies and the Mission of the Catholic University," in which he addresses the following issues: Catholic Studies and the rise of historical consciousness; Catholic Studies and the loss of a unifying philosophical vision in Catholic universities; Catholic Studies and the mission of Catholic universities; "Catholicity" and the promise of Catholic Studies; and, finally, as an addendum, Centers of Catholic Studies.

David Gentry-Akin teaches in the Collegiate Seminar and Religious Studies Departments at Saint Mary's College of California. His contribution, "Catholic Studies Programs: Catalysts for Reviving the Catholic Intellectual Tradition in Higher Education," considers a new moment in our consideration of the mission of Catholic colleges and universities. He contends that many of our institutions are failing their students in passing on the legacy of Catholic faith and the Catholic intellectual tradition. He suggests that to allow this erosion of Catholic identity to continue unchecked fails to honor the memories of the generations of faithful women and men who built these institutions on faith and at enormous sacrifice.

Finally, James A. Fisher, co-director of the Francis and Ann Curran Center for American Catholic Studies at Fordham University in New York City, offers experience and observation rooted in his own field, American Catholic Studies. He sees issues in play of broader significance for the evolving project of Catholic Studies nationwide. He suggests that "More significant than simply the growth of lay representation [in the faculty demographics of Catholic theology programs] is the much greater range of authentically formative experiences witnessed, especially those grounded not in religious life but in experiences of family, gender, sexuality, disability and other versions of cultural/intellectual difference from the historic norm authorized in Catholic institutions." He finds Catholic Studies implicated "in the discussion over Catholic identity just as it becomes in turn a potential site of transition-if not transformation-in the ways that Catholic knowledge is produced and authorized."

The essays in Parts II and III were first delivered as lectures on campus in the "Here Comes Everybody" series to inaugurate and celebrate the establishment of the Braegelman Program of Catholic Studies at The College of St. Scholastica in Duluth, Minnesota, during the first years of the emerging program generously endowed by the Benedictine Sisters of the St. Scholastica Monastery, founders of the College. Duluth's first Bishop, James McGolrick, accurately and honestly said in tribute to their founding Prioress, Mother Scholastica Kerst, "She built my diocese." The lectures themselves were made possible by a gift from an anonymous friend of The College of St. Scholastica to whom I here express the gratitude of all who have profited from that generosity.

Beginning Part II, writing from Caldwell College in New Jersey, Sister Elizabeth Michael Boyle, O.P., offers "Art & Agnosticism: God's Partners in Revelation, A Poet Explores the Landscape of Faith and Doubt." Here is an ambitious undertaking: a theological reflection on Boyle's own personal experience of what John Paul II may have meant in his 1996 "Letter to Artists" when he wrote, "The church needs the arts not primarily to illustrate scripture or dogma but as a different and genuine source of theology."

In "The Earth is the LORD's (Ps 24:1)," Sr. Dianne Bergant, C.S.A., of Chicago's Catholic Theological Union, looks to the time when the irresponsibility and impertinence of human self-centeredness will be replaced by a sense of respect and responsible stewardship, and the bottom line of monetary calculation of resources will give way to aesthetic contemplation of natural beauty, a contemplation not unlike that of Job: "I had heard of you by word of mouth, but now my eye has seen you" (42:5).

In his essay "Human Dignity and the Kingdom of God: A Russian Theological Perspective (Vladimir Solov'ëv)," my colleague at The College of St. Scholastica, Randall A. Poole, explores the universality of Russia's greatest philosopher as he considers his principal theme: human perfectibility.

"Theological Challenges to Community Organizing," by Lee Stuart, offers the clear perspective of one who has had a hand in the transformation of the Bronx from dying embers to glowing hope. And from the halls of Congress, James Oberstar reflects on both faith and service in his contribution, "Faith And Values in the Public Arena: An American Catholic in Public Life."

Mark McVann, F.S.C., begins Part III with "'The Misfit,' the Grandmother, and Genesis in Flannery O'Connor's 'A Good Man Is Hard To Find.'" He reads O'Connor's most famous, difficult, and even shocking short story as an illustration of the theology salvation. In this story, it appears that evil has triumphed unconditionally, but at the very height of this seeming victory of the forces of evil and chaos, a moment of transforming, salvific grace is granted to the two principals in the story. One accepts, the other rejects this grace.

Anthony Barrett is a seeker, too. His "The Search for Faith and Pascal's Wager" tells the story of a scholar's search. Anne-Marie Kirmse, O.P., in "Avery Cardinal Dulles, S.J.: From Convert to Cardinal," gives us the picture of another search that has yielded great treasure not just for the seeker, Cardinal Dulles, but for all of those he has taught in his long and significant career.

"Not Scandalized, Not Seduced," by Matthew Lickona continues the exploration from the point of view of a young and observant Catholic husband and father while Aurelie A. Hagstrom, in "Theology of the Laity: New Horizons and Recent Roadblocks," points to problems and possibilities in a developing church.

The authors gathered here, in and through their wide-ranging scholarly interests, begin to suggest something of the depth and breadth of the living Catholic Intellectual Tradition. They are leading the way in new and important discussions. These essays are offered in the hope that they reflect the goodness of the work of creation, which the Lord renews day by day. May their voices echo the voice of Jesus for the readers of this volume: "You are not far from the kingdom of God" (Mark 12:34).

William C. Graham
The College of St. Scholastica
Duluth, Minnesota

NOTES

1. In John's Gospel, Jesus says, "I am the way, and the truth, and the life" (14:6) echoing the promise make to Jeremiah the Prophet: "If you seek me with all your heart, I willlet you find me, says the Lord" (29:13).

2. Berard Marthaler, *The Creed: The Apostolic Faith in Contemporary Theology*, revised edition (Mystic, CT: Twenty-Third Publications, 1993), p. 96.

3. Works Cited: Feuerbach, Ludwig. *The Essence of Christianity*. Trans. George Elliot. New York: Harper Torchbooks, 1957. Hume, David. *The Natural History of Religion*. Ed. H.E. Root. Stanford, CA: Stanford University Press, 1956.

4. *Weekday Prayer Book* (New York: Rabbinical Assembly, 1962), 42.

5. Bert Ghezzi, *Mystics and Miracles: True Stories of Lives Touched by God* (Chicago: Loyola Press, 2002), 127.

6. Ibid.

7. Cited by James L. Empereur in *The National Catholic Reporter*, "Liturgy: the challenging call to a new direction," Feb. 13, 2004, 9.

8. Ian G. Barbour, *Religion and Science: Historical and Contemporary Issues* (San Francisco: HarperCollins, 1997), 6, 7.

9. Jane Tompkins, in an Afterword to Susan Warner, *The Wide, Wide World* (New York: The Feminist Press, 1987), 584, quoting a citation from Anna B. Warner, *Susan Warner* (New York: G. P. Putnam's Sons, 1909), 354. The novel first appeared in 1850, and was a literary sensation. None had ever sold better in the United States. Critics praised it, and fourteen editions followed in two years. It became one of the best sellers of the nineteenth century in the U.S. and in England.

10. John Baptist de La Salle's Meditation 193.3, cited in *"Touching Hearts: the greatest miracle you can perform,"* in *Lasallian reflections on mission* (vol. 1, no. 4, February 2004), 1.

11. Ibid., Meditation 43.3.

Part I

American Catholic Studies: Theory and Practice

SEVEN ATTITUDES AND APPROACHES
THAT MAKE A COLLEGE CATHOLIC

William C. Graham

What are the elements that identify Colleges as Catholic? Vatican II directs the steps and efforts of educators and campus ministers in the Declaration on Christian education, *Gravissimum educationis* (GE 10): "The hoped-for result is that the Christian mind may achieve, as it were, a public, persistent, and universal presence in the whole enterprise of advancing higher culture, and that the students of these institutions may become truly outstanding in learning, ready to shoulder society's heavier burdens, and to witness the faith to the world . . . ."

I propose that there are seven ways we can be about that Herculean task so that the distinctive identity of our Catholic institutions be recognized and celebrated as we work with our students on their journey to growth in wisdom and grace.

FIRST:

We must teach our students that life is messy. Ambiguity confronts us all. The Church seems to teach this truth at every step even though there are Catholics among us who dispute it. They tend to look on 1957 as the best of all possible ages and suggest that we return there. However, we cannot. Even if Mr. Peabody and his Way-Back Machine could transport us to that time long ago, we know that the advances in health care alone would make us want to stay in our own age. But with advances in health care come moral trials. Moral theologians and ethicists cannot keep up with the pace of medical technology. We understand that just because we can do something does not mean we should do it. But what morality looks like in 2006 is not as simple as it seemed in 1957. It will not be that simple again. Paul VI of happy memory recognized that truth in 1968 when, in *Humanae vitae*, he wrote that "the recent course of human society and the concomitant changes have provoked new questions. The Church cannot ignore these questions, for they concern matters intimately connected with the life and happiness of human beings" (1).

Considering that "this new state of things gives rise to new questions" (3), Paul notes that the Papal Commission he expanded, originally set up by John XXIII in March 1963, "to examine views and opinions concerning married life, and especially on the correct regulation of births" (5), found that "within the commission itself, there was not complete agreement concerning the moral norms to be proposed." He reports that he then "intently studied the whole matter, as well as prayed constantly to God" (6). His prayer and study spread over the course of two years. The Pope recognizes that ambiguity does indeed confront us all when he later notes, "It is to be anticipated that perhaps not everyone will easily accept this particular teaching" (18). He also notes, when giving pastoral directives, that "there is no doubt that to many it will appear not merely difficult but even impossible to observe" his teaching which he asserts "is a promulgation of the law of God Himself" (19).

Many Catholics take issue with the teaching of *Humane vitae*, even some Catholics who have not read the encyclical but disagree with what they think it may have said or have heard or read about it. They may attribute to its author a greater sense of clarity than he himself would appear to claim. They would do well to study the teaching and see the ambiguity pointed out here even as Paul links his teaching to the very law of God while recognizing that many will find it either difficult or impossible to observe. In *The Courage to Be Catholic*, George Weigel writes that Pope Paul "evidently, was willing for a time to tolerate dissent on an issue on which he had made a solemn, authoritative statement, hoping that the day would come when, in a calmer cultural and ecclesiastical atmosphere, the truth of that teaching could be appreciated."

Avery Cardinal Dulles even notes a certain sense of ambiguity or lack of clarity flowing from the Second Vatican Council: "Like most other councils, Vatican II issued a number of compromise statements. It intentionally spoke ambiguously on certain points, leaving to the future the achievement of greater clarity" ("The Basic Teaching of Vatican II," in *Sacred Adventure: Beginning Theological Study*, by William Graham). We do not serve students well if we suggest that there is black and white where they may truly be variegated shades of gray.

This attention to ambiguity highlights the Catholic college or university's absolute dedication to academic freedom. Educators in these institutions often claim that academic freedom is more intact in a Catholic university than it is in many places which are responsible to an arbitrary administration or board of directors. Academic freedom derives from the Church's intellectual tradition, its respect for the power and dignity of the intellect, and the confidence the Church has always placed in the good faith and conscience of the faithful, that is, in the dignity of the human person. Thus, the truly Catholic university would be totally intolerant of academic coercion in any of its guises.

WHICH BRINGS US TO POINT TWO:

Not everything is ambiguous. Richard N. Ostling points out that in Huston Smith's new book, *The Soul of Christianity: Restoring the Great Tradition*, Smith writes that "discounting invisible realities" is the "modern mistake" promoted by an intolerant secularism which sees only empirical, scientific knowledge as valid (see http://www.stnews.org/ Books-2541.htm). Ostling heads his article "A fence around faith," which calls to mind the description variously attributed to Augustine or Flannery O'Connor of doctrine as a fence around a mystery. Inside the fence we are certain of the truth. We can dig as deep as we can manage, and can continue finding new depths and beauty, and perhaps unexpected ramifications to this same truth—this is why prayerful meditation will never exhaust the possibilities and theologians will never be out of business. The mysteries are infinite and our minds and capacities to absorb or ponder them are finite.

So, we must teach students to distinguish one voice from another. Today's students have been raised in a culture which prizes tolerance and diversity. Those who do not have a firm grasp on what true tolerance or real diversity look like will sometimes suggest that all voices are equal. But students in Catholic colleges should be taught to think and judge with the Church (*sentire cum Ecclesia*). They can learn to appreciate that someone in a chat room on the internet does not speak with the same authority as a professor in a classroom, and that a televangelist may have an interesting interpretation but not one that necessarily squares with a Catholic approach to Scripture. An intellectually mature Catholic asks questions and seeks answers. And she keeps at it until death.

By provoking ourselves and our students into a consideration of voices, a Catholic College or University gives priority to the building of community, to modeling a healthy and vital community, to supporting one another in genuine love, to praying together formally and informally, and to uniting with one another in crises. If our students experience a Catholic community during their university years, that experience will transform their hopes and their lives ever after.

POINT THREE:

We must be active in guiding students through the study of scripture. Timothy Radcliffe, the former Master of the Order of Preachers, writes in *What is the Point of Being Christian?* that "we should be aware that the gospel invites us to a liberty and happiness which should swim against the expectations of our culture, and may look positively eccentric." He reminds us that "Christianity invites us to a peculiar freedom and happiness, which is a share in God's own vitality" (29). We cannot really know this truth without being students of the Gospels and of all the Scripture. But interpreting the Scriptures is not as easy as consulting the Manhattan Yellow Pages or reading *The Daily News*.

For example, the calming of the storm about which we read in Mark 4:35-41: this is a fascinating story revealing the power and person of Jesus to his terrified disciples. Consider briefly the message for readers that may be found in it. In his essay "Biblical Study: A Brief Introduction" (In *Sacred Adventure: Beginning Theological Study*, by William C. Graham), Mark McVann, F.S.C., asks "How was it possible for Jesus to sleep through a violent storm with the boat filling up with water? Why would the disciples wake Jesus to ask him, in effect, to save them, and then be amazed when he actually does it?" Clearly, this story of the mighty work on the lake needs an interpretation.

McVann asks, "What, then, might Mark want us to understand from this story?" He points out that from the earliest days of Christianity, the boat is a symbol of the Church. Also, we know that persecution was a dangerous feature of life for the first Christians. Further, we know that the first Christians looked forward with great anticipation to the return of Jesus in power and glory, but in the interim mourned his absence: "But even though Jesus was gone, had he abandoned them? This is the question Mark addresses in this story."

McVann concludes that in the "Calming of the Storm," Mark is telling a story in which the disciples, fearful because Jesus is "absent" (that is, asleep), panicked in the storm, a symbolic reference to persecution. Jesus awakes and calms the storm. Despite his apparent absence, he has not abandoned them, and he calms the "storm" of their fears of persecution. They should have known all along that they had not been abandoned, and this is why Jesus scolds them in v. 40. The disciples "have experienced the *mysterium tremendum*, the tremendous mystery of an encounter with the divine. They have seen revealed the power of God to save life from death, which will be revealed fully in Jesus' resurrection, which this story points anticipates: Jesus, asleep (sleep is a Christian symbol of death), wakes up (rises from the dead) and is revealed as the Lord of divine power and majesty." Not only is the Lord in the boat with us, it is his boat. We are called to trust and to row.

Learning to read the Bible in a responsible and intellectually respectable way is the work of a lifetime. We must show our students the way in a manner that will nurture, comfort and challenge them even as it quickens them in hope.

POINT FOUR:

We must stress the importance of the sacraments, especially baptism, the eucharist and reconciliation. Baptized Christians need to be reminded of the special dignity that belongs to us who rise, radiant, from the waters. It is clear from the prayers that we say that the Church thinks we are "God's holy people, set free from sin by baptism" (Blessing of the Water), and "a new creation . . . clothed . . . in Christ" (Clothing with a Baptismal Garment), as well as "children of the light" (Presentation of a Lighted Candle).

But we live today in a Church scarred and stained by sin, a church whose bishops, many charge, have squandered the Church's moral authority. Some suggest that the crisis will shipwreck us. But Radcliffe reminds us that "we should not be fearful of crises. The church was born in a crisis of hope. Crises are our *specialité de la maison*. They rejuvenate us. The one that we are living through now is very small" (16). The crises facing us are both external and internal. The external crises (where the Church is persecuted, for example) will strength our witness; the internal crises (the clergy sex abuse scandal, for example, a burning and resented phenomenon in the Church) convict us of flawed witness and call us to repentance. Radcliffe sees a fundamental paradox in Christianity in that our foundational story, the Last Supper, "tells of a moment when there was no story to tell, when the future disappeared. We gather as a community around the altar and remember the night that the community disintegrated: our founding story is of the collapse of any story at all, and our community looks back to when it fell apart" (15). The Apostle Paul quickens us in hope for "what God has prepared for those who love him" (1 Cor. 2:9) which Vatican II tells us we enjoy in preview gathered around the eucharistic table, "in a foretaste of that heavenly liturgy which is celebrated in the holy city of Jerusalem toward which we journey as pilgrims" (CSL 8). This "is a sacred action surpassing all others; no other action of the Church can equal its efficacy" (7).

We come to the table, then, Sunday by Sunday, not "as a constraint on our freedom," or as a product of "Catholic legalism and of a culture of control," but "as a sign of our stable belonging in this liquid and mobile world," and our attention to our obligation is a sign of God's fidelity (Radcliffe 199).

But there are bumps along our holy road, events that cause us to falter. In *Humanae vitae*, Paul VI suggests that when sin "exercises its hold," we "are not to lose heart," but have "recourse to the mercy of God, abundantly bestowed in the Sacrament of Penance" (25). How fortunate are we to belong to a Church that prays what it believes: "God, the Father of mercies, / through the death and resurrection of his Son / has reconciled the world to himself / and sent the Holy Spirit among us for the forgiveness of sins." And what a gift to belong to a Church whose priests can pronounce with authority over a penitent, "Through the ministry of the Church / may God give you pardon and peace, / and I absolve you from your sins / in the name of the Father, and of the Son, + / and of the Holy Spirit" (prayer of absolution).

POINT FIVE:

We must teach our students Church history. Perhaps some of them share Henry Ford's attitude that "history is just one damn thing after another." But they can be called to a more sophisticated view. Radcliffe suggests that when Peter and Paul were martyred, "many Christians betrayed each other. It seemed as if the Church was on the verge of collapse." But those first Christians endured and "It is probable that the Gospels, especially Mark's, were the fruit of grappling with this crisis" (16). Many Catholics seem to think that ours is the only age in which the Church has suffered distress. Attention to our history, beginning with the Acts of the Apostles, will disabuse them of that notion. Further, historians have shown that there are at least fifty years of tumult in the wake of each of the Church's ecumenical councils, but there will certainly be a longer period of confusion in the wake of Vatican II given the fact that millions more people today can read and thus comment and disagree, and the communications revolution has not just facilitated but revolutionized the conversation.

POINT SIX:

We must instruct students in and promote the practice of Catholic Social teaching. Radcliffe points to his fellow Dominican Herbert

McCabe who asserts that political action is just "the social visibility of faith" (p. 33, citing *Law, Love and Language* [London, 2003], p. 159). Some suggest that social justice is to religion what love is to marriage. James, in his epistle, instructs us about the relationship of faith and religion to social justice: "What does it profit, my brethren, if a man says he has faith but has not works? Can his faith save him? If a brother or sister is ill-clad and in lack of daily food, and one of you says to them, 'Go in peace, be warmed and filled,' without giving them the things needed for the body, what does it profit? So faith by itself, if it has no works, is dead. But some one will say, 'You have faith and I have works.' Show me your faith apart from your works, and I by my works will show you my faith" (2:14-18).

Cardinal Dulles helps us to understand that from the Reformation until Vatican II, the Church tended to regard its mission as exclusively religious, aimed at preparing individuals through faith, worship, and right behavior to attain external life. "Gradually, with the social encyclicals of popes such as Leo XIII and Pius XI, the church began to assume responsibility to teach the principles of a just social order, but this order was viewed in terms of conformity to the natural law rather than as an implementation of the gospel."

He notes that with Blessed "John XXIII and Vatican II, the emphasis shifted. The apostolate of peace and social justice came to be seen as a requirement of the church's mission to carry on the work of Christ, who had compassion on the poor and the oppressed. This changed attitude was eloquently expressed in Vatican II's *Message to Humanity*, released nine days after the opening of the council in 1962. It was more fully elaborated in the *Pastoral Constitution on the Church in the Modern World*, which described the church as endowed with 'a function, a light, and an energy that can serve to structure and consolidate the human community' (*GS* 42). Since the council, this trend has gained momentum. It was reflected in the encyclical of Paul VI, *Populorum progressio* (1967), and even more clearly in the synod document, *Justice in the World* (1971), which depicted the struggle for justice and the transformation of society as constitutive dimensions of evangelization" ("The Basic Teaching of Vatican II").

The *Pastoral Constitution on the Church in the Modern World* reminds us, "The social order and its development must constantly yield to the good of the person, since the order of things must be subordinate to the order of persons and not the other way around" (26). Pope John Paul II returned to that insight in Toronto in 1984: "The needs of the poor take priority over the desires of the rich; the rights of workers over the maximization of profits; the preservation of the environment over uncontrolled expansion; and production to meet social needs over production for military purposes."

John Paul II also writes, "But it will be necessary above all to abandon a mentality in which the poor—as individuals and as peoples—are considered a burden, as irksome intruders trying to consume what others have produced" (*Centesimus Annus*, 1991). We are bound to justice, as Archbishop John R. Roach reminds us: "For it is not only appropriate, but essential that Catholics be involved in working for social, political and economic justice. This is not an optional or peripheral part of our faith. Nor is it new. It is at the heart of our faith, and it is deeply rooted in the gospel" (*Reviving the Common Good*, 1991).

There is no escaping the primacy of justice as a life-building and church-sustaining virtue. We must teach our students to study the Church's rich legacy of social teachings and put it into practice.

AND, FINALLY, POINT SEVEN:

We must be for our students the very person of Jesus. Writing in *Humanae vitae*, Paul VI, directing comments to priests, teaches that husbands and wives "when deeply distressed by reason of the difficulties of their life, must find stamped in the heart and voice of their priest the likeness of the voice and the love of our Redeemer" (29). All Christians, not just those employed as pastoral ministers, are called to be conformed to Christ, remembering St. Athanasius (c. 295 - c. 373) who said, "He was made man that we might be made God." This insight becomes our prayer at each eucharist: "By the mystery of this water and wine, may we come to share in the divinity of Christ who humbled himself to share in our humanity" (preparation of the gifts). We are to model that hope in our care one for another, that together we "may grow in love" (Eucharistic Prayer II), that the Father "might see and love in us / what [he sees and loves] in Christ . . ." (Preface, Sundays in Ordinary Time VII).

IN CONCLUSION:

We see that *Ex corde ecclesiae* (13) succinctly states our mission: "Since the objective of a Catholic University is to assure in an institutional manner a Christian presence in the university world confronting the great problems of society and culture, every Catholic University, as *Catholic,* must have the following *essential characteristics:*

1. a Christian inspiration not only of individuals but of the university community as such;

2. a continuing reflection in the light of the Catholic faith upon the growing treasury of human knowledge, to which it seeks to contribute by its own research;
3. fidelity to the Christian message as it comes to us through the Church;
4. an institutional commitment to the service of the people of God and of the human family in their pilgrimage to the transcendent goal which gives meaning to life."

If we adopt the seven attitudes and approaches as suggested above, we should expect to be in full compliance with the aims of *Ex corde ecclesiae* which seeks to ensure that those who govern Catholic colleges and universities will make the Catholic faith tradition a living reality at the institutions they serve, thus reclaiming both character and mission. And then we can hope to hear the voice of Jesus say, "You are not far from the kingdom of God" (Mark 12:34).

NOTE

An early, abbreviated version of this article appeared in the *Catholic Colleges & Universities* section of *The National Catholic Reporter*, November 3, 2006.

THE VERY IDEA OF CATHOLIC STUDIES

Paul J. Wojda

As a discrete program of study within American higher education, Catholic Studies is little more than a decade old.[1] However, despite its youth—or more likely because of it—the phenomenon has already attracted more than a little controversy. Indeed, in some circles, particularly on the campuses of Catholic colleges and universities where such programs have been initiated, the very idea of Catholic Studies is enough to send some into giddy revelry and others into an apoplectic fugue, which would suggest that, whatever else may be said about it, Catholic Studies is no *mere* idea, but a palpable reality. The prime difficulty is definitional: just what is Catholic Studies, anyway? Some attempts have been made to size-up the phenomenon (I will consider three of them below), but such efforts at clarity are bedeviled by the absence of any consensus about how best to go about the task. Does one privilege the professed beliefs of programs as displayed in their mission statements and other official documents, usually penned by program founders, directors, and participating faculty? Or do the operative beliefs informing actual program practices—both curricular and extra-curricular—deserve more attention? (Getting at the operative beliefs would, of course, require some form of participant-observer research.) What about the historical and sociological studies of the shifts and trends in post-conciliar (mostly North American) Catholicism, and in Catholic higher education specifically: might they give us a more accurate fix on what Catholic Studies is all about? Of course, we might turn to the time-tested formal categories and methods employed within the academy itself for delimiting scholarly fields of inquiry. (That most Catholic Studies programs identify themselves as "interdisciplinary" makes this last option problematic.) We could, of course, simply conduct an opinion poll.

It is beyond the scope of this paper, as well as my abilities, to resolve these methodological difficulties. Rather, what I wish to suggest is that, whatever the approach or combination of approaches to getting a more accurate fix on the phenomenon of Catholic Studies, the interests and views of the students (and to some extent the faculty) who are actually being attracted to these programs ought to play a prominent part. It may seem odd to suggest that the interests of students should or even could be constitutive of a program's identity. After all, there must *be* a program to elicit student interest in the first place. On the other hand, only the most thoroughgoing rationalist would hold that student interest plays (or should play) absolutely no role in either the construction or development of such programs. In any case, enough time has now elapsed since the formal beginnings of Catholic Studies programs, and enough controversy about the character of such programs has emerged, to think that attending to what I will call the "originating experience" of students enrolling in these programs might help to clarify both the present and future shape of the Catholic Studies phenomenon.

Following a brief examination of three recent typologies of Catholic Studies, on which I intend my own reflections to build, I offer a systematic survey of these originating experiences based primarily on my own interaction with students who have expressed an interest in, and in many cases successfully applied to, the program I direct. The limitations of my reflections, and thus typology, will be obvious. I am clearly no disinterested bystander, and my own experience is partial at best.[2] On the other hand, one of my assumptions is that Catholic Studies will continue to be defined by and thus depend on the critical engagement with each other of the individuals and groups it comprises, not least of which are the students themselves. My conclusions, therefore, ought to be taken as an invitation to just such an engagement. The aim of such engagement, I further assume, is to move from controversy to dialogue, one of the chief tasks of those working within an intellectual tradition, Catholic or otherwise.[3]

TYPOLOGIES OF CATHOLIC STUDIES

Most of those who have attempted some general description of Catholic Studies have recognized its diversity and have therefore adopted a typological approach to their task. The three I review here have a great deal in common, though they differ with respect to their principles of selection and method.

Mark Massa, S.J., a co-director of the Center for American Catholic Studies at Fordham University, sees at least three "semi-distinct" models of Catholic Studies presently in existence.[4] The sources of his typology are not entirely clear, though he seems to be working with some combination of the "stated agendas" (mission statements?) of programs answering to each of his models, opinions of academics involved in Catholic Studies, and the dominant character of the scholarly work published by individuals working within each of his types. Massa's effort is avowedly informal (an 'initial typology' is his subtitle) and so he doesn't provide— nor would it be fair to criticize the absence of—more specific information about his sources and method.

Massa's first model, for which he confesses little interest or sympathy, is one he calls "restorationist," because faculty in this sort of Catholic Studies program are "heavily invested in the project of restoring the Catholic character of their institutions and are thus (fairly or unfairly) perceived as part of the broader 'restorationist' project of contemporary Catholicism."[5] Restorationist-type programs, claims Massa, seek to immerse students as deeply as possible into an unambiguously and "unabashedly Catholic culture" as an antidote to the uncertain or "secularized" Catholic identity with which they show up at its doors. Dogmatic theology of a neo-scholastic type tends to be the central academic discipline in this model, buttressed by both spiritual and liturgical formation, with study-abroad semesters in Rome a common feature. Massa's objection to this model is that it is historically naïve. "Structuring Catholic Studies programs around marathon readings of St. Augustine, St. Thomas Aquinas, and the papal social encyclicals—without a rigorous consideration of the methods of historical criticism, cultural theory, and the rigors of Enlightenment and postmodern critique—fails the litmus test of liberal arts education, including a Catholic liberal arts education."[6]

Massa's second model is, accordingly, more "historically" focused. "Programs in this 'historical mode' situate their intellectual and academic projects squarely within the larger post-Enlightenment historical project, which understands human reality itself as an historical stream in which social institutions, intellectual constructs, and even logical categories are immersed."[7] While Massa admires the rigorous quality of the scholarship promoted within the historically-oriented model (he mentions the work of John Tracy Ellis, Chris Kauffman, Jay Dolan, David O'Brien, and Philip Gleason, among others), he laments its failure to address the normative questions raised by its historical research. Questions about the truth of Catholic belief and practice are central to the core of Catholic experience itself, argues Massa, and thus to ignore them "leaves out crucial parts of the puzzle in understanding Catholic identity and belief."[8]

Not surprisingly, then, Massa concludes his typology by plumping for a third model, one that combines the historical (i.e., descriptive) and normative. Jewish Studies programs are, he proposes, a helpful analogue.

Massa acknowledges the institutional obstacles to sustaining such an interdisciplinary approach; long-standing "walls of separation" between departments of history, sociology, theology, and philosophy do not come down easily. (Massa proposes a "meandering porous fence" as an alternative metaphor here.) The outlines of this model are nevertheless visible in universities, many of them non-Catholic, where chairs in Catholic Studies have been endowed: Harvard and Yale a few decades ago, and more recently the University of Illinois-Chicago and the University of Toledo. Finally, claims Massa, comprehensive analysis of such events as the clergy sexual-abuse crisis, make this third "interdisciplinary model" only more attractive, if not necessary. "This national crisis needs social-scientific-demographic study, historical examination of institutional protocols and clergy formation, philosophical and theological analyses of ideas of priesthood and Church leadership and accountability, and much more besides, not necessarily as separate or separated disciplines, but as ongoing conversation partners—or perhaps even better, as stages in a cohesive intellectual project."[9]

Massa's typology is not without its merits, though it seems in the end less a description of models of Catholic Studies *programs,* actual or potential, than an argument for a certain kind of *scholarship*—one that more self-consciously combines descriptive and normative modes of inquiry—in the examination of Catholic identity or culture. A similar difficulty besets the typology developed by my colleague J. Michael Joncas, who seeks to "situate Catholic Studies within an American Catholic university's academic enterprise," by examining whether such a program would be better conceived as a "discourse," a "field," or a "discipline."[10]

By "discourse" he means an "ongoing" but largely unstructured "conversation about a common interest." As a discourse, Catholic Studies "simply marks out a conversation held by anyone interested in Catholic topics, ranging from believers in the pew concerned about clergy sexual abuse, through reporters covering a papal election and inauguration, through bishops testifying before congress on welfare legislation, to professors of theology, philosophy, history, sociology, psychology, literature, visual art, music, etc., exploring distinctively Catholic topics." As an *academic* discourse, then, Catholic Studies would largely be restricted to the latter participants.

A *field* describes a more delimited space and, importantly, set of activities. As an example, Joncas offers the "health field," which comprises such things as the training of physicians, the treatment of patients, and the issuing of insurance. Important for Joncas is the fact that, within a "field," the unity of the various activities, in the case of Catholic Studies their distinctively "Catholic" character, is not engaged, except pragmatically.

Thus, Catholic Studies as an *academic* field "might provide appreciation of Catholic church architecture to one group, history of Catholicism courses for seminarians, explore the papacy's policies toward the Jews during the Nazi era in an inter-religious dialogue, or sponsor retreats for law students," but the internal unity of these projects would not itself be a constitutive part of a Catholic Studies program under this description.

Joncas dismisses each of these two types in favor of Catholic Studies as an "academic discipline," which turns out on closer inspection to be a very similar, albeit more detailed version of Massa's third "historico-theological" type. While he offers no formal definition of a "discipline," Joncas situates Catholic Studies within the humanities (classics, history, modern languages, English, and, perhaps, philosophy and theology), primarily because it shares with them the goal of interpreting "cultural achievements." In fact, he continues, Catholic Studies will be interdisciplinary, drawing on what he terms the "meta-disciplines" of philosophy and theology, as well as (possibly) the social sciences, to investigate the "origins and development, present manifestations and characteristics, underlying structures, instincts, and loyalties of "Catholic Christian culture(s), and especially the "monuments" (literary, historical, aesthetic) thereof.[11] Like Massa, Joncas also looks to Jewish ("Judaic") Studies as a helpful parallel to what Catholic Studies is (or might be), and thus sees one of the primary goals of Catholic studies as the formation of a "community of academic inquiry with habits of mind understanding of and sympathetic to Catholic Christian culture(s) and their monuments."

Joncas also rejects the "restorationist" model of Catholic Studies, though not by that name, and not, like Massa, because he finds it historically naïve. Rather, he sees the emphases on moral and spiritual formation characteristic of that model as more properly the task of other institutions within the Church.

> Initiation into and practice of Catholic Christian belief and practice is properly the work of the [Catholic] [sic] Church through its ministries of pastoral care, involving initiation, mystagogy, catechesis, etc.; the appropriate venues for such pastoral care include parishes, retreat and spirituality centers, campus ministry, etc. . . . Development of Catholic Christian belief and practice is properly the work of the [Catholic] [sic] Church under the guidance of the Episcopal magisterium, involving preaching, teaching, works of charity, action for justice, witness, etc.; the proper venues for such development include the institutions mentioned above, as well as specialized organizations such as the USCCB with its multiple secretariats, universal and (arch)diocesan curial offices, parish administrations, etc.

As an *academic* discipline, therefore, Catholic Studies, while having primary appeal to Catholic scholars working intentionally within the Catholic tradition, would also have and welcome as its audience those without such loyalties, but sympathetic to Catholic Christian culture(s) for other reasons (e.g., cultural historians, non-Catholics or non-Christians committed to ecumenical or inter-religious dialogue, etc.).

Taken together, Massa's and Joncas' typologies are less a description of the Catholic Studies phenomenon than a normative vision of Catholic Studies as a fully-fledged scholarly activity, the contours of which are instantly familiar to those, Catholic or otherwise, already situated within the academy, Catholic or otherwise. As attractive as this vision may be, and an argument might be made that, whatever else Catholic Studies comes to mean, this vision ought to be the central or controlling one, it nevertheless falls short of accounting for the current reality of Catholic Studies, especially as it emerged over the last decade. In this respect, both Massa and Joncas engage the idea of Catholic Studies, not the thing itself.

A more compelling account is offered by Mary Ann Hinsdale, of Boston College, whose four-fold typology is based on her study of Catholic Studies programs across the United States (in anticipation of writing an introductory Catholic Studies textbook), site-visits to which included interviews with faculty, administrators and, "where possible," students.[12] Hinsdale limited the scope of her research to undergraduate Catholic Studies programs at Catholic Colleges and Universities, and in the case of those places she visited in person (sixteen of the roughly two-dozen investigated), made a point of speaking with faculty who were either ambivalent or opposed to Catholic Studies. Her resultant typology is based on what she discerned as the "major purpose or aim of a program," with the important caveat that no actual program fits one type exactly.

Hinsdale's first type, which she calls the *cultural studies* model, is a version of Massa's and Joncas' third type. "This approach to Catholic Studies regards Catholicism as an 'object' of study. It does not presume that either the students or the faculty that participate are Catholic. It studies the 'phenomenon' of Catholicism as a multi-faceted 'culture.'" While ostensibly "neutral" with respect to its subject matter, Hinsdale argues that, like other "area studies" programs, this model of Catholic Studies does advocate for the "intellectual heritage" of Catholicism, which in the minds of those working predominantly within this model is perceived as unjustly marginalized within the academic community. Hinsdale is attracted to this model as the best location for addressing issues of inculturation and ecclesiological pluralism, and in fact sees its advocacy-orientation as arising precisely out of the "internal pluralism" that emerges in the wake of the Second

Vatican Council (when questions of Catholic identity become particularly acute). On the other hand, Hinsdale laments the tendency of scholarship in this model towards "Catholic exotica," echoing Massa's criticism of work that, however historically insightful, never raises the important normative questions about Catholic beliefs and practices.

In contrast to the cultural studies model is the *apologetic* model, which disavows any neutrality in explicitly seeking to restore "a unified Catholic worldview," arguing not only for the "reasonableness and plausibility" of Catholic faith, but its *truth*. Such programs often define themselves over against "wishy-washy" theology/religious studies departments that are perceived as failing at this task. Anglo-Catholic and neo-Thomist sensibilities pervade the curriculum: Newman, Dawson, Chesterton, C.S. Lewis and T.S. Eliot (*honoris causa*), Gilson, Maritain, Pieper, Bernanos, Bloy. Formation elements, "retreats, clubs, publications, and worship experiences," are often incorporated into programs of this type. "Social justice" and "freedom" are not neglected concepts, Hinsdale notes, but their exemplars are typically those of unambiguous allegiance to Church authority (e.g., Thomas More, J.C. Murray, Dorothy Day, Peter Maurin).

A hybrid of these first two types is the *Catholic Intellectual Tradition* model, which Hinsdale finds to be characteristic of institutions where Catholic Studies is more a "concentration" or (at best) a "minor" rather than a self-standing program or department. The aim of this model is to "preserve and expand" a "long tradition of Catholic intellectual life," drawing heavily on the discipline of history, but including the arts, humanities, and even the natural sciences as well. "There seems to be a wider definition of Catholicism in this approach," writes Hinsdale, with the frequent inclusion in the curriculum of "marginated voices within Catholicism" (e.g., "women, African Americans, Native Americans, Latinos, working-class and poor Catholics"). Like the cultural studies model, this type also examines the "dark side" of the Catholic tradition (e.g., Crusades, slavery, anti-Semitism). However, Hinsdale notes that in programs of this type there is often lacking a "sense of Catholicism as a world religion," and an appreciation for "how it has been inculturated in non-western cultures."

Hinsdale's final type is one she calls the *formational* model, and is, she avers, usually an appendage to programs of the other major types. (Hence, like Massa and Joncas, Hinsdale can be seen as offering a three-fold typology.) In the formation model "there is an emphasis on building community among students (sometimes including their families) and faculty," often in the face of what is perceived as "an alien, increasingly secularized culture." Unlike antecedently existing programs in Peace and

Justice Studies, Catholic Studies programs under this model seek to ground "service-learning" on a more coherent intellectual structure of the Catholic tradition.

Hinsdale recognizes a variety of motives (she identifies five) and "ideological stances" (at least three) behind Catholic Studies programs,[13] which when combined with her four dominant types would bring the possible permutations of Catholic Studies models to sixty. Her attention to these additional dimensions adds considerable depth to her description as well as analyses of the Catholic Studies phenomenon. Among the most salient points of her analysis, at least for present purposes, is her conviction that the guiding vision of Catholic Studies need not be a univocal one. ("A coherent vision need not be a univocal vision.")

> It strikes me as unconscionable today to promote Catholic Studies as monocultural. The experience of American Catholicism is too rich to neglect the contributions of different ethnicities and regions that shaped its past and are shaping its present contours. I also find that what in many instances has brought Catholic Studies into existence—the assimilation of a marginated group into the dominant U.S. culture and the experience of fragmentation that has accompanied the loss of a Catholic subculture—is actually a *strength* to be capitalized upon (emphasis in original).[14]

Hinsdale's emphasis on the irreducible pluralism of (American) Catholicism, doesn't so much correct those of Massa and Joncas as provide them with needed depth *and* breadth. It also suggests an ear for the underlying dynamic responsible for the emergence of Catholic Studies in the first place. Importantly, and in my estimation laudably, Hinsdale also recognizes that this pluralism will require an acknowledgement that Catholic Studies programs will likely, and legitimately, differ depending on such contingencies as the size and demographics of its host institution, its regional location, student profile, and founding religious tradition (if any). In short, as Hinsdale concludes, no "one size fits all," or, to paraphrase the late Senator Moynihan, "all Catholic Studies is (invariably) local."

Such a conclusion does not render nugatory further attempts to identify the phenomenon of Catholic Studies as a whole. Much remains to be known, and said. In fact, in the concluding section of this essay, I take up another of Hinsdale's final recommendations, that "listening to students should be one of the primary starting points" for those interested and involved in Catholic studies, to build not only on her typology, but those of Massa's and Joncas' as well.

LISTENING TO STUDENTS

It is worth repeating that the following observations are both limited in scope and partial in perspective. For the past two years I have directed the M.A. Program in Catholic Studies at the University of St. Thomas, home to one of the first, and among the largest, Catholic Studies Programs in the United States.[15] The students attracted to this program, and whose views I summarize below, are thus *not* undergraduates, even though a fair number of St. Thomas Catholic Studies majors apply for admission to the M.A. program every year. The views of these students, in other words, might not be a reliable guide for those interested in understanding Catholic Studies as primarily or only an undergraduate phenomenon. Secondly, my own convictions about what Catholic Studies is and ought to be (the very idea of Catholic Studies), inevitably affects what I have heard students telling me (or what I have read in their application essays). With these caveats, however, I have found the following to be among the dominant interests among students considering a degree in Catholic Studies.

Enrichment. For a significant number of students, Catholic Studies offers the opportunity simply to enrich their understanding and appreciation of their Catholic faith. In some degree this is true of every student interested in Catholic Studies with whom I have spoken; however, those for whom enrichment—another term could well be "adult-faith formation"—is the primary interest are often put off when they encounter the academic challenges of the program (close reading of texts, seminar discussion, research papers, exams, etc.). That such individuals are attracted to Catholic Studies in the first place is perhaps a reflection of the failure of their own parishes (or dioceses) to offer meaningful adult catechesis, their search for which draws into question as perhaps too hasty Joncas' distinction between the formation proper to the church and the academy. However, even if Catholic Studies programs are not equipped to meet the needs of such individuals—and not every program will have the resources to do so—the existence of such an interest suggests that one service a Catholic Studies program might provide is the creation and/or bolstering of such adult-faith enrichment programs at the parish level, or perhaps in one of the many diocesan "theology on tap" events one increasingly finds across the country.

Apologetics. A small but not insignificant number of students tell me that Catholic Studies interests them as a place where they might hone their evangelization-skills, which they intend to direct both at their fellow Catholics (of the lukewarm variety) as well as at Protestant and secularist co-workers. These are individuals who crave more than simply personal enrichment. They want to share their faith. Not surprisingly, many of them are newly converted, or "reverted" Catholics, with an interest in the clarity and coherence of doctrine, whether in part or whole. While individuals with apologetic interests tend to be more willing, and able, to undertake the historical, philosophical, theological, and literary study required of students in our program, their interests in evangelical outreach clearly drive their classroom pursuits. The precision and (presumed) completeness of neo-scholastic theology find a ready audience here.

It is worth reflecting here on what may be the single most likely explanation for the rising expression of interest in both enrichment and apologetics among many Catholics: the publication of the *Catechism of the Catholic Church* in 1993. For the first time in more than a generation, American Catholics have been able to take in hand, literally, the broad sweep of Catholic doctrine and practice, organized in a clear and compelling form, with the throw-weight of magisterial authority to boot. For many Catholics, especially those with "enquiring minds," encounter with the *Catechism* is surely an experience of intellectual awakening, providing their first inkling of the riches of the Catholic tradition and leaving them with a taste for more. If such persons are drawn toward the "restorationist" point of view that Massa, Joncas, and Hillsdale find so problematic, it may well be that "restorationist"-type programs (and other outlets, e.g., EWTN) understand this experience and are only too happy to provide the structure and clarity the newly awakened crave.

Foundations. A small number of students coming to the M.A. program in Catholic Studies are interested in further scholarly study, most often in the humanities, but also in the social sciences and fine arts. These individuals are not necessarily interested in the study of any particular subject matter, or even of something "distinctively Catholic." Indeed, they are typically coming fresh out of an undergraduate program in which they have spent the last two years fulfilling "major" requirements. Rather, what interests them is the broad, interdisciplinary focus of Catholic Studies, the opportunity to orient themselves with respect to the Catholic intellectual tradition as a whole—in its philosophical, theological, and literary expressions—prior to descending into the fragmented specialization of doctoral study.

These are normally the brightest and best-prepared students in the program, quite accustomed to the demands of academic life, and unencumbered by the burdens of family or work that beset the majority of students. These are also the students most likely to pursue the sort of advanced study singled out by Massa, Joncas, and to some extent Hinsdale, if only because they are the ones who will be earning the degrees that grant them access to the academic levels in which such work is engaged and validated. Such students, I would propose, will play a key role in sustaining the academic seriousness of Catholic Studies programs, but at this point in the history of Catholic Studies, it is unrealistic to expect them to constitute the majority.

Integration. By far the most common sentiment I hear from students drawn to the Catholic Studies M.A. program is a desire to integrate their Catholic faith into their lives as a whole. In many cases it is a question of bridging a gap between the affective, practical, and intellectual dimensions of their faith; but more often than not it is to bring the affective, practical, and intellectual to bear more coherently on their work and family life. Many students in our program have been recommended by their parish priest, and I can imagine that the prompting to do so grew out of an awareness that the sorts of questions these individuals were bringing to spiritual direction, or simply by repeatedly cornering the vicar at coffee and doughnuts after Sunday Mass, demanded a more extensive and systematic response than is possible in these contexts. The majority of students in our program are, in fact, professionals of one sort or another (business, law, medicine). For some, the pursuit of a Catholic Studies degree has meant a change of vocation, usually towards education. For most, however, the chance to engage the Catholic intellectual tradition, to discover their "love of learning" within their "desire for God," is its own reward.

Do these interests have anything in common? I believe they do. It is what I referred to above as an "originating experience," and my simple proposition is that no account or typology of the Catholic Studies phenomenon can be adequate that fails to address this experience. What every student interested in Catholic Studies whom I have listened to, or whose application essay I have read, expresses, without exception, is the sense that they perceive and intend the world as *Catholic* Christians, and are intrigued and fascinated by the prospect of continuing to do so; are intrigued and fascinated, that is, by what it means and requires to both be and become a *thinking* Catholic. There is both a joy and excitement to this, and most importantly a deep intellectual hunger.

There are, of course, multiple explanations for the sources of this intellectual awakening, and it may well be different for each student. Hinsdale's suggestions that the loss of a Catholic subculture among second- and third-generation Catholic immigrants, or the marginalization of Catholic scholarly interests in the academy, are surely correct, and bear more detailed scrutiny. Certainly we ought not overlook the emergence, over the past four decades, of an educated Catholic laity. Catholic higher education has doubtless had a lot to do with this, and rather than lamenting the state of theology (and I would add philosophy) departments at

Catholic colleges and universities, we might see Catholic Studies as a sign of their success in provoking in students a desire to become more articulate *Catholics*. Whatever its origins, it is this intellectual hunger, I propose, that lies at the heart of the current growth of Catholic Studies. As it matures, efforts to define more precisely the subject matter(s), method(s), and aims of Catholic Studies will continue to be an important task of Catholic Studies itself, and attending to this hunger will be necessary if its growth is to remain real. Just what Catholic Studies is to be, and it is unlikely to be any *one* thing: of that, we have as yet hardly any idea.

NOTES

1. Thomas M. Landy puts the beginning of Catholic Studies around 1997. See "Catholic Studies at Catholic Colleges and Universities," in John R. Wilcox and Irene King, eds., *Enhancing Religious Identity: Best Practices from Catholic Campuses* (Washington, D.C.: Georgetown University Press, 2000), 218-225. However, see the account by Don Briel of the origins of the Catholic Studies program at the University of St. Thomas, in which the origins of that program, among the first and largest, are slightly earlier. "Catholic Studies at the University of St. Thomas," *idem.*, 226-234.

2. I am unaware of any empirical data collected on the attitudes and views of Catholic Studies students, or faculty.

3. See Richard McKeon, "Dialogue and Controversy in Philosophy," *Philosophy and Phenomenological Research*, Vol. 17, No. 2 (Dec. 1956), 143-163.

4. Mark Massa, S.J., "American Catholic Studies: An Initial Typology," *U.S. Catholic Historian* 23 (Spring 2005), 45-52.

5. Massa, 45. Richard McCormick (and others) have referred to the same trend as "reconstructionism." See Richard A. McCormick, *The Critical Calling: Reflections on Moral Dilemmas Since Vatican II* (Georgetown University Press, 1989), *xviii.*

6. Massa, 47.

7. Massa, 47.

8. Massa, 49. As an example, Massa points to Robert Orsi's highly regarded study of Catholic belief and practice, *The Madonna of 115th Street: Faith and Community in Italian Harlem, 1880-1950* (New Haven: Yale University Press, 1985). As a brilliant evocation of the "tribal, *domus*-centered religion of the immigrants," Orsi's study is nevertheless flawed, argues Massa, because it fails to ask whether the sort of Catholicism on display ("priestly, therapeutic popular piety") represents "what the Church meant and means by 'Catholic Christianity.'" Massa thinks it doesn't because the "priestly" shape of Italian immigrant Catholicism during these years is "almost totally devoid of that 'prophet edge' that Christianity and Judaism have always accepted as basic to their message." *Idem*, 50.

9. Massa, 51.

10. J. Michael Joncas, "Thoughts on Catholic Studies," unpublished ms., 6 September 2005. All quotations are from this non-paginated manuscript.

11. *". . . The distinctive methodological stance of "Catholic Studies" as an academic discipline will be a recognition of the irreducibly multi-disciplinary character of its inquiry and its desire to integrate the findings of multiple humanistic, (possibly) social scientific, and meta-disciplinary insights into its work"* (emphasis in original). He elabo-

rates on how this might work using Augustine's *De Doctrina Christiana* (On Christian Doctrine): ". . . classics could help us translate the text from Latin to English, indicate A's particular form of Latinity, provide parallels to this type of liter-ature, etc.; history could help us situate the work in A's life and times and also indicate what influence the work had on later Christian and world thinkers . . . ; English could help us understand the rhetorical conventions and structuring of the work, A's use of symbolism and the move-ment of his thought . . . " etc.

12. Mary Ann Hinsdale, IHM, "Catholic Studies at BC? Continuing the Conversation" (unpublished ms.), address delivered at the Catholic Theological Society of America Annual Meeting, June 9, 2001. All references are to this text.

13. The motives are: 1) the answer to "Catholic identity;" 2) disillusionment/ disenfranchisement with post-modern scholarship (a.k.a., nostalgia); 3) a way to deal with religious illiteracy/loss of "a culture"; 4) evangelization ("handing on the faith"); and 5) the pursuit of knowledge (Catholicism is a world religion). The ideological stances: 1) conserving (a *past* culture, tradition, history); 2) dialogical (interacts with culture, moving toward a new synthesis); 3) pluralist (toleration with little or no analysis/evaluation).

14. Like Massa and Joncas, Hinsdale recommends Jewish Studies programs as a potential source of experience and insight for Catholic Studies programs. Her claim that parallel experiences with the gradual assimilation of immigrant ethnic/religious groupings into a dominant American culture, however, gives her recommendation a grounding and texture that Massa's and Joncas' lack.

15. The M.A. Program was founded in 2001 and currently enrolls approximately sixty students, the large majority of them part-time. The program was founded and directed for its first five years by Dr. Mary Reichardt of the English Department at the University of St. Thomas. For more information, consult the program website at http://www.stthomas.edu/cathstudies/masters/.

CATHOLIC STUDIES
AND THE MISSION OF THE
CATHOLIC UNIVERSITY

Richard M. Liddy

A faith that places itself on the margin of what is human, of what is therefore culture, would be a faith unfaithful to the fullness of what the Word of God manifests and reveals, a decapitated faith, worse still, a faith in the process of self-annihilation.

(John Paul II, *Ex corde ecclesiae*, 44)

This evening I received a newsletter called "Dimensions" from the Thomas More Center for the Study of Catholic Thought and Culture at Rockhurst University in Kansas. Among other news the letter announces upcoming courses in Catholic Studies, including a new course entitled "Catholic-Jewish-Muslim Interaction in the Middle Ages." This is just another indication, it seems to me, that Catholic Studies is an idea whose time has come.

Catholic Studies as a program in American universities had one of its significant beginnings in the early 1990s at the University of Saint Thomas in Saint Paul, Minnesota. Today that is virtually the flagship program in Catholic Studies with over 100 students majoring in Catholic Studies, a program in Rome, etc. Concomitantly, other programs have sprung up around the country. For the last two years the Curran Center for American Catholic Studies at Fordham University has hosted a meeting of Catholic Studies programs and the meeting has been attended by representatives of programs at both Catholic and secular institutions. I counted nineteen programs represented, but certainly there are more.

Not all the programs are named such: at Fordham the program is specifically one in American Catholic Studies; at Villanova there is a program in Augustinian Studies and Humanities; at Duke there is the beginnings of a Catholic Studies program under the religious studies program; etc. Then there is the Lumen Christi Institute in Chicago, which is independent of the University of Chicago, but in fact influenced by faculty at the University of Chicago. The common denominator seems to be the study of Catholicism as historical fact and, in some cases, a creative and theological orientation.

A number of these programs are undergraduate programs with minors or concentrations in Catholic Studies, but there are also a few, like our own at Seton Hall University, which has a major in Catholic Studies. (The University of Saint Thomas also has an Masters program in Catholic Studies.) The undergraduate major at Seton Hall—often a second major—consists of 36 credits with 6 basic courses and 6 electives. The basics include *Introduction to the Catholic Vision, Catholicism and Literature, Catholicism and Art, Catholic Social Teaching.* The remaining electives are chosen from concentrations in the Catholic intellectual tradition or the Catholic cultural tradition and are generally located in other departments: English, History, Classics, etc.

In this article I would like to address the following issues: 1) Catholic Studies and the rise of historical consciousness; 2) Catholic Studies and the loss of a unifying philosophical vision in Catholic universities; 3) Catholic Studies and the mission of Catholic universities; 4) "Catholicity": the promise of Catholic Studies; and 5) finally, as an addendum, centers of Catholic Studies. As will be obvious in this paper, I am indebted to the thought of Bernard Lonergan in my orientation towards Catholic Studies.

1) CATHOLIC STUDIES AND THE RISE OF HISTORICAL CONSCIOUSNESS

Bernard Lonergan in his writings sometimes employed the notion of "vertical finality" to explain the emergence of a new consciousness, a new feeling or awareness that here and there slowly gathers in intensity until a new social movement emerges. The existence of Catholic Studies programs would seem to be an instance of such an emergence. Nor is this kind of an emergence unique in the world of academia. Women's studies, American studies, African-American studies and various types of cultural studies would seem to be similar emergent trends. Typically, many faculty like to teach in such programs because they go beyond traditional curricular categories and embody current interests and questions.

But why Catholic Studies? And the retort can simply be: Why not?

After all, Catholicism has had and continues to have an enormous influence in world history. A recent book by Thomas Woods entitled *How the Catholic Church Built Western Civilization* (Regnery, 2005) captures for many a deep and lasting influence. Why not study that influence and that history? Nor need that study be uncritical: the flaws of the church as well as its triumphs can be studied in depth.

Such a world of historical study is still catching up with many Catholics. As a movement, critical historical study began, chiefly in Germany, in the latter part of the eighteenth century. It focused first on the ancient Greek and Roman classics and then, gradually, on the Jewish and Christian Scriptures. In fact, one could say that this movement of historical consciousness only caught up with a major part of the Catholic community at the Second Vatican Council with its acceptance of critical historical scholarship in the study of Scripture, etc. In many ways, Catholic Studies represents only a continuation of this movement of historical consciousness as researchers now study, for example, the immigrant communities that have came to America and have had such a major effect on the common life of America. The Cushwa Center at Notre Dame has been at the forefront of training scholars in these areas and Fordham's program in American Catholic Studies continues that trend. In my own area of New Jersey, Seton Hall University is sponsoring tours of local Catholic Churches in Newark, Jersey City and surrounding areas as people seek to reconstruct the roots of their own identity. Such study of "Catholic cultures" is a promising area of historical research. In a recent trip to Argentina I was struck by the particular brand of Catholicism there, a specific historically conditioned brand with its particular devotions, emphases, etc.

But such facts can be justifiably studied merely from an historical point of view with no intention of having a more immediate influence on contemporary practice. Thus, for example, one can study the work of Saint Thomas Aquinas without invoking Aquinas to shed light on contemporary issues. To quote Bernard Lonergan:

> When the study of Aquinas was enjoined on all students of philosophy and theology, what was envisaged was the assimilation of the basic tenets of Thomistic thought. But the first concern of historical scholarship is not to set forth and convince readers or hearers of the profundity of an author's thought, the breadth of his vision, the universal relevance of his conclusions. That sort of thing may be allowed to pad a preface or to fill out a conclusion. But the heart of the matter is elsewhere. It is a long journey through variant readings, shifts in vocabulary, enriching perspectives—all duly documented—that establish as definitively as can be expected what

the great man thought on some minor topic within the horizon of his time and place and with no great relevance to other times and places. Only from a long series of such dissertations can the full picture be constructed—a picture as accurate as it is intricate, broad indeed but with endless detail, rich in implications for other times if only one has the time to sort them out, discern the precise import of each, and infer exactly what does and does not follow. (*Philosophical and Theological Papers 1965-1980,* Toronto: University of Toronto Press, 2004, 281)

So one could say that Catholic Studies is the result of the Enlightenment catching up with Catholics, as with Vatican II a decidedly historical and empirical frame of reference took over from a more classical frame that articulated itself in terms of scholastic philosophy. This is one dimension of the emergence of Catholic Studies in the United States: a greater sensitivity to historical roots and a greater desire among many to uncover those roots. Such Catholic roots are studied both at Catholic universities and at secular universities and such a fact leads us to ask how Catholic Studies can be related to the specific mission of Catholic universities.

2) CATHOLIC STUDIES
AND THE LOSS OF A UNIFYING PHILOSOPHICAL VISION

But first I would point to another line from Bernard Lonergan: "Mere history is not theology." In other words, Catholic studies as history is not enough for the creative side of the Catholic vision, that is, a theology not only rooted in the past but as oriented toward the creation of the future. Let me use a bit of history to illustrate this.

For just as, with the Second Vatican Council, historical consciousness began to swamp Catholic universities, there also began to disappear from Catholic universities a unified philosophical framework, that is, the framework of scholastic philosophy. For without a doubt, what gave a certain unity to the whole Catholic academic enterprise in the early part of the twentieth century was the neo-scholastic philosophy that provided a framework for a unified Catholic world-view. As Philip Gleason put it in his masterful *Contending with Modernity: Catholic Higher Education in Twentieth Century America*, scholastic philosophy, not theology, was the lynchpin that held the whole academic structure together. Even today, I meet graduates of our Catholic universities who tell me that the most significant element in their undergraduate education was the "metaphysics" or the "logic." How many credits in philosophy were they required to take in those days? Twenty? Thirty? "That stuff taught you how to think," they will say to me. And as Gleason brought out in his book, such scholastic philosophy represented an impressive group of thinkers throughout the world—of the caliber of Etienne Gilson, Anton Pegis, Jacques Maritain.

> It was, in fact, a very large and important school which at its height supported 25 specialized journals throughout the world and engaged the commitment of thinkers the quality of whose work makes it impossible to dismiss the whole phenomenon as party-line philosophizing, however much that characterization might apply to many of those who taught it to American collegians. (116)

And the noted scholar David Tracy paid tribute to the role such neo-scholastic philosophy in Catholic colleges played in the world of American academics in general.

> People in this country too easily forget simple things, for example that it was the philosophy departments of Catholic universities that kept philosophy pluralistic in this country. They weren't taken over, as so many secular departments in this country were until recently, by analytical philosophy. It's been the philosophy departments of the great church-related, chiefly Catholic, institutions that kept alive philosophical forms that can help one think about religion and give one ways to approach theology. This is an intellectual benefit for the culture as a whole, as well as for the Catholic Church. (*America*, October 14, 1995, 18)

It was in fact, then, Catholic philosophy that unified the academic mission of Catholic universities in those days, as even psychology courses treated questions of "body and soul" and scholastic terminology seeped into other courses as well. But it was not to last. The unified Catholic mission of Catholic universities was swamped by modern empirical scientific/historical methods and the questions among committed Catholics in higher education since the 1970s have been: "Have we thrown the baby out with the bathwater?" "How can we avoid relativism?" "Is there any possibility for a unified vision of the whole academic enterprise in the Catholic university?" "Can the mission of the Catholic university ever again influence the academic curriculum?" Bernard Lonergan recognized that the dissolution of classical culture threatened a unified viewpoint among Catholics.

> So it is that modern culture is the culture that knows about other cultures, that relates them to one another genetically, that knows all of them to be man-made. Far more open than classicist culture, far better informed, far more discerning, it lacks the convictions of its predecessor, its clear-cut norms, its elemental strength. (*A Second Collection,* Toronto: University

of Toronto Press, 1996, 92)

Nevertheless, it is important to note that the prevalence of historical consciousness in Catholic universities over the past forty years has not been without theological foundation. For Christianity is an inherently historical religion. It is rooted in particular times and places and it has always taken the cultures of particular times and places seriously. Neoscholasticism as it was generally presented was incapable of integrating modern discoveries in science and historical consciousness into a unified world view. Vatican II's recognition of the autonomy of the various disciplines, such as the discipline of history, is a direct result of changes in Catholicism's developing stance with regard to modern culture. Where previously there had been a pronounced tendency to stand apart and condemn the whole modern project, the tendency of Vatican II was much more pastoral and discerning. While not plumping for an uncritical embrace of all things modern, the tendency of contemporary Catholicism is to discern the wheat from the chaff, the tinsel from the silver, the counterfeit from the gold. But how to do that? That's the trick.

3) CATHOLIC STUDIES
AND THE MISSION OF THE CATHOLIC UNIVERSITY

What then does an historically grounded Catholic Studies have to do with the mission of the Catholic university? Could Catholic Studies conceivably be related to a Catholic and unified vision of the academic life of the university? I think it can. But to do that it has to have at its disposal an adequate philosophy, capable of integrating scholasticism's intention of linking faith and reason within contemporary culture. It needs a philosophy sophisticated enough to deal with modern historical and scientific methods and to integrate such methods into an overall vision of humanity in the world today: a humanity that from a Christian point of view is created in the image and likeness of God and destined for eternal union with God. What is needed is something like Newman's "science of the sciences," that is, a philosophical theology that can bring all the disciplines in the university into a unified theological vision.

Such was Bernard Lonergan's vision of metaphysics as integrating, purifying and transforming all the disciplines. For that the modern scientific and historical disciplines—fragmented, each in its own "silo"—need integrating into a comprehensive and inspiring vision is certainly a felt need, not only among Catholics but also among others in the academic world. And that the various disciplines need some philosophical purifying is also obvious to many. Psychology, sociology or economics that treat the human person merely as an animal responding to stimuli—or less—need to be brought within a more dignified vision of the human person. So also, a contemporary humanism needs to bequeath hope to the contemporary world.

And so there is need for philosophical theology in a Catholic Studies program: that is, for a theology, as the Latin puts it, in *oratione directa*, that is, in direct speech. Having studied the past, we dare to make direct statements about the present and what's worth creating in the future. Such a systematic theology can stand as a framework or vision statement, not only for the Catholic Studies program, but for the whole mission of the Catholic university.

4. FROM CATHOLIC TO CATHOLICITY:
THE PROMISE OF CATHOLIC STUDIES

Let me give you an example of what I mean. John Haughey, S.J., at the Woodstock Theological Center, Georgetown University, has initiated a program on the Catholic mission of Catholic universities that focuses on the "catholicity" of the disciplines: and even more, on the faculty teaching those disciplines. That is, "catholicity" with a small "c"—whatever heads for wholeness. The workshops that Haughey convenes typically begin with asking faculty—whether Catholic or not—what brought them into the disciplines they are teaching. A particularly engaging teacher? A moment of insight? A realization that one could contribute in a particular way? This autobiographical account is very important for it engages people in their own reasons for becoming a teacher in this or that area—"the dream" that sparked their academic journey.

A further element in the workshop consists in posing the question: how does what you are doing in your discipline contribute to the common good? What is "the whole" to which your academic work contributes? (Haughey tells the story of the business school teacher who, against reigning academic preferences, researched the role "vengeance" played in the workplace.) The point is to name the "whole" towards which my work is tending: that towards which my own work, along with others in other fields, contributes.

It is this vision of "catholicity" with a small "c" to which Catholicity with a capital "C" must contribute. It is out of such concern with the wholeness of the disciplines and the public good to which they should be contributing that particular questions for Catholicism can be put: What is the society we are building? What kind of people are we becoming? And how can Catholic faith and belief contribute to such goals?

How can the Catholic vision of the Triune God, the Incarnation of the Word, the gift of the Holy Spirit, be related to our human activities? Can such a vision make a difference?

The point here is to ask: How do Catholic Studies relate to "catholicity" and vice versa? Could Catholic Studies contribute by not only detailing the historical contributions of Catholics to social justice but also by outlining a vision of society-wide cooperation that could "change the face of the earth?" Could Catholic Social teaching, rooted in Catholic faith and belief, make a difference in the future that with our neighbors we seek to build?

5) AN ADDENDUM: CENTERS FOR CATHOLIC STUDIES

At Seton Hall our efforts in Catholic Studies have focused largely on faculty development with faculty from various departments and of various beliefs regularly gathering for dialogue on humanistic and religious issues. These dialogues have been very well received. One faculty member called them the best academic experience she had had at the university.

But how to guarantee that such experiences be regularly available to the faculty? At Seton Hall we have found that the formation of a Center for Catholic Studies gives us the leeway for creating such opportunities for faculty development. The formation of a center allows for funding outside the normal university structures while at the same time fostering cooperation on various projects with various parts of the university. Not only does the center oversee the running of the undergraduate program, but it allows for efforts at dialogue in various directions. Currently at Seton Hall the Center for Catholic Studies includes the Chesterton Institute for Faith and Culture, the Bernard J. Lonergan Institute, the Institute on Work, and the Micah Program for Senior Executives. All these efforts are interdisciplinary and represent the Church through this Catholic university reaching out to dialogue with various aspects of modern culture. The creation of the Center for Catholic Studies gives us the flexibility to support these other centers and to contribute to a unified vision of the human person and society rooted in the Triune life of God—within a complex world with its many disciplines, professions and areas of concern.

CATHOLIC STUDIES PROGRAMS: CATALYSTS FOR REVIVING THE CATHOLIC INTELLECTUAL TRADITION IN HIGHER EDUCATION

David Gentry-Akin

Just outside the Hesburgh Memorial Library at the University of Notre Dame, near the reflecting pool and below the famous mosaic often humorously referred to "Touchdown Jesus," is an impressive bronze likeness of Father Theodore Hesburgh, CSC, president emeritus of this great Catholic university. At the base of the statue, one finds these words of Father Hesburgh: "A Catholic University should be a *beacon,* bringing to light, in modern focus, the wonderfully traditional and ancient adage, 'faith seeking understanding', it should be a *bridge* across all chasms that separate modern people from each other, and it should be a *crossroads* where all the intellectual and moral currents of our times meet and are thoughtfully considered." It is my thesis that Father Hesburgh's words constitute an excellent charter for any Catholic institution of higher learning, that such institutions are more desperately needed by our culture than at any time in the past, and that many of these institutions in the United States are also in grave peril of losing touch with the very source of their founding inspiration. Even if they do survive as institutions, they may survive only as shadows of their former selves, and may fail entirely to make the vital contribution to the renewal of our culture that they were once uniquely equipped to make.

THE EROSION OF CATHOLIC CULTURE SINCE VATICAN II

It is well documented that, since the Second Vatican Council ended in 1965, American Catholic culture has undergone dramatic changes and weathered more than a few crises. Concurrent with the end of Vatican II, the assimilation of American Catholics into the mainstream of public life in the United States was considered complete. The election of the first president of the United States to be of the Roman Catholic faith, John F. Kennedy, is often referenced as being symbolic of that assimilation. The deliberations of the Second Vatican Council were marked by a wonderful spirit of optimism about the world and a willingness to engage the world in all of its diversity that was, by and large, welcomed by American Catholics. The church began to change, and many of the cultural markers that had once clearly identified a distinctive Catholic sub-culture in the United States began to disappear: the celebration of Mass in Latin, the prevalence of devotions like eucharistic adoration and benediction, the rosary and novenas, abstinence from meat on Fridays and the strict fasts observed during Lent, the distinctive habits worn by Catholic Sisters, etc., etc.

The point here is not to decry the loss of these cultural markers or to suggest that we could overcome our present crisis by reclaiming them in an uncritical way, as some might argue. Rather, whatever our perspective on the dramatic changes in Catholicism since the Second Vatican Council, it is crucial to recognize that the erosion of Catholic culture that followed the collapse of the "thick" sub-culture prevalent before Vatican II has brought us to a new moment, with new challenges, in the history of the American church and of American Catholic Higher Education. As is well documented, after the Second Vatican Council, institutions of Catholic higher education embarked on a program of "opening to the world" that led them to diversify their curricula, their faculties, and their student bodies. In most cases, sponsoring religious congregations ceded ownership and control of these institutions to Boards of Trustees composed of mixed groups of lay people and representatives of the sponsoring congregation. In an effort to escape the so-called "ghetto mentality" that is often thought to have characterized Catholic Higher Education before the Second Vatican Council, these institutions made an option to compete in the mainstream of American higher education and to strive for "excellence" as it is defined in the mainstream.

Prior to the late 1960s, Catholic colleges and universities, of course, offered multiple majors and had many fine faculty who had a profound impact on many generations of students. Most of these institutions, however, were liberal arts colleges that judged their success, not by the number of majors they offered or by the number of advanced degrees they awarded, but by the extent to which they were successful in passing on the Catholic faith and the Catholic intellectual tradition to the next generation. They were concerned, of course, with academic excellence, but they were also preoccupied with a desire to form women and men of deep character and enduring faith commitment, women and men who would make substantial contributions of a human and moral nature to the church and to the wider culture. After the mid-1960's, these institutions adopted new norms of excellence that had less to do with the degree to which they promoted a particular worldview or communicated a unique ethos, and more to do with the number of majors they offered, the number of advanced degrees they awarded, and the percentage of their faculty who were highly published or otherwise recognized in their respective fields. All of those, it could be argued, are good things, but none of them will necessarily contribute anything to the transmission of Catholic culture to the next generation.

All of this brings us to a new moment in our consideration of the mission of Catholic colleges and universities. While there have been many gains as a result of the choices that have been made in the past forty years, there have also been some serious losses, as documented in books such as James T. Burtchaell's *The Dying of the Light* and, more recently, in Melanie M. Morey's and John J. Piderit's *Catholic Higher Education: A Culture in Crisis.* Documents of the Holy See, such as the Apostolic Constitution *Ex Corde Ecclesiae*, published by John Paul II in 1990, have called us to examine the extent to which, in our desire to embrace the modern world, we have been uncritical in our assimilation of contemporary culture and, further, have sacrificed or downplayed some elements of our own tradition in order to find acceptance and respectability in that culture.

THE CATHOLIC INTELLECTUAL VISION

As Thomas E. Woods argues in his recent book, *How the Catholic Church Built Western Civilization,* the church's contribution to the preservation of civilization, the development of the university, to science, art and architecture, Western and international law, economics, social thought and practice, and morality is of monumental proportions. As Woods notes, "All of these areas: economic thought, international law, science, university life, charity, religious ideas, art, morality—these are the very foundations of a civilization, and in the West every single one of them emerged from the heart of the Catholic Church."[1] The problem we face, however, in our contemporary milieu is that, on the one hand, these contributions have been so sanitized of their religious context that few of our students have any idea of what the church has given to society. On the other hand, the contribution that these fields of inquiry—now alienated from their religious roots and suffering from historical amnesia—might make to the ongoing development and elaboration of the Catholic tradition is also diminished. The present challenge for the Catholic intellectual tradition and those who are committed to it is precisely to seek to recover these connections and revitalize the conversation between the Catholic tradition and the disciplines in such a way that the religious tradition and the disciplines themselves are both made richer for the encounter.

THE LEGACY OF CATHOLIC HIGHER EDUCATION

The story of Catholic education in this country is one of such staggering vision, commitment, and sacrifice on the part of many generations of faithful people—women and men religious, lay, and clerical alike—that it can only be described as "heroic." They founded institutions of higher education to give immigrant Catholics, and others who found themselves on the margins of society, access to higher education, and thus to the possibilities of a better quality of life in the United States. But, just as importantly, they founded these institutions in order to hand on—in all of its beauty, wisdom, and vitality—the Catholic faith to future generations. While they sought to give their students access to "the American Dream," they were equally committed to bequeathing to their students a love for, and a grounding in, the Catholic faith that would serve them well throughout their lives. What they sought to hand on was not merely Catholic theology or the Catholic religion understood in isolation, but rather what might be best described as the Catholic Wisdom Tradition— a tradition deeply rooted in human and Christian values that offers not only doctrinal teaching or moral guidelines, but more importantly a philosophy of life and a perspective from which to examine any question posed by one's existential circumstances or the culture at large.

In spite of all of the financial pressures facing American Catholic Higher Education, there is much evidence that many of our institutions continue to be faithful to their social justice inspiration. We continue to educate many first-generation college students from poor and working class backgrounds, and to provide those young women and men with an education far superior to what they could find in the public sector, both in terms of the caliber of instruction and the level of individual attention that each student receives. Are we, however, being faithful to the task of handing on a knowledge, love, and appreciation of the Catholic faith to all of the students who have come through our doors, Catholic and non-Catholic alike? Or have we merely surrendered to the "forces of the marketplace," seeing our students merely as "consumers" who will not elect to enroll in our institutions unless they are given "what they want"? Such a strategy may assure economic survival in the short term, but it is a recipe for spiritual and intellectual suicide in the long term. In the race to the bottom, to the lowest common denominator, every institution will simply look like every other, and will increasingly have to struggle to maintain any unique identity.

OUR FAILURE AS EFFECTIVE AGENTS
FOR THE TRANSMISSION OF CATHOLIC FAITH AND CULTURE

It is the contention of this article that many of our institutions, for varied and complex reasons, are failing their students in regard to the passing on of the precious legacy of Catholic faith and the Catholic intellectual tradition. Some of the right-wing backlash that many of us experience on our campuses can be attributed to our failure in this regard. While I am not always sympathetic with the tactics employed by those often identified as being "on the right," I find myself, increasingly, to be in sympathy with their essential and most urgent concern: Catholic Higher Education is going the way of the many institutions of higher learning in our society which were once faith based institutions but which have long ago ceased to be so. At so many of these institutions, Catholic culture is no longer the healthy, vibrant, and dynamic force on campus that it once was. To allow this erosion of Catholic identity to continue unchecked is to completely and utterly fail to honor the memories of the generations of faithful women and men who built these institutions on faith and at enormous sacrifice.

The reasons for this failure are many and complex. Young people no longer come to college in the homogenized cohorts of an earlier era, ready to participate in the kinds of prayer, faith sharing, theological exploration, and ministry opportunities that once characterized the Catholic college campus. It could once be assumed that most of the young people coming to us had a foundation in the Catholic faith—intellectually, affectively, socially, and culturally—that would allow them to be engaged in higher level theological discourse, and this is, sadly, no longer the case. If Catholic colleges and universities are going to fulfill their responsibilities today, then we must admit that our students come to us with a deficit in religious literacy not unlike the deficits we find in other areas, like mathematics or composition and rhetoric. Just as we have implemented remedial programs to assist students with deficits in math or English, so we may have to implement remedial programs in Catholicism. Some would decry this approach as the "dumbing down" of college education, but it is complete abdication of our responsibility to blithely indulge our desire to teach advanced courses in theology when our students do not even have the basic tools that would enable them to contextualize and to appreciate the advanced subject matter to which we seek to expose them. Consistent with the need to provide remediation but also to uphold college level standards so that a college degree continues to hold currency, we must develop strategies for taking students "where they are," giving them the tools to succeed, and then challenging them to do serious college level work.

With the abandonment of the scholastic, neo-Thomistic paradigm prevalent before the Second Vatican Council, curricula in Catholic colleges and universities became so diversified so that, in many institutions, the core curriculum became little more than a set of "distribution requirements" in which different disciplines were represented, thus assuring that students would be exposed to different modes of inquiry, but with little or no advocacy of any kind of integral vision. In the push to multiply majors that was part and parcel of the effort to go "mainstream," Catholic institutions succumbed to the pressures of specialization that are endemic to contemporary academe, and this, too, contributed to the demise of the endeavor to communicate to students a cohesive vision of life rooted in the best of the Catholic Wisdom Tradition. In order to staff the proliferation of majors, faculty were increasingly hired because of their competence in an academic specialization, with little or no attention given to whether they were prepared to contribute anything of significance to the ongoing project of the development and promotion the Catholic intellectual tradition. All of these changes were well intentioned and it could be argued that many of them contributed to the enhanced academic excellence of these institutions, but at what cost vis a vis our most sacred trust: the handing on of the Catholic Wisdom Tradition? Can we engage in an honest self-assessment and assert that our founding mothers and fathers would find that what we are doing today is consistent with their original vision and inspiration?

STRATEGIES FOR ADDRESSING OUR PRESENT SITUATION

If one accepts the basic outline of my argument thus far, one is left with the question as to what can be done at this juncture. As argued above, many Catholic institutions are highly "diverse" in terms of the composition of their faculties and student bodies. While there are ways in which it can be argued that this diversity is a strength, that exposing students to multiple perspectives strengthens their critical thinking skills and equips them for living and working in an increasingly pluralistic world, this approach also has its weaknesses. Will students leave our institutions with a sense of what the Catholic intellectual tradition can contribute to helping them find meaning and purpose in the world, or will they leave equipped only with the kind of relativistic philosophy that is endemic to contemporary academe? Are we serving our students well if all we have given them, ultimately, is an appreciation for diverse perspectives and a sense of tolerance for individual views? Is this philosophy really anything more than a form of secular humanism? What perspective, what set of values, is going to give unity to our curricula and a sense of identity, common purpose, and community to our campuses? If not our Catholic faith, then what? Our fidelity to our founding mothers and fathers and our commitment to the well being and future happiness of our students demands more of us. *Ex Corde Ecclesiae* offers four essential principles that could be fruitfully employed as criteria for examining the degree to which we are being faithful to the Catholic intellectual vision: 1) the search for an integration of knowledge, 2) a dialogue between faith and reason, 3) an ethical concern, and 4) a theological perspective.[2] These are the hallmarks by which a Catholic college or university culture can be identified.

Since the publication of *Ex Corde Ecclesiae,* a proliferation of books has appeared exploring the question from various perspectives, relating success stories, and examining long-range strategies for the maintenance and renewal of the religious identity of faith-based institutions of higher learning. Among the texts worthy of mention are *The Challenge and Promise of a Catholic University* (1994) edited by Theodore M. Hesburgh; *As Leaven in the World: Catholic Perspectives on Faith, Vocation, and the Intellectual Life* (2001) edited by Thomas Landy; *Enhancing Religious Identity: Best Practices from Catholic Campuses* edited by John Wilcox and Irene King (2000); *Examining the Catholic Intellectual Tradition,* volumes one (2000) and two (2002), edited by Anthony J. Cernera and Oliver J. Morgan; and *Quality With Soul: How Six Premier Colleges and Universities Keep Faith with Their Religious Traditions* (2001) by Robert Benne. A number of institutions around the country—among which Boston College (Boston, Massachusetts), Sacred Heart University (Fairfield, Connecticut), the University of Notre Dame (South Bend, Indiana), and the University of Saint Thomas (Saint Paul, Minnesota) are worthy of special note—are developing bold and promising new initiatives to respond to the crisis in Catholic Higher Education. At the University of Notre Dame, for example, under the presidential leadership of Father John I. Jenkins, CSC, a new project is underway— led by Erasmus Institute Director Father Robert Sullivan—for developing new ways of identifying, training, and recruiting Catholic scholars. Another project, the *Catholic Traditions Initiative,* is "a comprehensive educational program that will help faculty of all religious traditions incorporate Catholic intellectual, theological, and spiritual traditions into their work in various academic disciplines."[3]

The problem can obviously be tackled on many fronts: efforts to augment the resources and enhance the quality of Campus Ministry Programs and Residence Life programs can be very helpful, but to stop there might only result in simply reinforcing "the general trend in American culture to marginalize religious questions to restricted areas of inquiry and public commitment."[4] Ultimately, however, the heart of an educational institution is to be found in its curriculum and in its faculty. If the Catholic tradition is not present there, in a vibrant way, all other efforts are sure to be marginalized and, therefore, only minimally effective. In an earlier era, the Catholic college faculty was distinctive from that of a secular institution in virtue of the presence of strong Catholic philosophy and theology departments and curricular requirements, but Catholic thought did not stop there, and could also be found to permeate courses taught in other disciplines, such as literature or the arts. Thus, the student was challenged, implicitly and explicitly, to think about the connection of faith to all aspects of the life of the mind and to material reality in all its forms.

CATHOLIC STUDIES: AN INTERDISCIPLINARY VENTURE

The core curriculum, of course, is the primary vehicle through which an institution can endeavor to communicate its ethos, mission, and values to its students, and vigorous efforts must be made to design and implement core curricula that are inspired by the principles of the Catholic Intellectual Tradition.

An institution can gauge the presence and vitality of the Catholic intellectual tradition on its campus by the degree to which the footprint of that tradition is discernable in its Core Curriculum, but it must be acknowledged that the Core Curriculum of an institution is under great pressure to cover many areas of contemporary inquiry and to respond to many constituencies and so it may not be able to carry the task alone. Anyone who has ever served on a Core Curriculum Task Force can attest to the challenges and difficulties inherent in attempting to craft a core that will be responsive to all of the exigencies of a given institution. In the past fifteen years, however, very interesting experiments have been popping up at institutions across the country with a new phenomenon called "Catholic Studies." These programs, when they are truly interdisciplinary in design and led and staffed by faculty who are deeply rooted in the tradition and balanced in their approach, offer the best hope for trying to bequeath to students an organic sense of the Catholic intellectual vision. They are the best hope for freeing Catholicism from its current "ghettoization" in Theology or Religious Studies departments and requirements and Campus Ministry or Service Learning programs. They are the best hope for arousing the appetites of faculties from across all disciplines for an engagement in the challenge and the promise of the Catholic intellectual project.

Far from the prevailing conventional wisdom, a Catholic Studies program is *not* a program in Catholic theology. It is *not* a reactionary program that seeks to offer an "orthodox" alternative to what is being taught in the theology or religious studies department of a given institution. It does not seek to replace or duplicate the crucial function of a theology department within the Catholic university. It does not replace or render superfluous the need for comparative religious studies of diverse traditions such as Judaism, Islam, Hinduism, or Buddhism in our increasingly diverse and dangerous world.

A Catholic Studies program is, rather, one in which the unique resources of the Catholic wisdom tradition—intellectual, moral, social, and aesthetic—are given pride of place and are referenced and developed in light of what they can teach us about what it means to be human and to be religious in our contemporary world. The courses that one might legitimately find in a Catholic Studies program could include the treatment of the Catholic contributions to the worlds of literature, history, the arts, the natural and social sciences, and the professions. In such a program, one might find that content as diverse as the fiction of Flannery O'Connor or Walker Percy; the role of Pope Pius XII in the Second World War; a contemporary Catholic perspective on the creation/evolution debate, the contemporary ecological crisis, or economic globalization; Carl Jung's appreciation—from an anthropological and psychological perspective—of the Catholic Mass; and the contribution of Catholic Social Teaching to the practice of the professions of law, medicine, or business.[5]

A Catholic Studies program is an effort to recover a sense of the integral vision of Christian humanism that is at the heart of the Catholic tradition, and to bring that vision to bear on conversations across all of the disciplines being studied in a college or a university. A Catholic Studies program, at its best, will explore the intersection of knowledge that is to be found when the wisdom of the Catholic tradition comes into contact with all of the various fields of intellectual endeavor. What does the Catholic wisdom tradition have to say to each of these fields of inquiry? And in what ways do those fields of inquiry challenge the Catholic tradition to explore new questions that will contribute to its own vitality and ongoing development?

To be sure, a Catholic Studies program must certainly be rooted in the Catholic philosophical and theological traditions, but from the perspective of those traditions it seeks to do exactly what Father Hesburgh describes as the mission of a Catholic university: to be a *beacon* for the integration of faith and reason, a place within the university where questions of faith and reason are given privileged status; to be a *bridge* that seeks to bring all people of good will together around a consideration of what the Catholic tradition has to offer to the exploration of the most urgent questions confronting our world; to be a *crossroads* where all of the intellectual and moral currents of our times can be thoughtfully considered from the perspective of the Catholic wisdom tradition.

CATHOLIC STUDIES AS A STRATEGY FOR CURRICULAR RENEWAL AND FACULTY DEVELOPMENT

A Catholic Studies program can also have important institutional benefits for a Catholic college or university and its faculty. It can create a space within in an institution for moving beyond the "ghettoization" of Catholicism in the academy and the "silo mentality" that is often endemic to the other disciplines that make up the contemporary college curriculum. It can create an environment in which the myths surrounding Catholic teaching—myths under which even otherwise highly intelligent people often labor—can be dispelled. It can create an opening for further conversation and dialogue that can lead to fruitful developments in all the disciplines and in the Catholic tradition itself. The creation of a Catholic Studies Program also provides administrators with an important opportunity for shaping the faculty in ways that will enhance its potential for contributing to the mission of the institution over the long haul. The need to staff a program of Catholic Studies can provide the college or university with the opportunity to hire Catholic scholars in all of the disciplines who will contribute not only to the building up of the program itself but who will also contribute, by virtue of the teaching and research interests that they will bring to their respective departments, to a greater understanding of, and a consequent respect of and hospitality for, the Catholic intellectual tradition among their own departmental colleagues.

CATHOLIC STUDIES AND RELIGIOUS AND CULTURAL ECUMENISM

Catholic Studies is, by definition, an interdisciplinary field. What has the Catholic tradition contributed to the fields of literature, history, art, architecture, music, the natural and social sciences, and the practice of the professions? In addition to its primary role as a means of handing on Catholic faith and culture to the next generation, a Catholic Studies program can also have a distinctly ecumenical role. Through the Catholic Studies program, Catholic scholars can be invited to dialogue with people of other faiths or with people of good will who eschew faith altogether, with people who are trained in a variety of disciplines and who are interested in the dialogue of faith and culture, people who seek to bring their experiences and insights to the Catholic Wisdom Tradition so that those experiences and insights can both critique, and be critiqued by, the tradition. While a Catholic Studies program will undoubtedly find itself in the role of explaining or defending the faith in a contemporary culture that is increasingly ignorant of and hostile toward it, such a program, if it is to have any scholarly integrity, must avoid the temptation of being purely apologetic in nature. It must be willing to confront and examine the "shadow" side of Catholic faith and culture; to examine those times in the history of the church in which the church has failed to live up to its own deepest insights and self-understanding. Thus, a Catholic Studies program might sponsor dialogues between Catholic and Jewish scholars, between Catholic and feminist scholars, between Catholic scholars and representatives of the scientific academy, or between Catholic scholars and members of the lesbian and gay community.

THE RENEWAL OF THE CATHOLIC INTELLECTUAL TRADITION AND HOPE FOR THE FUTURE

The thrust of a Catholic Studies program which hopes to be a catalyst for the renewal of Catholic intellectual and cultural life on our campuses must be on bringing the wisdom of the Catholic Tradition to bear on all those concerns and issues that are of urgency in our times. As the Fathers of the Second Vatican Council tell us in the opening lines of *Gaudiam et spes:* "The joys and the hopes, the griefs and the anxieties of the [people] of this age, especially those who are poor or in any way afflicted, these are the joys and hopes, the griefs and anxieties of the followers of Christ. Indeed, nothing genuinely human fails to raise an echo in their hearts."[6] Those who are committed to the future of the church must have enough faith in the resiliency of the tradition to allow it to be interrogated by the experience of people who have encountered it in painful ways. Very often people have been hurt or alienated from the Church because the tradition was poorly, inadequately, or only partially communicated to them. The rich context for dialogue that a vibrant Catholic Studies program can offer will provide people with an opportunity to explore, understand, and appreciate the Catholic Wisdom Tradition in all of its multi-faceted dimensions. And, the Catholic tradition itself will be enhanced by such dialogue. We will learn better how to communicate the truths of the gospel and the patrimony of the Catholic Faith.

NOTES

1. Thomas E. Woods, Jr., *How The Catholic Church Built Western Civilization* (Washington, DC: Regnery Publishing Company, Inc., 2005), 221.
2. Pope John Paul II, *Ex Corde Ecclesiae*, paragraph 15.
3. *Notre Dame Now: Development News from the University of Notre Dame.* Fall 2006.
4. Don Briel, "Catholic Studies and the University of Saint Thomas" in John Wilcox and Irene King, *Enhancing Religious Identity: Best Practices from Catholic Campuses* (Washington, DC: Georgetown University Press, 2000), 227.
5. Thomas Landy, in his article "Catholic Studies at Catholic Colleges and Universities,"
notes that De Paul University in Chicago listed, at one time, no fewer than 85 courses in its Catholic Studies Program, including such topics as "Catholicism in Africa," "Catholic Faith and Musical Expression," "The Catholic Church in World Politics," "Economics and the Common Good," "Catholicism and Race," and "The Life and Times of Saint Vincent De Paul." At Santa Clara University in California, Landy notes, elective courses include "Dante," "Theology and Science," and "The Church in China." At LaSalle University in Philadelphia, courses included "The Cult of the Virgin and the Saints: Art, Architecture, and Religion" and "Creation and Evolution." See Thomas Landy, "Catholic Studies at Catholic Colleges and Universities," in John Wilcox and Irene King, *Enhancing Religious Identity: Best Practices from Catholic Campuses* (Washington, DC: Georgetown University Press, 2000), 221.
6. Second Vatican Council, *Gaudiam et spes*, paragraph 1.

THE (LONGED-FOR) VARIETIES OF CATHOLIC STUDIES

James A. Fisher

Catholic Studies is unusual among interdisciplinary academic projects for its self-referential character. In traditional interdisciplinary enterprises like American Studies—arguably the oldest and the one with a history of which I am familiar—there is certainly a self-referential element evident in such perennial queries as "what is *American* about American Studies?" Though it has been decades since the conceit of "American exceptionalism" shaped inquiry in the field, even then practitioners were challenged to seek connections with the broadest range of disciplines. Recent political debates over the centrality of ethnic, gender, and queer studies (to name just a few subfields) are always accompanied by practical and methodological discussions over, say, the prospects or desirability of a coherent American Studies practice grounded in the collective strength of its diverse foundations. The field thrives in its self-perceived un-centeredness: its boundaries are perpetually challenged.

Catholic Studies has evolved in different fashion. In Catholic colleges and universities, Catholic Studies is largely driven by a single concern that blends pastoral, political, ecclesiastical and ideological dimensions: "How do we preserve the Catholic identity of our colleges and universities?" At such places Catholic Studies is asked to re-constitute a core religious identity seemingly imperiled by forces far too numerous to list. This newer field has increasingly privileged a single constituent discipline—theology—and has moved toward consensus on the value of a unifying vision of a historic "Catholic culture" that is grounded in an approach to history different than those taken by the professional cultural historians I know. In the case of those Catholic Studies endowed chairs that have popped up on public and private non-Catholic campuses in recent years, the politics of donor relations have often produced a surprisingly analogous "mission" to present a unified vision of Catholic thought and culture as a saving alternative to secularism. Such positions however will likely feature over time more diversity (two good examples being the recently established Monsignor Thomas J. Hartmann Chair of Catholic Studies at Hofstra University and the Virgil Cordano Chair in Catholic Studies at UC Santa Barbara, occupied by Professors Julie Byrne and Ann Taves, respectively) and less concern with identity issues that suffuse the Catholic Studies phenomenon at what critics (or cynics) might call "historically Catholic" colleges and universities.[1]

I'm neither a theologian nor a theorist of any stripe so my reflections here are profoundly limited in applicability even as the sense of urgency in preserving "Catholic identity" at Catholic colleges intensifies. I cannot pretend to offer a coherent approach to Catholic studies or a "vision" for the future; nor do I know what is found in practice elsewhere beyond discussions with friends and colleagues and from an occasional campus visit. I can only offer experience and observation rooted in my own field, American Catholic Studies. When I accepted an endowed chair position focusing on American Catholicism at Saint Louis University in 1994 I was scarcely aware this was likely the first academic position ever formulated in "American Catholic Studies." Though the label itself had not yet been invented the job was advertised in such a way as to encourage candidates with backgrounds in interdisciplinary fields to apply. The fact that the position was to be housed in a theology department was of little concern: I was an untenured Associate Professor of American Studies at Yale at the time, with a "courtesy" joint appointment in Religious Studies; it was time to move on. I was lucky to have other options present themselves in American Studies, but this was the height of the culture wars and I found appealing the notion of working from a broader cultural foundation in Catholic and especially Jesuit tradition. What's in a name? I figured I could move to the nation's heartland and continue—in a Jesuit setting—the work in American Catholic cultural studies I had begun in the distinctly non-Ignatian locales of New Brunswick, New Jersey (history graduate school) and New Haven.

That part worked out fine. The tough stuff was in negotiating a local sphere of influence for an avowedly experimental approach to the study and teaching of the American Catholic experience. Much of it was on me: I could be loud and belligerent (then surely more than now!); the explanation that it was a Jersey thing only went so far. There were also local issues that pre-dated my arrival that belong to the generic category of departmental/personal politics; every academic setting produces its own version of this master narrative. But there were also some issues in play of broader significance for the evolving project of Catholic studies nationwide. Saint Louis University was founded in 1818: as of 1994 the institution had never hired anyone to teach and write about Catholicism that was not either a priest or (more recently and much less often) a member of a Catholic women's religious community; categories that had expanded in recent years to include inactive or laicized priests and ex-seminarians. Even the small but very lively cohort of Protestant faculty was ordained to ministry in their own traditions.

It took me a while to notice this fact and even longer to discern its importance. What was true in 1994 may well be even truer in 2006: Catholic intellectual authority in America is inseparable from the "formation" process in which "Catholic knowledge" has almost invariably been grounded. Such has been the case since the nineteenth century in the U.S.; much longer in other places. This is not exactly headline news but the implications remain largely unattended. "Clericalism" is a familiar but inadequate label for this historic and enduring phenomenon, this "Catholic sociology of knowledge" for want of a pithier handle. It means that the seminary (or novitiate) remains a site of memory; a point of reference; a ground of being: even for those who have never seen one. The fascination/horror with which American Protestants historically viewed these sites of Catholic formation is a stock ingredient of nineteenth century U.S. cultural history but amazingly we know almost nothing about the ways non-clerical or non-vowed Catholic intellectuals have negotiated their own understanding of seminary/novitiate as sites of formative *absence*.[2]

I don't know many priests that actively promote clericalism: what we find instead in this awkward, poignant moment of transition is a cohort of Catholic intellectuals—clerical and lay alike—that have for over four decades now been engaged in dialogue within the post-conciliar church; a dialogue that has been rich and moving but generally conducted in an idiom grounded in the church's residual ability to shape the means of knowledge-production. In practice—given the dwindling number of active priests and women religious teaching in Catholic-related fields at colleges and universities—this Catholic sociology of knowledge is sustained by civilians who increasingly assume the burden of passing the tradition on to the next generation. American Catholic intellectual culture remains grounded in this unique culture of formation, yielding in the cultural lag a kind of "clericalism *sans* clergy."

A REVIVAL TEMPERED BY LAMENTATION

The "long generation" of Catholic intellectuals shaped by the council—and particularly by its spirit of unprecedented lay-clerical collaboration—is now waning. The Catholic "lost generation" (roughly coinciding with the Baby Boom of those born between 1946 and 1964) produced but a tiny cohort of self-consciously Catholic intellectuals, lay or clerical. The 1990s witnessed a student-driven upsurge in things Catholic on both secular and religious campuses that is ongoing, evidenced in lively liturgical settings and in popular community service programs validated by the church's social teachings. This Catholic revival has been tempered, however, by a kind of ritual adult lamentation over the absence of adequate formation in Catholic doctrine and tradition witnessed in young people. In the meantime the faculty demographics of Catholic theology programs—the most concentrated source of faculty contribution to Catholic studies—have changed substantially.[3]

More significant than simply the growth of lay representation is the much greater range of authentically formative experiences witnessed, especially those grounded not in religious life but in experiences of family, gender, sexuality, disability and other versions of cultural/intellectual difference from the historic norm authorized in Catholic institutions. As historian Scott Appleby wrote in 1999, this shift "forms the backdrop of the brouhaha brewing between some bishops and some Catholic theologians over the implementation of *Ex corde ecclesiae*, the pope's encyclical on higher education." This cultural lag is also evidenced at the curricular level: Catholic Studies finds itself implicated in the discussion over Catholic identity just as it becomes in turn a potential site of transition—if not transformation—in the ways that Catholic knowledge is produced and authorized.[4]

The fate of "Catholic identity" at colleges and universities is uneasily linked to these less than fully-acknowledged developments. The efforts of many culture warriors to enshrine a vision of Catholicism as antidote to the norm-less secular variant of identity politics cannot disguise the reality that Catholic intellectual life *is itself* wracked by identity politics. Catholic Studies is presumably distinguished from all the secular interdisciplinary enterprises that preceded it by virtue of its quest for wholeness not fragmentation; community not tribalism; tradition not deconstruction. These values do not however necessarily immunize Catholic Studies from the same perils of ideology that previously beset fledgling projects in gender, ethnic or queer studies— beginning with the ideology of essentialism, the modernist remnant that drove the identity politics of these putatively "post-modern" academic phenomena. Any religious tradition will feature an essentialist dimension but the enduring legacy of neo-scholasticism in Catholic parlance—coupled with the current church mode of retrenchment—fuel a special brand of essentialism that is evident in Catholic Studies strategies from the most doctrinaire or "restorationist" to the truly imaginative.

ANALOGICAL IMAGINATION AS FOUNDATIONAL

Perhaps the most compelling Catholic Studies model in practice at present is built on a rich tradition that isolates an "analogical" or "sacramental imagination" as foundational for Catholic culture as well as theology, thus giving promise to the integrated holistic model sought by proponents of a separate (if not separatist) Catholic identity. Someone might construct a fascinating narrative tracing the development of this tradition in postwar American Catholic thought in key texts, from the subtly allusive (William Lynch, S.J., *Christ and Apollo*, 1960); to the magisterially systematic (David Tracy, *The Analogical Imagination,* 1981); to the welter of popular and scholarly works of Andrew Greeley bracketed by *The Catholic Myth* (1990) and *The Catholic Imagination* (2000). While Greeley occupies a room or two of his own in American Catholic intellectual life, his multitude of works in that decade bore a remarkable affinity with a characteristic polemic driving the Catholic studies project: in Greeley's formulation "Catholics imagine differently." Attentiveness to such difference has resulted in useful interpretations of works of visual art, in particular, by Greeley and dozens of others attuned to the "sacramental" dimension in film, painting and sculpture by Catholic artists.[5]

Practitioners of Catholic Studies follow the lead of Lynch, Tracy, Greeley and others when they contrast the analogical Catholic imagination with Protestantism's putatively "dialectical" sensibility. "I often illustrate the theory," wrote Greeley in 1999, "by noting that Catholics have angels and saints and souls in purgatory and statues and stained glass windows and holy water, and an institutional church that itself is thought to be a sacrament. Protestant denominations, on the other hand, either do not have this imagery or do not put so much emphasis on it." Lynch and Tracy were (are) anything but polemicists: Greeley is another story; for him the "dialectical" tradition with its characteristic image of a remote sovereign God means that Protestants "will be more likely to despair of society ever being anything but God-forsaken and sin-ridden and hence will be less optimistic and less supportive of social change." This bizarre assertion—grounded in his survey data—virtually nullifies the entire canon of scholarly writing on U.S. history but it certainly provides an eminently "teachable" moment: the passage invariably generates a spirited response from Protestant undergraduates![6]

The point is not to single out Greeley (who is among the most vivid characters in American Catholic history): even he hastens to acknowledge "rarely does one encounter a religious imagination that is purely analogical or purely dialectical." I am arguing however that an essentialist rhetoric (drawn from multiple sources) privileging a distinctly "Catholic imagination" pervades Catholic studies discourse—so far as I can discern—at most institutions with ties to the church. The works of Lynch, Tracy and Greeley may be wholly absent from the curricula in such programs: I cite them simply as historical sign-posts in the evolution of a sensibility whose origins long predate these works but which help us locate themes at play in programs with an interest in promoting a distinctive Catholic-Christian ideology. The interests of Catholic identity are served in the classroom through engagement with the works of religiously-inspired artists and writers that shaped Western culture for two millennia. This move also opens a window to the sources of Catholic thought, in particular the natural law tradition which integrally links culture and theology, aesthetics and spirituality. My Fordham colleague Mark Massa, S.J., to cite but one Catholic studies practitioner, is highly adept at guiding students as they seek to ground modern texts in these sources.

A representative sampling of this approach may be found in the handsome journal *Logos: A Journal of Catholic Thought and Culture*, a publication sponsored by the Catholic Studies program at the University of St. Thomas. The journal—like the field of Catholic Studies generally—is un-self-consciously "Eurocentric" if it is still possible to employ the term in descriptive not polemical fashion. A 1987 film Danish/French film, Gabriel Axel's *Babette's Feast* (from a story by Isak Dinesen), provides one of the most widely-touted visual representations of the putative dichotomy between Catholic and Protestant sensibilities, played out here on the culinary front. A screening of *Babette's Feast* is a staple at the annual summer colloquy of Collegium, a lively program founded in 1992 to promote the integration of faith and the intellectual life at Catholic colleges and universities. Collegium, which became part of the Association of Catholic Colleges and Universities in 2002, is open to faculty members and graduate students of all religious traditions teaching or studying at Catholic institutions. Collegium is very much in the "Catholic imagination" camp and has been an important player in the Catholic Studies movement.[7]

The major downside of the "Catholic imagination" school, in my judgment, is in its reconstruction of boundaries wrought of *ideology* to replace those that failed in *history* to prevent the creative borrowings, hybrid theologies and all manner of promiscuous cultural interaction with

Protestants (white and black) and Jews that produced so much of the good stuff with which urban American Catholics were particularly gifted. While I understand that Catholicism is (as a priest-contestant on *Wheel of Fortune* once put it) "a major global religious institution" the students in Catholic Studies programs live and work in a culture that undermines the formulation "Catholics imagine differently" at every turn; so too does a study of American Catholic history. The "Catholic imagination" school extols, for example, the creative contributions of many individual converts to Catholicism without ever addressing the cultural history of the conversion experience itself and its central role in shaping the American Catholic tradition. Converts are particularly revealing as much for what they *bring* as what they *find* on arrival. From Orestes Brownson to Dorothy Day to Thomas Merton, these bring conversion *narratives*, the closest thing to a native (Protestant) cultural form in the American experience and a source of enormous spiritual and cultural authority that resonates powerfully with students of all backgrounds.[8]

The conversion narrative is not a genre with roots in a discretely Catholic imagination. The moment one invokes the "Augustinian tradition," for example, one enters dangerously mixed company; there is little more futile than the effort to extricate the Catholic from the "reformed" strain of this tradition as found in American conversion narratives. In teaching Catholic Studies we always look forward to class periods devoted to Part Two—the conversion narrative—of Dorothy Day's *The Long Loneliness*. The only Catholics found in this section are Day's infant daughter; a scolding nun and "that young Catholic girl in the hospital who gave me a medal of St. Therese of Lisieux." Yet there is no more powerful account of the human heart's yearning for communion than found in this text, especially in light of the author's elisions to suit 1950s Catholic taste. As if the text were not poignant enough—with its account of Day's effort to preserve her relationship with common-law husband Forster Batterham while responding to the ineluctable call of the spirit—these are sub-textual elements: hints that she stayed with Batterham an additional eighteen months after Tamar was born (not six as her biographers report); her struggles with individual Catholics; her lingering doubts even after Baptism; her habit of making "devotional" reading of such distinctly "dialectical" works as William James' *Varieties of Religious Experience*. All these serve as harbingers of the eclectic, boundary-crossing and highly innovative "personalist" spirituality that would not only mark the Catholic Worker tradition for decades to come but would help transform American Catholicism itself. *The Long Loneliness* is a text that invites us to dwell on the journey as well as its outcome; it's in the journey that student readers find meaning while Catholic Studies ideology hurtles us toward the destination.[9]

As the British scholar Paul Giles wrote in 1999, American Catholicism functions "as a form of hybridity, modulating the very different (often antagonistic) forces with which it has come in contact." William James's' *Varieties* was the key text not only in Dorothy Day's conversion but in the (Protestant-inflected) formation of Alcoholics Anonymous in 1935; yet it was a St. Louis Jesuit, Ed Dowling, who "modulated" the recovery program's nascent spirituality into a "faith that works" (just as perhaps the woman in Day's hospital room "modulated" her inherited animus against Catholicism). I often have students read Anne Lamott's best-selling 1999 conversion narrative, *Traveling Mercies*. Though Lamott's spiritual journey leads to a Presbyterian church in Marin City, California, she too takes spiritual counsel from a Jesuit (to whom the book is co-dedicated). Critics will surely charge that the unbounded eclectic spiritual marketplace touted here is precisely why we *need* to shore up the bulwarks of Catholic identity. But there is another way of seeing that upholds this principle of "hybridity" as in fact *constitutive* of American Catholic identity itself.[10]

In this light our students evince a freer and easier handle on Catholic identity: they generally respond with openness and charity to expressions of human complexity and tend to favor authenticity over ideological purity. When Mark Massa and I team-taught Flannery O'Connor's luminous story "The Displaced Person," for example, we prompted students to locate the "sacramental imagination" represented in the story by "Father Flynn" but we also explored together issues of race, sex, class, region, and the passions that haunted Southern Protestantism. To honor only the first theme and ignore the rest threatens to ignite a kind of Catholic studies by-the-numbers, appealing only to those already comfortably ensconced in their certitude, a danger we may not wish to encourage. I teach in both Catholic Studies and American Studies contexts and the contrast between the Catholic students in these cohorts can be striking: do we risk attracting to Catholic Studies students already amenable to a pre-approved and less than challenging notion of "the Catholic imagination?"[11]

Our contention is that this ideological construction of an innately "Catholic imagination" offers *one* fruitful way among many to read books and look at pictures, to be sure, but is scarcely the only way of Catholic looking, or Catholic-looking way. It stands here as merely the most conspicuous among any number of related approaches through which Catholic Studies treats identity issues by seeking to redraw clearly defined boundaries. This reductive temptation always lurks for those of us Catholics of a certain age especially when we seek to operate in an irenic if not crowd-pleasing mode. When I show lecture audiences of "mature" Catholics clips from *On the Waterfront*, the superlative 1954 film depicting the struggle of a dockworker in the Port of New York and New Jersey to surmount the violent tribalism of the waterfront, it's always easier to succumb to temptation and treat the film like an inspirational documentary extolling the "Catholic imagination" in both form and content. In the middle of the film Karl Malden as "Father Pete Barry" gives an impromptu fiery sermon in the hold of a steamship over the prone body of a longshoreman slain by mobsters for defying the waterfront's code of silence. The body, the priest and an elderly long-suffering dockworker are then hoisted up on a rack as if ascending to heaven, confirming for many the film's Catholic *bona fides*.[12]

"Pete Barry's" soliloquy was in fact drawn directly from a fiery address the real-life Jesuit "waterfront priest" John M. ("Pete") Corridan delivered in Jersey City in 1948; the cinematic version of this speech *does* offer the most vivid depiction of Catholic social teaching-in-action ever seen on film to that point. But there is also an often brutal back story to tell involving Corridan's struggle against powerful figures in the New York Archdiocese and his fruitful collaboration with an entirely non-Catholic creative team including the great director Elia Kazan, who nursed a grudge against New York's Francis Cardinal Spellman for his alleged role in the "well-organized conspiracy" of the church's "upper cadre" and the Breen Office—the film industry's self-censorship apparatus—to bowdlerize Kazan's director's cut of Tennessee Williams' *Streetcar Named Desire* in 1952. In discussing the scene in the ship from *On the Waterfront* Kazan later explained: "that's the way you get out of the hold of a boat; there's no other way . . . . But they said no, it's the priest taking his soul up to heaven. The fact is, I'm not in the least religious."[13]

Without asking folks to relinquish their Catholic-romantic reading of this and other works of the imagination, an authentic vocation to Catholic Studies teaching demands that the *struggle* be treated with as great care as the "reception" of the artwork. *On the Waterfront*, to take just one apt example, was the product of a creative collaboration wrought of one such great struggle. There is an ideological reading of the film valorizing Catholic social action; then there is a historical inquiry which yields a much more complex, more interesting and ultimately more human story about individuals reaching out across boundaries of religion and ideology to wrest art from experience.

Our discussion points toward another key term in the Catholic historical sociology of knowledge: *vocation*. Though there is really nothing left to stop us, we have yet to authorize a Catholic intellectual vocation grounded in alternative cultures of formation: Catholic sensibilities shaped for example in vernacular idioms or in the kind of eclectic inter-disciplinary scholarship that ordinarily propels new academic initiatives. "Sensibilities" is our key word here: it would encompass an array of cognitive differences; differences in learning styles and modes of expression; differing experiences of ethnicity/gender/sexuality; differing views of the relationship between Catholic Studies teaching and scholarship and the church; and many other differences whose expression in practice surely would complicate the "coherent vision" motif driving many programs in Catholic Studies. The upside might find a Catholic Studies that looks more like Catholicism.

The fate of Catholic Studies in Catholic colleges is fraught with implications. We can cling fearfully to a declension model rooted in the secularizing experience of historically Protestant schools which ignores (among *many* other differences) the extraordinary vitality of rigorous Catholic secondary schools, or we can do better by promoting the recovery of our shared tradition's incredibly variegated expressions and sources. There are tremendous scholarly resources on Catholic history and culture from which to draw even as we encourage new scholarship that is more deeply engaged with broader cultural and political issues facing Catholics. To better appreciate this complexity we might also revisit some of the very figures and sources that were appropriated in developing the "Catholic imagination" school. William Lynch, for example, preceded *Christ and Apollo* with *The Image Industries*, a work that offers a fascinating meditation on the relationship between popular culture and theology not invested in a discretely "Catholic imagination." The "creation of a really human world of beauty and sensibility," Lynch insisted, "has never come from anything less than thousands of indeterminate sources." Lynch's fascination with the machinery of mass culture could not have anticipated the phenomenon of Andrew Greeley Enterprises, Ltd., but surely there is a place in Catholic Studies for exploration of the Catholic imagination as commodity capital. As Greeley astutely and persistently reminds us Catholics "like being Catholic." We might pursue that insight to all the realms of culture and commerce where Catholics explore "freedom of the imagination," for William Lynch the "preoccupation of the saint and of every true artist."[14]

Then there is David Tracy's recent effort to "develop a theory of the religious fragment . . . something that sparks into the realm of the infinite yet disallows a totalizing approach." We might follow Tracy's lead in relinquishing the desire for a "totalizing approach" to Catholic Studies, which he surely never intended to encourage in writing *The Analogical Imagination* (whose subtitle, after all is "Christian Theology and the Culture of Pluralism"). Pluralism in Catholic Studies teaching and schol-

arship need not be mistaken for a division in the Body of Christ. A renewed engagement with the varieties of Catholic experience might well
recast the question: whose Catholic identity is truly at risk? Or to paraphrase the title of a celebrated 1940 book by sociologist Robert Lynd,
what is Catholic knowledge for?[15]

IN CONCLUSION

Since we began with the dilemma of Catholic Studies as a distinctly
self-referential interdisciplinary project we might conclude with an
account of one modest effort to explore if indirectly the relationship
between Catholic Studies and a subject that would customarily be located elsewhere, in this case in the field of disability studies. On October 27,
2006 the Francis and Ann Curran Center for American Catholic Studies
hosted "Autism and Advocacy: A Conference of Witness and Hope," a
daylong event that represented perhaps the first attempt to mobilize spiritual resources in advocacy for and by persons on the autism spectrum.
The conference brought together theologians, parents, advocates, persons
with autism, pastors and students as a witness against the claim that
autism is fundamentally shaped by the experience of social isolation and
withdrawal.[16]

We decided to foreground the links to Catholic Studies as directly as
possible, beginning with a narrative of shared adventure with our nine-
year old autistic son Charlie in learning to ride bikes *together*. We tried to
ground the story in our understanding of Catholic social teaching's
emphasis on relationships and the dignity of the human person, before
suggesting that sometimes that tradition is not sufficiently adapted to
embrace the experience of persons with profound *differences* that merit
great attentiveness *as* differences. We suggested that autism, like Catholic
Studies, is a subject far too complex to be approached from any single
angle of vision. The conference program gave hint of a version of
Catholic Studies resolutely interfaith in orientation and inclusive in ways
that even embraced theological "neurodiversity," a term with which we
will all grow familiar as increasing numbers of students on the autism
spectrum enroll in colleges and universities.

Autistic self-advocate Kassiane Alexandra Sibley offered a critical
reflection on theological language (we're all "broken" selves) often
employed to demonstrate solidarity—through Christ—with suffering persons but which can too easily mask enduring inequities that limit the freedom of disabled persons to shape their own theological vocabularies
("I'm not broke and don't need fixin,'" asserted Ms. Sibley). A session on
Catholic education and the autism spectrum highlighted the prophetic

dimension of Catholic schools by linking a singular program for students on the autism spectrum (at Brooklyn's Xaverian High School) with the spirituality of inclusion and embrace of difference. This was a meaningful session for me because I've always been conscious of the difference in my experiences as a student with Attention Deficit Hyperactive Disorder (ADHD) at Catholic and public schools, the kind of difference that Catholic Studies might fruitfully explore as we encourage such programs to embrace neurodiversity in practice and principle. William James treated theological neurodiversity more than a century ago in *The Varieties of Religious Experience*, a book whose condemnation by "antimodernist" Catholics could not quarantine its irrepressible spirit of inquiry, of curiosity and joy, attributes worthy of emulation by practitioners of Catholic Studies.

NOTES

1. I am aware of the small body of survey and overview literature on the evolution of "Catholic Studies." I have chosen not to engage that literature in this brief essay since to do so would result in a very different work; there is enough of the historian left in me to wait for a more comprehensive literature to emerge before proffering evaluations beyond the "idiosyncratic" presented herein.

2. See especially Jenny Franchot, *Roads to Rome: The Antebellum Protestant Encounter with Catholicism* (Berkeley: University of California Press, 1994); there is a rich lit-erature treating the experiences of those who *left* religious life (or "left" the church, sometimes to return). See for example Debra Campbell, *Graceful Exits: Catholic Women and the Art of Departure* (Bloomington: Indiana University Press, 2003).

3. For one impressionistic treatment of the generational issues see James T. Fisher, "Clearing the Streets of the Catholic Lost Generation," in Thomas J. Ferraro, ed., *Catholic Lives/Contemporary America* (Durham, NC: Duke University Press, 1997), 76-103.

4. Appleby is quoted in Paula Powell Sapienza, "Catholic Intellectual Life: An Opportunity for the Church to Continue to Learn," in Thomas M. Landy, ed., *As Leaven in the World: Catholic Perspectives on Faith, Vocation, and the Intellectual Life* (Franklin, Wisconsin: Sheed and Ward, 2001), 27.

5. William F. Lynch, S.J., *Christ and Apollo: The Dimensions of the Literary Imagination* (New York: Sheed and Ward, 1960); David Tracy, *The Analogical Imagination: Christian Theology and the Culture of Pluralism* (New York: Crossroad, 1981); Andrew M. Greeley, *The Catholic Myth: The Behavior and Beliefs of American Catholics* (New York: Charles Scribner's Sons, 1990); Greeley, *The Catholic Imagination* (Berkeley: University of California Press, 2000).

6. The story grew stranger at a Fordham conference on Anti-Catholicism in New Yorkon May 24, 2002. At lunch I reported to Father Greeley on the enthusiasm of Saint Louis University students—Catholic and Protestant alike—for his account of the *Catholic* imagination. I then informed him that Protestant students usually failed to recognize their own tradition in his account and was about to add that Catholics did not understand how the two traditions could be said to differ so sharply when he asserted: "They're wrong: I have the data." The first Greeley quotation above is found in John Neary, "*Twin Peaks* and

Columbo: Two Ways to Imagine God," in Landy, ed.,   *As Leaven in the World*, 105. Neary is himself a gifted interpreter of these "two ways" and his essay is a good representation of the approach in a distinctly Catholic Studies context. The second quotation is from Andrew M. Greeley, *The Catholic Myth: The Behavior and Beliefs of American Catholics* (New York: Charles Scribner's Sons, 1990), 48.

7. www.stthomas.edu/cathstudies/logos; www.accunet.org/collegium

8. See Patrick Allitt, *Catholic Converts: British and American Intellectuals Turn to Rome* (Ithaca: Cornell University Press, 1997).

9. Dorothy Day, *The Long Loneliness: The Autobiography of Dorothy Day* (New York: Harper, 1952), 113-62.

10. Paul Giles, "American Catholic Arts and Fictions and the New Catholic Scholarship," *U.S. Catholic Historian* 17 (Summer, 1999), 1-8; see also Giles's' definitive study of the "Catholic imagination" thematic in American literature: *American Catholic Arts and Fictions: Culture, Ideology, Aesthetics* (New York: Cambridge University Press, 1992); John Samuel Tieman, "The Origins of Twelve-Step Spirituality: Bill W. and Edward Dowling, S.J.," *U.S. Catholic Historian* 13 (Summer, 1995), 121-35; Anne Lamott, *Traveling Mercies: Some Thoughts on Faith* (New York: Pantheon Books, 1999); William James, *The Varieties of Religious Experience: A Study in Human Nature* (New York: Longmans, Green and Co., 1902).

11. Flannery O'Connor, "The Displaced Person," in *A Good Man is Hard to Find and Other Stories* (New York: Harvest Books, 1955), 196-252.

12. The *On the Waterfront* saga is treated in full in James T. Fisher, *Covering the Water front* (forthcoming from Cornell University Press in 2007).

13. Elia Kazan, *Elia Kazan: A Life* (New York: Alfred A. Knopf, 1988), 432-43; Michel Ciment, *Kazan on Kazan* (New York: Viking, 1974), 110-112. Kazan's retrospective animus toward Spellman was surely aggravated by the prelate's much more overt attacks on his 1956 film *Baby Doll*, which the Cardinal denounced from the pulpit of St. Patrick's Cathedral. See Richard Schickel, *Elia Kazan: A Biography* (New York: HarperCollins, 2005), 212-13, 248-50, 31-35.

14. Many Catholic intellectuals remain enamored of the declension model as found in such works as George Marsden, *The Soul of the American University: From Protestant Establishment to Established Nonbelief* (New York: Oxford University Press, 1994); William F. Lynch, S.J., *The Image Industries* (New York: Sheed and Ward, 1959).

15. Lois Malcolm, "An Interview with David Tracy," www.religion-online.org/showarticle.asp?title=2269

16. The conference presentations are available on video at www.fordham.edu/cs click "Media."

Part II

Art, Earth and Dignity: Faithfully Shaping the Common Life

ART & AGNOSTICISM:
GOD'S PARTNERS IN REVELATION
A POET EXPLORES THE LANDSCAPE
OF FAITH AND DOUBT

Elizabeth Michael Boyle, O.P.

Art, revelation, faith, agnosticism—with a little science tossed in—
what a theological salad! The ambitious task I've set myself reminds me
of a story John Ciardi used to tell when he was poetry editor of *The
Saturday Review.* One very persistent woman kept bombarding him with
submissions of religious verse straight out of the Hallmark School of
Theology—all of which the editor politely rejected. Undaunted, she finally submitted a sonnet entitled grandly, "God." This time Ciardi's standard
pink slip provoked an angry protest: "Obviously you're an atheist!" she
fumed. "No wonder you don't like my poetry!" Ciardi replied: "Madam,
believe me, it is out of deepest respect for the deity that I decline to pub-
lish your poem entitled 'God.' I simply cannot resist the impression that
your talent is not equal to your subject matter."

I confess and do not deny that indeed my talent is not equal to my subject matter. What I offer here is merely my own personal experience of
what John Paul II meant—in his 1996 Letter to Artists—where he said:
"The church needs the arts not primarily to illustrate scripture or dogma
but as a different and genuine source of theology." As far as I know, John
Paul never made a similar claim for agnostics, but I suspect there were
times when he found agnostics easier to understand than some practicing
Catholics. Being an amateur, I feel free to make my case speaking the
plain English so scrupulously avoided by professional theologians. Then
I'll illustrate my main points with some very accessible poetry. Unlike the

poet Billy Collins, for whom the label "accessible" evokes the image of a ramp for the handicapped, I'm quite comfortable being understood. Perhaps the first step in that direction would be a clarification of the terms *revelation, art* and *agnosticism* as I intend to use them.

Among lay Catholics whom the Church has not yet deigned to educate, there persists a regrettable tendency to limit the meaning of "revelation" to doctrinal statements enshrined in scripture. Throughout history, however, the term revelation has always denoted something more than the mere transmission of a "message," even a message as attractive as the Good News. "Revelation," says Karl Rahner, "embraces not only doctrinal statements based on scripture, but every action and event in which God acts creatively to bestow grace and utter an illuminating word."[1] According to this definition, then, God has uttered pre-verbal illuminating words in the works of creation and continues to utter non-verbal illuminations in the discoveries of science and of art. It is forty years since Paul Tillich brilliantly illuminated how the arts neither invent nor transcribe revelation, but rather mediate God's self-communication to us. According to Tillich, the gospels themselves are such a mediation in the form of expressionistic art.[2] The term revelation means the transmission, not of information about God, but of an experience of God's very life. Such knowledge can never be confined to a book, not even if God had written one.

Perhaps that's one reason why Jesus never wrote a book. In an interview with Bill Moyers the Canadian novelist Margaret Atwood, an agnostic, commented on this fact:

> The oral tradition has to be communicated by a person to a person or a group of persons. So it is the breath, which is the spirit, the spirit moving from one person to another . . . (that communicates Jesus's message). Possibly Jesus wanted to keep his spirit, the spirit of what he was saying . . . to keep it fluid rather than fixed and permanent and therefore dead.[3]

Evolutionary theology underscores this concept of revelation as something alive and therefore changing. According to Dominican Cletus Wessels, "revelation is not a thing but a dynamic relationship between a human community and an inexpressible presence. God's self-revelation has been unfolding for fifteen billion years . . . therefore, it is appropriate that the revelation of God's presence be perceived as not an unchanging doctrine but as the dynamic, on-going reality of a deepening relationship between God and the human community."[4] Human communication, as we know, is achieved not when a message is sent but when it is received. So too, divine revelation requires a living, responsive encounter. Rahner's definition of revelation, therefore, includes all the acts of creation, science, art, personal and communal history, and pre-history through which humanity encounters life-giving intimations of holy truth.

Not all revelations are created equal, of course. Ordinarily, the romantic musings of a teenager do not inspire the same level of credibility accorded the startling metaphors of a mystic or the cautious formulations of a professional theologian. Moreover, a person's whole intellectual and psychological history can modify his/her interpretation of God's self-communication. But the greatest obstacle to hearing God's word accurately is neither education nor the lack of it. The greatest obstacle to genuine revelation is human ego. The scholar's arrogance and sophistication can get in God's way as often as the peasant's ignorance. For this reason, the most reliable interpreters of holy truth are the truly selfless. In fact, the state in which the mystic receives a revelation is usually referred to as "ecstasy," which means literally "standing outside the self."

In Hebrew the word *holy* means "other." "My thoughts are not your thoughts, my ways not your ways: it is Yahweh who speaks" (Is 55:8). We encounter the holy whenever—in a state of receptivity to truth or beauty, in the act of study or creative work or prayer—we forget ourselves in the presence of unmistakable otherness: something beyond what our senses register, beyond what our minds can grasp. Stephen Jay Gould, the agnostic paleontologist, seems to understand this Hebrew connotation of *holy* when, completing his masterwork on evolution, he says:

> Something almost unspeakably holy—I don't know how else to say this—underlies our discovery and confirmation of the actual details that made our world and also, in realms of contingency, assured the minutiae of its construction in the manner we know, and not in any one of a trillion other ways, nearly all of which would not have included the evolution of a scribe to record the beauty, the cruelty, the fascination, and the mystery.[5]

Notice that Gould's encounter with the holy in his study of science leads him to *an act of gratitude for the evolution of the artist to record the beauty and the mystery of it all.*

Stephen Jay Gould is my kind of agnostic. I'd like to stipulate that for me the term agnosticism refers to that healthy iconoclasm that refuses to worship certainty. (That's why an agnostic refuses to be an atheist, i.e., someone who is positive there is no god.) Accepting only the truths that can be demonstrated, the agnostic holds that ultimate truth is unknowable. My favorite agnostic, Thomas Aquinas agrees: "This is the final knowledge of God: to know that we do not know God."[6] Thomas went to great pains to demonstrate that the human mind can know that God is, but not what God is.

Agnosticism serves revelation by rescuing us from idolatry. It's true, we don't see too many golden calves on sale these days, but there's plenty of idolatry going on. It's no accident that the Decalogue gives first place to: "Thou shalt not have strange gods before me." One subtle form of idolatry is Biblical literalism. The most common form is the worship of a god made in our own image. Lately we favor the theology of divine election whose cult worships the dogma of American superiority. It is this theology of election which even now sends our children off to die in an un-winnable war, believing passionately in God's preferential option for capitalism. Strange gods indeed. We could use a little agnostic uncertainty these days, couldn't we?

The agnostic's questions urge us not to rest in rigid concepts of God, thus forcing our image of God to evolve as we mature in faith and knowledge. The poet Kathleen Norris expresses it beautifully in "Little Girls in Church."

Now it begins, the search for a God who has moved on . . .
The pillar of cloud you saw march across the plain
Will pass you by
Some younger child will see it.
It was given so easily and now you must learn
To ask for it back.
It's not so terrible;
It's like the piano lessons you love
And hate.
You know how you want the music to sound
but have to practice, half in tears
without much hope.

Art, like evolutionary faith, is a search for a God who is constantly moving on. *Art*, by which I mean all the arts, requires, above all, a unique search for the heart of the natural world and an intimate participation in the invisible spirit which animates it. As a gift of the same Spirit who inspired the scriptures, art enjoys the gift of tongues. The arts translate penetrating visions into accessible languages of shape and sound and color that involve and enhance all other forms of revelation. When they are ideally revelatory, the artist's verbal and non-verbal poems are interactive, evoking our own encounter with the divine life within us.

Fortunately, 20th century findings in cosmology and quantum physics have begun to teach science and technology the languages of art and mysticism. Social psychologist Diarmuid O'Murchu sums up the phenomenon: "We are outgrowing the subject-object relationship (with reality) and embarking upon a new intersubjectivity."[7] My only argument here is with the adjective "new." An intersubjective relationship with other-than-human phenomena echoes the intuitions of poets as early as the psalmists who heard the trees exalt their creator and the everlasting hills murmur their desire.

Like revelation, artistic knowledge is not a thing but a relationship. The poet or mystic who seeks knowledge as communion rather than knowledge as mastery is different from the scientist who approaches his task with a determination to master and control. The artist and the mystic approach natural phenomena to enter into communion with the mystery at its source. Across the centuries, poets, artists, musicians have intuited the dynamic interior life of matter that has been exposed by scientific technology only recently. To an even greater degree, the mystics have exemplified this way of knowing, not by analysis, but by way of participation. According to Einstein, "mysticism is the power of all true art and science."[8]

There's an important difference between the artist and the mystic, however. Creative experience culminates in expression. Mystical experience culminates in silence. An agnostic believes rightly that the human mind cannot grasp ultimate truth. But the artist knows from experience that you can be grasped by it. And the true artist's product is always an attempt to replicate that revelatory event. I'm fond of saying that the poet is a failed mystic.

When I look at an artifact or listen to a piece of music that moves me, I try to get back to the moment that inspired it. Only once have I seen a painting that seemed to be about the mystical experience before the painting. We're all familiar with the paintings of Fra Angelico—especially the famous Annunciation where the angel steals the show. A few years ago, I saw a banner by the Dominican artist, Thoma Swanson of Columbus, which shows the artist in the act of painting that scene. He's just started on the face of the Virgin, and her eyes are looking into him so deeply that he can't go on. I spent the afternoon with Fra Angelico and wrote this poem called:

Annunciations

Before each moment art can capture
comes a greater moment unrecorded.
Before the Word takes form
in wood, or stone, or pigment,
a flashing second taunts the sight
with stunning recognition—then retreats
leaving the soul to make a shape for longing.

Before his Virgin heard the angel's voice
this artist heard a different voice speak color:
the air around her head chimed gold—and waited while
her breathing stilled the rush of alien wings. And when
she simply looked at him
all seven colors on his palette
chorused vibrant white.

Before he mixed the sand with lime and
raised a sturdy trowel to
smooth the frescoed surface
for the stroke of his reluctant brush
their gaze carved art's penultimate vision
into a space so sacred
no angel dared intrude.

Before the reader concludes that I have it in for angels, let's consider an angel who expresses my whole thesis so far. In "Angel with Palette," Marc Chagall has given the angel paints and brushes to illustrate explicitly his belief that the artist is a messenger from God. Not every artist wants the job, of course, but the angel in this painting has Chagall's face; it is his spiritual self-portrait.

Here Chagall expressly accepts his role as a mediator of God's self-communication to the human community. The angel hovers hugely at the center of the canvas; but in the upper left corner is the village, and in the other darkened corners, we see a pair of lovers and a farm animal feeding from a manger. Chagall's work exemplifies eminently the theologian's definition of revelation as: "the experience of the presence of God unfolding from the universe as perceived by the community through historical and symbolic events."[9] Chagall consciously and eminently fulfills the role the artist shares with the prophets, i.e., interpretation of history through the cultural roots of the people.[10]

The artist does not always know that he/she is doing that. The revelatory artist does not simply illustrate an idea that's fully-formed in the mind. The act of painting or sculpting or writing leads the creative person into a way of seeing something in a new way. Chagall's work with the subject matter of the crucifixion is a good illustration of the creative process. Early in his career, when he began painting the crucifixion, his intentions were completely aesthetic, completely secular. He chose the crucifixion as the most conventional, ubiquitous image he could think of to demonstrate how cubist techniques could transform something boringly familiar into something dramatically new. His cubist crucifixion is not really about Christ; it's all about cubism. It had as much to do with divine revelation as a Picasso nude.

By 1938, when Chagall painted White Crucifixion, however, reality had intruded rudely on the aesthetic concerns of a Russian Jew. As his fellow Jews were being exterminated, Chagall painted his way to a vision that showed Christ himself at the center of the holocaust. In this startlingly new rendition of a familiar image, we see Christ surrounded by his fellow Jews with a Jewish prayer shawl covering his nakedness. What distinguishes this crucifixion from traditional renderings of Calvary is the fact that Jesus is not the only one suffering. In fact, God and humanity are suffering together. Through Chagall, we can see dramatized the whole mystery of divine suffering which has compelled the interest of theology lately.

The White Crucifixion was painted the year after Chagall completed a triptych of crucifixion scenes whose center panel, entitled "Resurrection," has become known as the Red Crucifixion. Again you can see Jesus surrounded by Jewish people and liturgical objects, but what you might not notice is the fact that the artist himself is in the picture. He is hanging upside down beside Jesus with his palette in one hand. With the other hand he is touching the wounded body of Christ.[11] Chagall's Red Crucifixion shows the artist united to the divine compassion. According to religious historian Karen Armstrong the only thing that can unite the major religions of the world and save them from each other is not theological compromise, but compassionate action.[12]

To sum up where we are so far: revelation can be any act or event in which we experience genuinely the gift of God's self communication. Art—the creative expression of this experience—can be one of God's instruments of revelation. The agnostic's questions also mediate that self-communication. Agnostics help to purify our faith of literalism, of solipsism, of triumphalism, of the temptation to make God in our own image. Through the skeptic's questions, we are forced to face what God is not. The act of writing poetry, composing music, or engaging in the visual and performing arts not only records these illuminating moments, it forces the creative person into the darkness beyond them. That Emily Dickenson wannabe who wrote the poem called "God" would have written a better poem had she spent some time in the agnostic's darkness—as Emily did. Then even John Ciardi might have found her verses revelatory.

From here on, I'd like to present a series of demonstrations showing how artistic activity mirrors and often predates that other form of revelation we call science. I'll start this demonstration with an amusing story. Back on my campus in New Jersey during National Poetry Month we have an annual reading by members of the faculty and staff who write poetry. We delight in attracting participants across disciplines. One year, we led off with a professor from the art department appearing for the first time. John was a slight, soft-spoken, somewhat nerdy looking fellow who began reading a slight, somewhat nerdy poem about a significant year in his childhood when a pet bunny came into his life at Easter time. It was a charming, sentimental, frankly ho-hum narrative until all of a sudden, the little boy murdered the rabbit. It seems that between spring and winter the blinking bunny had become boring. So the boy took him out in the snow and beat him to death. The poet's description of this event was extremely graphic.

Suddenly, a vividly-revised version of the nerdy professor electrified his listless audience. Obviously, there were two professor John Kaufmans in that room, the visible-physical John Kaufman, plus the less physical but more real John Kaufman who had just leaped out of the poem. John's interior self did not become visible to him when he beat the bunny to death, however. It was years later when he re-created the episode as a poem that he began to probe its universal spiritual significance in the poem's final stanzas.

More importantly, when John read the poem aloud, new images of our own alarming possibilities invaded the collective imagination. We recognized the bunny-basher in each of us: that selfish part of us who demands that every living thing prove its usefulness. We acknowledged silently the capacity for violence in children. We shivered together as the hairline border between innocence and evil, between our private sins and their cultural consequences, quietly dissolved. No one in that room doubted his/her need for redemption. These connections and other unexpressed fears reverberated in our shattered psyches. We felt an almost tangible nexus between the pair in this childhood crime scene and every innocent victim of "respectable" forms of aggression from Brooklyn to Baghdad.

This was a shocking revelation about us, but what did it reveal about God? I for one saw in that slain rabbit a Christ figure, a vivid image of God's own vulnerability. I felt God wounded by the primal, irretrievable act in which the Creator entrusted this beautiful world to the whims of human freedom. I submit that to feel such connections is an emotional knowledge that is genuinely revelatory. Indeed, the anecdote tells us something about the power of poetry, but I said I would be demonstrating how artistic vision anticipates the revelations of science. What's scientific here? Much later I came across a scientific report about current research that seems to describe exactly what the dead bunny released into the room. Scientists have recently photographed something called "mirror neurons" in the brain. Mirror neurons are brain cells that "flare" whenever a primate beholds another primate performing an action he too is capable of performing.[13] In the act of reading his poem John Kaufman showed us primates a symbol of what all humanity is capable of. So when I wrote a poem about the experience of hearing his poem, I called my version:

Mirror Neurons Flare

The day John Kaufman killed the Easter Bunny
perspectives changed forever.
In the drowsing lecture hall
Art History's softly-modulated voice
assumed a sudden terror.
Art majors—en masse—transferred to
Criminal Justice and Forensic Psychology.
and for the first time in history
a pink-eyed quadruped threatened campus security.
The day John Kaufman killed the Easter Bunny
a nameless pet emerged to take his place beside
Blake's Tyger
Marianne Moore's plumed basilisk
Elizabeth Bishop's armadillo
and Mark Doty's golden retriever.
Yes, that was the day a simple declarative sentence
stained fresh snow with bright indelible blood and
laid clammy hands on our decorous academic guts
instantly demolishing stereotypes, ennui, delusions of innocence and
attention deficit disorder,
Oh, the day John Kaufman killed the Easter Bunny
Was a red-letter day for poetry at Caldwell College.

Before you begin to fear that my next poem will feature a serial killer, let me offer a nicer Christ figure with a more optimistic example of how an artistic experience can reveal the best in us. In one version of the Cirque de Soleil, the show opened with a spectacular solo called "Icarus." Standing at the top of the soaring tent, the aerial artist opened huge white wings, then suddenly plunged to within inches of the floor. Slowly his limp body was drawn up to hang with wings outstretched like Christ on the cross. As I watched this performance, my "mirror neurons" flared as I recognized something deathless in the human psyche. I recorded my reaction in this short poem.

Cirque de Soleil

Reaching forever upward
into remembered skies

the body of Icarus plunges
straight for the earthbound crowd.
Trapped in a tangled net,
he hangs above them, cruciform.
Then, deep inside each of us
flight revives. Icarus never dies.

It has taken almost two millennia of theologizing to demolish the distance between the God up there and the God within, between the God of Genesis and the God of the New Cosmology. For me, the aerial artist of Cirque de Soleil demolished that distance in a few seconds.

Many times a scientist unconsciously uses language that is almost biblical. Physicist David Bohm's definition of matter is a case in point. He says: "Matter is nothing but gravitationally-trapped light."[14] Think of it: God said "Let there be light!"—and in that single word uttered everything else in the universe, including my body and yours. The physicist's statement of literal fact sounds like poetry. It also sounds like Cletus Wessels' speculation about the mystery of Resurrection: "I believe that after death our bodies are transformed into energy, into light."[15] I had reason to recall this beautiful possibility a few months ago when I found myself suddenly trundled into an operating room. For several days, surrounded by aides and interns from many countries, the only words I heard in my native language suggested that I might not survive. Strangely, I felt the very opposite of frightened. Because of Wessels' idea of Resurrection, I felt neither fear nor even curiosity—rather a quiet anticipation that the gravitationally trapped radiance of my person was about to be set free from my mortal body. I lived to write this little poem about it.

Lovers and Other Strangers

A man whose face I've never seen
is invading my body
with eyes and hands
I have never loved.
How can I
abandon myself so completely
knowing we will never
meet again?
Because the Love whose face
no one has seen
Is
and is coming soon
to transubstantiate my flesh
to light.

In this case, my creative experience came after reading theology inspired by scientific knowledge. In fact, historically the vision of artists, poets and mystics has often predated scientific discovery. Two artists familiar to us for their distinctive styles offer examples of how revelatory art has anticipated scientific revelation, Vincent Van Gogh and his contemporary Paul Gaughin. We all recognize Van Gogh's cypresses and starry night, in particular because of the way they seem to be vibrating on the canvas. Art historians applaud Van Gogh's brush stroke as the introduction of a new technique in painting. What is more significant for our purposes is the fact that Van Gogh in painting what he sees, is the first to illustrate the scientific fact that there is no such thing as "solid matter," that everything is living, dancing energy. His canvases correspond exactly to Hildegard of Bingen's visions centuries earlier and what modern microscopes revealed to physicists decades later.

Van Gogh famously abandoned the biblical literalism of his parent's church, but that did not, in his own words, "keep me from having a terrible need of—dare I say the word—religion. Then I go out at night and paint the stars."[16] Van Gogh painted in a way that deliberately "divinized" his two greatest sources of revelation: nature and the poor. Hence, in "The Sower,"[17] the sunlight that drenches the wheat fields also creates a halo around the head of the farmer. And the way Van Gogh uses color to unite heaven, earth, and humanity vividly adumbrates the homilies of our contemporary eco-theologians.

In a little-appreciated painting by Van Gogh's contemporary, Paul Gaughin, "Yellow Christ," the artist was making a deliberate statement about the continuity between divine and human suffering. But a century later, we could also use Yellow Christ to make a religious plea for environmental responsibility. By making the body of the Crucified the same color as the earth, the artist has (consciously or unconsciously) made a statement about the earth herself as a suffering body.

When an artist enters into communion with a landscape or an object, she enters into communion with the universe. When she paints a face, she enters into communion with humanity. Scientists call this phenomenon holon theory, that is, the idea that the whole of any physical entity is contained in every part. Holographic photography now confirms this long-held holon theory. As Jane Hirshfield demonstrates in her anthology of forty-three centuries of sacred poetry by women "holon experience has been recorded in the poetry of virtually every religious tradition."[18]

Holon theory has moral consequences. Reflection on holon theory compels us to a wider, deeper sense of accountability: because the whole is contained in every part, I am accountable for the global consequences of my actions—and inactions—accountable to humanity, to the forests, the rivers, to every one of the 5000 species who disappear every day into the giant maw of an economy that demands over-consumption of fraudulent necessities.

Contemporary technology gives the scientist access to the molecular, subatomic, quantum levels of all that we used to call "solid matter." What scientists are discovering in this previously invisible world confirms the intuitions of ancient poets. For example, a recent article in *The Science Times* records how the subatomic particles of the whole human person respond to loss, "When a person grieves, the cells of the body grieve also—the molecules, the atoms grieve also." This scientific statement gives new meaning to the phrase, "deeply moved," doesn't it?

Centuries before a molecular biologist actually photographed that deep mourning of the atoms, the poet Virgil heard other-than-human weeping and wrote: "*Sunt lacrymae rerum.*" Literally, "There are tears in things." As a poet Virgil could hear those tears. Now micro-photography has belatedly discovered them. Eco-theologians tell us it is up to us to wipe them away.

In the forest
where no ear listens
the tree falls
without a sound.
So say the monolingual philosophers.

But the tree knows better.
In each shriveled leaf
uptorn root
and still-born blossom
the tree, like other poets,
hears distinctly
the music of the tears in things.

In one forest
no tree falls
without an echo in song.

I have to confess to feeling a guilty thrill every time the poets steal the march on scientists. This happened not long ago when *The Science Times* reported as "news" the discovery in a physics lab that there's a still point at the heart of all motion. For an Eliot scholar, those words "still point" rang a bell and touched off a series of associations.[19] One of the first things I learned about Eliot's *Quartets* is that whole pages are lifted almost verbatim from John of the Cross. So the poem begins

T.S. Eliot, you old plagiarist!
Outdone yourself at last—

stolen the words
right out of the mouth
of the future.
At the still point of the turning world,
Neither flesh nor fleshless,
a white light, still and moving
At the still point there is only the dance.
Three quarters of a century later
quantum midwives cry:
The whole system is undergoing
a coordinated movement like a ballet dance.
Helium spinning at white heat
gives birth to a freezing supersolid.
Neither gas nor fluid a new
state of being!
"It's going to make us rethink
our whole concept of 'solid.' "[20]
But you were there first, old friend,
burning in the dry ice of faith
freezing one half degree above
absolute zero
spinning toward the still point
where your partner disappears
into the dance, the only solid
in our fragile universe.

By now I trust the reader agrees that some artists are God's partners in revelation just as true prophets are. Not all artists qualify, of course. How do I identify a "revelatory" artist? I think I'd limit the title to artists whose work is an habitual act of faith. When Jesus enjoined his disciples to have faith so as to move mountains, he was not urging them to adopt a correct theology; he was urging them to open themselves to the power of God. The artist opens herself to the word of God when she *listens* to her medium. Painters listen to color; sculptors listen to stone. A poet listens to words the way a cardiologist listens to ultrasound. She understands that power in language which has so far eluded linguistic analysis but which medical research has come to respect. We associate the psychological power of words to heal with the poetry of vocal prayer. Reciting the words of a prayer doesn't change God—but listening to the words of our prayers can change us. Sometimes this power is strong enough to make us stop asking God to fix things and answer the prayer ourselves.

Elie Wiesel offers a dramatic example of the power of language to restore faith. We are all familiar with that heartbreaking scene in *Night* where the young boy witnesses the death of a child hanged from a scaffold. The narrator utters the chilling words: "God died on that tree."[21] Ever since, Wiesel has been widely regarded as an atheist. Nothing could be further from the truth. In more than one interview, Wiesel identifies himself as a believing Jew. Asked, "How did you reclaim your faith?" he replies: "I kept on saying the prayers even after I believed there was no one listening. First the words spoke for me. Then they began to speak to me. Finally, they spoke me. The words of the prayer spoke who I am. The words themselves were a kind of presence."[22]

Presence is the ultimate form of revelation. Wallace Stevens in one of his enigmatic epigrams says: "The world is presence and not force. It fills the being before the mind can think." The creative act can mediate this kind of presence as I discovered once when I was alone in a cabin in the woods writing. Something began to intrude on my thoughts and I abandoned what I was writing to record exactly what was happening:

Untitled

Moving across the blank page
the sound of my pencil
creates a silence
the wake of a tiny ship.

The silence becomes a person
more real to me than myself
a companion looking over my shoulder
smiling a little at the poem
that has ceased to matter.

Nothing I shall ever write
can be more true
more trustworthy
than this faceless presence
beside, beyond
inexorably within.

The wise ones called you Unpronounceable.
He called you Abba.
Now they tell us to call you
Quantum Vacuum, Empty Fullness.
Whatever.

Language neither creates nor destroys
this moment

this moving stillness
whose white sails carry me
through darkest waters
unerringly home.

Well, you expect that kind of statement from a poet. Here's one from a fairly respectable scientist who acknowledges Presence as a valid form of knowledge: "That deeply emotional conviction of the Presence of a superior reasoning power which is revealed in the incomprehensible universe—this forms my idea of God."[23]

These are the words of Albert Einstein. It's quite astonishing to have a scientist of his rank go on record with language that acknowledges a "deeply emotional conviction," a kind of knowledge that cannot be put under a microscope. Notice, however, that he carefully specifies: "My idea of God." That's all we have, any of us. "To know that what is impenetrable to us really exists, manifesting itself as the highest wisdom and the most radiant beauty, this feeling is at the center of all true religiousness. In this sense, and in this sense only, I belong to the ranks of devoutly religious men." Einstein, by his own admission, is a deeply religious agnostic.[24]

Speaking of Einstein reminds me that I have said nothing so far about the art form that is perhaps God's greatest partner, music. Of Mozart Einstein said that he did not compose music; he simply discovered what had been waiting for him there from all eternity.

Music reveals not only the highest thing we can say about God, but also the best that we can say of ourselves. Stephen Jay Gould, a professed agnostic, nevertheless belonged to the Handel Society in Cambridge and loved to sing all the great masses and oratorios in their repertoire. In a panel discussion on the possibilities of intelligent life elsewhere in the universe, Gould was asked:" If you met an extraterrestrial, how would you communicate?" He answered: "I'd play Bach's Mass in B Minor as a way of saying, 'This is the best we can say for ourselves. Listen!'"

Listening to Mozart, Einstein felt the same presence that he felt emotionally in his laboratory and his study. Einstein's love for the spirituality of music inspired the fantasy with which I will now conclude. In this poem Einstein celebrating his recent anniversary by listening to his favorite composer.

NOTES

1. Karl Rahner, *Theological Investigations,* trans. Kevin Smyth (Baltimore: Helicon, 1966), 4:255.

2. Paul Tillich, *Systematic Theology,* three vols. in one (Chicago: Chicago University Press, 1967), 2: 133.

3. "Bill Moyers on Faith and Reason," PBS (July 28, 2006).

4. Cletus Wessels, *Jesus in the New Universe Story* (Maryknoll, New York: Orbis Books, 2003), 68.

5. Stephen Jay Gould, *The Structure of Evolutionary Theory* (Cambridge: Harvard University Press, 2002), 1342.

6. *De Potentia,* q. 7, a. 5, ad. 14, cited in *The Human Wisdom of Saint Thomas: A Breviary of Philosophy from the Works of Saint Thomas Aquinas,* arranged by Joseph Pieper, trans. Drostan MacLaren (New York: Sheed and Ward, 1948), 99.

7. Diarmuid O'Murchu, *Evolutionary Faith: Rediscovering God in Our Great Story* (Maryknoll, New York: Orbis, 2003), 13.

8. Cited in *The Jewish Mystics,* Louis Jacobs, ed. (London, 1982).

9. Wessels, 60-65.

10. Wessels, 64-65.

11. All Chagall paintings referenced are in the catalog of the Marc Chagall Exhibit at the San Francisco Museum of Modern Art, July 26-November 4, 2003.

12. Karen Armstrong, *The Spiral Staircase: My Climb Out of Darkness* (New York : Anchor Books, 20005), 304.

13. Sandra Blakeslee, "Cells That Read Minds," *The New York Times* (1 January 2006).

14. David Bohm, *Wholeness and the Implicate Order* (New York: Routledge and Kegan Paul).

15. Wessels, 134.

16. Cited in Dana Silverman, *Van Gogh and Gauguin: The Search for Sacred Art* (New York: Farrar, Straus and Giroux, 2000).

17. Silverman, 114-115.

18. Jane Hirschfield, ed. *Women in Praise of the Sacred: Forty-Three Centuries of Spiritual Poetry by Women* (New York: Harper Perennial, 1995), xix.

19. T.S. Eliot, from "Burnt Norton," *The Complete Poems and Plays* (New York: Harcourt Brace and Company, 1952).

20. "Only in Quantum Physics: Spinning While Standing Still," *The New York Times* (21 September 2004) F3.

21. Elie Wiesel, *Night* (New York: Hill and Wang, 2006), 45.

22. "The Tragedy of the Believer," Interview with Krista Tippett, *Speaking of Faith* (National Public Radio, 13 July 2006).

23. Cited in the Einstein Exhibition at the American Museum of Natural History (New York: November 15, 2002-August 10, 2003).

24. Albert Einstein, "Strange Is Our Situation Here on Earth," in *The World Treasury of Modern Religious Thought,* ed. Jaroslav Pelikan (Boston: Little Brown & Co., 1990) 204.

THE EARTH IS THE LORD'S (PS 24:1)

Dianne Bergant, C.S.A.

INTRODUCTION

Time and again we have heard it said that we are in the midst of a paradigm shift (Küng & Tracy, 1989). Our scientific-technological achievements have thrust us out of the confines of classical western civilization into a new age, but our advances in devising a corresponding worldview have not kept pace. Our inauguration into the scientific era may have taken place as far back as the 16th or 17th century, when several great minds first began to understand the physical forces at work in the universe. As scientists invented new technologies that could manipulate and control the environment for human advantage, a very significant theological shift began to take place. The eschatological expectation of fulfillment seemed to be on the horizon and its achievement seemed to be within the power and reach of human beings. God may have been the original creator, but it seemed that human genius could now bring forth the 'new creation.' Progress took on a quasi-divine appearance and this was exaggerated by the undeniable good that it produced. Human life was enriched; human dignity was enhanced; and human beings seemed to hold their destiny in their own hands.

The world has seen that technology could lead to its destruction just as well as it might lead to its fulfillment. Western civilization certainly could not return to a pre-scientific perspective, but neither had it devised an alternative way of understanding its achievements or imagining its future. In many ways we perceive life as if we were still living in the world of the past. The patterns of growth and prosperity which have provided many of us with the benefits of material comfort can no longer be sustained at the same rate or for the same number of people. One reason for this is that we are depleting our available material resources and are doing little or nothing to replenish them. Another is that we are more aware that our prosperity has often been procured at the expense of other's human rights.

None of these various changes happened over night. We may have been catapulted into the modern age, but we advanced toward the moment of entry only gradually. A paradigm has been defined as "an entire constellation of beliefs, values, techniques, and so on shared by the members of a given community" (Kuhn, 1970:175). Since our former ways of understanding the world, society and human endeavor no longer seem adequate to meet and interpret the realities facing us, we are certainly facing a shift in paradigm.

Perhaps we have not realized the gravity of the environmental issue because we were not attentive to the limits of the natural wealth of the world. The world has been prodigal in surrendering its treasures to us. Or if we have been conscious of nature's limits, we may have disregarded them because we believed that the wealth was ours for the taking. After all, are we not superior to all of creation? Have we not been told to subdue the earth and have dominion over the fish and the birds and every living thing? (cf. Gen 1:26, 28). This kind of thinking was even illustrated formerly in some textbooks by means of a pyramid showing mineral creation at the base of the figure, vegetation just above it, sentient creation slightly higher still, and humankind at the top. In this way we learned that the lower levels of the natural world were created to serve the ends of the higher. How well this was illustrated; how well we learned it; and how wrong it has been!

Environmental concern has inspired many religiously inclined people to look anew at their own faith traditions, or the faith traditions of others, in the hope of discovering there both inspiration and direction for more ecologically sensitive thinking and behavior. At times this search has uncovered elements within the faith that have formerly played only minor roles in the lives of believers, e.g., the responsibility of stewardship implied in the duty of serving and guarding the garden of Eden (Gen 2:15). At other times elements from Eastern religions, native religions, or heterodox religious sects have been incorporated into the conventional religious worldview resulting in spiritual enrichment, but also, occasionally, in theological eclecticism.

A major theological response to this issue came in 1988 when the World Council of Churches sponsored a consultation at Annecy, France, which attracted scholars espousing various liberation and other political theologies. All of the participants came to realize that the theme of liberation can be applied to questions dealing not only with the human family, but also with all life forms and, indeed, with the earth itself. The report of this consultation, delivered to the World Council, was remarkable for its "emphasis on linking concerns of ecological sustainability with concerns of social justice;

on moving beyond oppressive understandings of God; on recognizing the deleterious effects of exclusively Western understandings of development on the peoples of Asia, Africa, Latin America, and Oceania; on recognizing the importance of science for contemporary Christian thought; on recognizing biblical resources for affirming what the World Council has called the integrity of creation" (Birch 1990:290).

Recognition of the fundamental integrity of all of creation may be commonplace in the domains of the physical and life sciences, but it is relatively new to most branches of theology, with the exception of process theology (Cobb, 1982:111-134; Daly, H., 1989:190-203) and some forms of ecofeminism (Daly, L., 1990:88-108; Merchant, 1983; Primavesi, 1991; Ruether, 1975:186-211). The Annecy report offers the following as a definition of the phrase 'integrity of creation': "The value of all creatures in and for themselves, for one another, and for God, and their interconnectedness in a diverse whole that has unique value for God, together constitute the integrity of creation" (Birch, 1990:277). Should such a definition be universally accepted, its ramifications would be felt in both science and theology.

Despite the present failure of theology generally to embrace such an ecological perspective, the Annecy report maintains that biblical narratives do in fact provide us with a distinct understanding of creation's intrinsic integrity. If this claim is true, then perhaps what appears to be an anthropocentric (human-centered) type of worldview has been imposed by the biblical reader rather than implied by the biblical author (Bergant, 1991:5) and new interpretation should be made. Such an optimistic understanding of the biblical tradition is a direct challenge to any view that lays primary blame for our ecological difficulties at the doorstep of the Scriptures themselves (White, 1967:1203-7). It is also opposed to various anthropocentric biases brought to biblical interpretation by readers, be they androcentric (male-centered) or gynocentric (female-centered).

Most interpreters contend that the Bible displays a fundamentally theocentric (God-centered) perspective within which the principal value of creation lies less in its usefulness to humans (instrumental value) than in the fact of its existence from God (intrinsic value). No one would deny that creaturely limitations make it impossible for us to measure reality from anything but a human point of view. However, it is quite another thing to maintain that humankind is itself the actual measure of everything. The intrinsic value of creatures is presumed in biblical passages such as the creation narratives (Genesis 1-3), the account of the Noachic covenant (Genesis 9), the YHWH Speeches (Job 38-41), and various other poetic sections (e.g., Psalm 104, Eccl 3:1-9, etc.) The world has not been created merely for our use. The Bible is very clear on this point. We may have been told "to subdue and have dominion" (Gen 1:26, 28), "to serve it and to guard it" (Gen 2:15), but the primary relationship we have with the rest of creation is less mechanistic than it is organic. New readings of biblical material show this.

THE BIBLE AND ECOLOGY

The first chapters of the Book of Genesis contain two separate and very distinct accounts of creation (Bergant, 1991:8-12). Actually, only the Priestly account (Gen 1-2:4a) should be called a cosmogony. The Yahwistic version (Gen 2:4b-25) lacks a description of the creation of the universe and begins with the appearance of various forms of life on an already established earth. Similarities and borrowing notwithstanding, Israel's cosmogonic traditions are significantly different from those of other ancient Near Eastern societies, for, among other features, they lack theogonic myths. The God of Israel is uncreated and infinite. The underlying focus of the Priestly account of creation is the undisputed and unshared creative power of God, clearly a theocentric conviction. Still, the stature of humankind as portrayed within this fundamental theocentric tradition suggests a kind of anthropocentric interest. Human beings are privileged among the rest of creation.

The structure of the unit describing the creation of living beings suggests that the verses reporting human creation are a literary insertion into the pattern. The creation of human beings appears to have been originally an independent motif (Westermann, 1984:22ff). In the description of the creation of water animals and birds of the air, three divine actions are mentioned: "God said . . . God created . . . and God blessed" (vv. 20-22). The blessing, "Be fertile and multiply and fill the water . . . and . . . the earth," is a commission to the animals to populate their appropriate habitat. Part of this pattern is repeated in the description of the creation of the land animals: "God said . . . God made" (vv. 24-25). There is no mention of blessing. The report of the creation of humankind (vv. 26-27) is followed by what the pattern would suggest is the blessing of the land animals: "God blessed them . . . Be fertile and multiply and fill the earth (v. 28). As it stands, this blessing is expanded to include a commission directed to the human beings: "subdue it; and have dominion" (v. 28). Since the Israelites believed that YHWH alone was the source of fertility, this account of the creation and blessing of animals and of humankind may have been a polemic against the popular ancient Near Eastern divinization of fertility. If this is correct, the absence of a blessing for the land animals supports the view that originally there was such a divine declaration which has now been incorporated into the blessing and commission of humankind.

There are other noticeable disparities in this literary unit. The verb forms are different (cohortative, "Let us make" [v. 26], which expresses self-deliberation or consultation rather than jussive, "Let the water teem . . . Let the earth bring for" [vv. 20; 24], which expresses direction). Also, humans are made "in our image, after our likeness" (v. 26) rather than "according to (their) kind" (vv. 21; 24f). Such a break in structure and such peculiarity in literary style were ways of calling attention to something in the narrative, in this case, the uniqueness of the creation of humankind.

Although they are closely associated with the land animals with which they share the same habitat, only the human couple are made in the image/likeness of God, a motif with clear royal connotations. They alone are given a commission to govern as king and queen with the responsibility to "subdue" and "have dominion" (v. 28), a charge appropriate to royal individuals. There are Mesopotamian myths that tell of a god forming a mental image and then creating another god according to that image. It seems that Israel reinterpreted this theme, characterizing its monarch (a human creature rather than a deity) as an image of the god. This explains why Israel's king was referred to as the 'son of the god,' ruling in the land and over the land in the place of the god (Bentzen, 1955:43). Since an image represented the locale and extent of the sovereignty of the deity and not that of the image itself, this kind of royal authority was provisional and contingent on the good will of the god.

Scholars currently agree that the narrative of the flood and the eventual recession of the waters is a second creation story, coming from the same theological tradition and highlighting much of the same theology as found in Genesis 1. In fact, in the traditions of many early civilizations, the flood narrative was identical with the creation narrative. The destructive flood was really the primeval flood, and the individual saved was the first created human being. This suggests that both creation and flood were viewed as primeval happenings, not as historical events. Israel's flood account contains some of the very vocabulary found in the creation report. The abyss (*tehom*) was in place before God separated the waters (Gen 1:2). This same abyss burst open causing the flood (Gen 7:11), and was closed when God decreed its end (8:2). Both narratives mention a wind (*ruâh*) that swept over the cosmic abyss (1:2; 8:1). It was God's intent that the animals "be fertile and multiply" (1:22; 8:17). The same blessing with the commission to rule over the animals is given to humankind in both passages (1:28; 9:1-2).

Much has been written about the covenant that God made with Noah (9:8-17). Actually, the covenant was between God and the earth (v. 13, 16), between God and *all* living beings (vv. 9-10, 12, 15, 17). This was not merely a divine covenant with human beings and through them the rest of creation. The covenant was really a promise that chaotic waters would never again return to destroy creation. The bow in the sky was an eternal sign of that promise. This bow was probably the weapon of the divine warrior, who was victorious over the forces of primeval chaos. This point is supported by several Mesopotamian artifacts depicting the arrows in the god's quiver as lightning bolts. Hanging the bow in the sky was a sign that the primeval war was over and all of creation could rest secure. Like the divine rest after creation (2:2-3), retirement of the bow heralded the establishment of order.

Clearly, the Israelite worldview underlying the Priestly account of creation was theocentric, not anthropocentric. Any reading of the narrative that would suggest autonomous human sovereignty or absolute dominion overlooks the implications of Israel's royal theology. The monarchy (primeval man and woman) was entrusted with God's world, to manage its riches and to foster the forces of life within it, not to ravish it in order to accomplish its own goals. We cannot use the biblical accounts of creation to justify environmental exploitation.

CREATION THEOLOGY IN THE BOOK OF JOB

The affinity of creation theology to the wisdom tradition of Israel has long been recognized. However, in such study creation regularly has been considered one theme among many, and usually one of secondary importance rather than the basis of all theology as is proposed here. Furthermore, when not dismissed as a mythological account of primeval origins, creation is typically considered a feature of literary expression (e.g., nature poetry or imagery that characterizes something other than nature itself). This is not the point of view of the present article. Here, the lens through which material from the Book of Job will be examined and the standard against which it will be evaluation will a perspective sensitive to the integrity of creation, not one flowing from the bias and tyranny of unyielding anthropocentrism, which has held sway for so long.

Who does not know the story found in the Book of Job? After long and apparently pointless argument with his unsympathetic visitors, Job turns to God and demands some kind of explanation of the suffering that has unexplainably overwhelmed him. God does respond, but with questions rather than answers, and the questions address the design and operation of the natural world and not the specifics of Job's afflictions. As we marvel at the vistas of creation painted by the God's interrogation, the distinctive form of the questions itself that God uses should not be overlooked. These are not requests for information. They are ironic questions that serve to correct Job's shortsighted perception of his ability to grasp some of the mysteries of life in general and his life in particular. "Where were you when I founded the earth? . . . Have you ever in your lifetime commanded the morning and shown the dawn its place? . . . Do you know about the birth of the mountain goats? . . . Do you give the horse his strength, and endow his neck with splendor? (Job 38:4,12; 39:1,19).

These are rhetorical questions meant to lead Job to a depth of understanding far greater than any level of knowledge mere answers would provide. The marvel of this questioning technique is seen in its ability to bring Job to real wisdom despite, or perhaps because of, the indirectness of the approach. God asks questions about cosmic nature and Job gains insight into human nature.

Perhaps the most neglected characteristic of this multifaceted biblical book is the revelatory significance of nature depicted therein. Nature is not the principal marvel that is showcased here. It is the awesome God who is manifested through the natural world. In other words, the artistry of God can be seen in the splendor of the universe; God's wisdom, in its delicate balance; God's imagination, in its diversity; God's providence, in its inherent fruitfulness. The natural world was not only born of the creativity of God, it also bears the features of this creativity. Every property of creation mirrors something of the Creator. It is not enough to say that creation is the medium through which God is revealed. In a very real sense, the medium is itself the revelation. Job states this in his final response, where he testifies to having seen something of God, not merely the splendor of creation (42:5).

The wonders of creation that are paraded before Job were not unknown to him before this extraordinary revelation. By and large, they constituted the everyday world that he knew, but which he did not understand; the ordinary world within which he lived, but which he seems to have taken for granted. This breathtaking, even mystical, experience of creation has catapulted him out of his narrow confines of anthropocentrism into the vast expanses of mystery. It has brought him to realize that human history unfolds within the broader context of the natural world, and not vice versa. Job comes to see that the natural world does not merely serve the ends of human history. His encounter with the ineffable Creator-God has led him to this new insight. It is an insight that transforms him from a self-pitying victim of circumstances to a human being who has endured the struggles of human finitude and emerged chastened, yet nonetheless a mystic.

In his last response to God, Job admits that he has been converted to God's point of view, even without comprehending it. The God whom he previously knew and to whom he had been faithful was a God of righteousness, one who had recognized Job's integrity and apparently had rewarded him for it. The God whom Job now knows is the mysterious power who brought forth the world, as a man begets or as a woman gives birth, and who is somehow revealed in and through that wondrous world. This is a God who can provide for the entire resplendent universe without being distracted from the specific needs of fragile human beings. God can do this, because God's designs are grander than, yet still include, human history. God has taken human suffering, the most pressing concern of human life, and has situated it within a broader context. That context is material creation in its entirety. The YHWH speeches have shown Job that, in the midst of measureless natural grandeur, the ambiguity of human life can be confronted with the honesty and humility that it requires, an honesty and humility that can admit to and accept the limited capacity of human comprehension. Creation itself has expanded Job's vision and called him to a deepening of faith that goes beyond understanding.

The Book of Job demonstrates the profound human struggle between anthropology and cosmology, between human-centered interests and cosmocentric realities. It pits the search for understanding against the enormity of the universe in such a way that the human spirit is enraptured, and not broken. The commonplace yet strangely unfamiliar natural world awakens amazement at its wonders and leaves the humbled gazer aghast. Having called on God to put things right in his particular life, Job was led by the magnitude of creation beyond himself, there to see that he could not fathom the laws by which God governs. In the end, cosmology does not defeat anthropology; rather it opens its arms to welcome back its prodigal son.

The implications of such a transformed attitude are profound as well as wide-reaching. The shift from an anthropocentric to a cosmocentric worldview requires not only a new way of understanding the universe itself, but also a reexamination of many, if not most, of the tenets of the faith. Notions such as frugality and sufficiency in our use of natural resources, the viability of human life and the earth's ability to sustain it will all play an indispensable role in theological thinking. The irresponsibility and impertinence of human self-centeredness will be replaced by a sense of respect and responsible stewardship, and the bottom line of monetary calculation of resources will give way to aesthetic contemplation of natural beauty, a contemplation not unlike that of Job. "I had heard of you by word of mouth, but now my eye has seen you" (42:5).

WORKS CITED

Bentzen, Aage (1955) *King and Messiah* (London: Lutterworth Press).

Bergant, Dianne (1991) "Is the Biblical Worldview Anthropocentric?" *New Theology Review* 4:5-14.

Birch, Charles, William Eakin and Jay B. McDaniel, eds. (1990) *Liberating Life* (Maryknoll: Orbis Books).

Cobb, John B. Jr. (1982) *Process Theology as Political Theology* (Manchester: University Press).

Daly, Herman E. and John B. Cobb, Jr. (1989) *For the Common Good: Redirecting the Economy toward Community, the Environment, and a Sustainable Future* (Boston: Beacon Press).

Daly, Lois K. (1990) "Ecofeminism, Reverence for Life, and Feminist Theology," *Liberating Life* (Maryknoll Orbis Books): 88-108.

Kuhn, Thomas S. (1970) *The Structure of Scientific Revolutions*, 2d ed. (Chicago: University Press).

Küng, Hans & David Tracy, eds. (1980) *Paradigm Change in Theology* (New York: Crossroad).

Merchant, Carolyn (1980) *The Death of Nature: Women, Ecology and the Scientific Revolution* (San Francisco: Harper & Row).

Primavesi, Anne (1991) *From Apocalypse to Genesis: Ecology, Feminism and Christianity* (Philadelphia: Fortress Press).

Ruether, Rosemary Radford (1975) *New Woman/New Earth* (New York: Seabury).

Westermann Claus (1984) *Genesis 1-11: A Commentary* (Minneapolis: Augsburg).

White, Lynn (1967) "The Religious Roots of Our Ecological Crisis," *Science* 155: 1203-7.

HUMAN DIGNITY AND THE KINGDOM OF GOD: A RUSSIAN THEOLOGICAL PERSPECTIVE (VLADIMIR SOLOV'ËV)

Randall A. Poole

On Sunday, March 1, 1881, Tsar Alexander II of Russia, known as the "tsar-liberator" because he had emancipated Russia's serfs in 1861, was assassinated by terrorist revolutionaries who called themselves the People's Will. The first bomb, a type of homemade grenade, was thrown at the emperor's carriage and disabled it, but left Alexander unharmed. He insisted on walking back to the crowd to check on casualties. A second bomb exploded directly in front of him, blowing off his legs. He died within a few hours.

Later that month Vladimir Solov'ëv, today widely regarded as Russia's greatest philosopher and famous already then despite his youth, gave a public speech in which he appealed to the new tsar, Alexander III, to show Christian mercy on the regicides who had killed his father. In particular, he asked that they be spared the death penalty, which he regarded as an unconscionable violation of human dignity. Solov'ëv's plea was poorly received by both his audience, who in effect booed him, and by Alexander III, who when he heard of the speech ordered the philosopher to "refrain for a certain time" from lecturing in public.[1] This was a mild measure, but Solov'ëv felt it necessary to resign his positions at the Ministry of Public Education and St. Petersburg University. Thenceforth he lived as an independent scholar and publicist, devoting himself to writing. As for the terrorists and their fellow conspirators: they were hanged, six altogether. It was the last public execution in Russia. The crowd was enormous, some eighty thousand. There was no proper drop to the scaffold, only stools

that had to be kicked away and were too low for a quick kill. The execu-
tioner was drunk, as was common (and understandable), and botched the
job. One of the terrorists had to be re-hanged.[2] Though it is unlikely, it is
nice to think that Solov'ëv may have had some small influence in bringing such spectacles to an end.

LIFE AND WORKS

   Vladimir Sergeevich Solov'ëv was born in Moscow in 1853, the son of
Sergei M. Solov'ëv, the leading Russian historian of his generation. After
receiving a classical gymnasium education, he graduated from Moscow
University in 1873. In November of the following year he defended his
master's thesis, *The Crisis of Western Philosophy: Against the Positivists*,
his first book.[3] It anticipated the broader Russian revolt against positivism
by about twenty years and made Solov'ëv into something of a celebrity.
He began lecturing at Moscow University, but in June 1875 went abroad
for research on gnosticism and mysticism at the British Museum. There
he had a mystical experience (his second) of Sophia, the Divine Wisdom,
who directed him to travel to Egypt. In the desert he saw her again.
Returning to Moscow in the summer of 1876, he resumed teaching and
wrote his second book, *Philosophical Principles of Integral Knowledge*
(1877).[4] Within a year he moved to St. Petersburg to take a position in the
Ministry of Public Education. In early 1878 he delivered his famous
Lectures on Godmanhood to audiences of nearly a thousand that included Dostoevsky.[5] In April 1880 the young philosopher defended a brilliant
doctoral dissertation, *Critique of Abstract Principles*, and then began
teaching at St. Petersburg University.[6] "The author of four books in six
years was twenty-seven years old," as Paul Valliere observes.[7]
   These early works, all highly theoretical, advance the main outlines of
Solov'ëv's philosophical system. It was a metaphysics of the "unity of
all" (*vseedinstvo*), which conceived the cosmos as the manifestation or
"other" of the divine absolute in the process of its own becoming or self-
realization.[8] The unity of all, the return of (perfected) creation to the creator, was to be achieved through Godmanhood (*bogochelovechestvo*),
which refers to humanity's divine potential and vocation, the ideal of our
divine self-realization in and union with God. Human beings, created in
the image and likeness of God, are called to actively work for this ideal,
that is, for the Kingdom of God and universal transfiguration in the unity
of all, in which all will be one in God. Humanity is the key link in this
metaphysics of cosmic redemption, the mediating principle between God
and world. The self-realization of each individual person is at the same
time a step toward the divinization of the cosmos. Indeed the great theme

of Solov'ëv's philosophy is human perfectibility.[9]

Compared to the theoretical focus of his first four books, Solov'ëv's works in the 1880s took a somewhat different direction. They focused on various aspects of his project for establishing a worldwide "free theocracy," which would reunify Eastern and Western Christianity under the spiritual authority of the Roman pontiff and the imperial dominion of the Russian tsar, all in preparation for the Kingdom of God on earth.[10] Disappointment with Russia as the prospective agent of universal theocracy, and more generally with the external forms of his theocratic ideal, led Solov'ëv to return to philosophy proper in the 1890s. This period culminated with a major treatise on ethics and social philosophy, *Justification of the Good* (1897).[11] His final work was *Three Dialogues on War, Progress and the End of World History, with a Brief Tale of the Anti-Christ* (1899-1900).[12] He died on 31 July 1900.

GODMANHOOD AND THE MEANING OF ABSOLUTE HUMAN VALUE

The central idea of Solov'ëv's philosophy is *bogochelovechestvo*, translated as Godmanhood, divine humanity, or the humanity of God. *Bogochelovechestvo* is an abstract noun formed from *Bogochelovek*, God-human or God-man, a name for Christ. The concept's overall meaning is conveyed by the teaching of St. Athanasius and other church fathers that "God became man so that man might become God."[13] This formula consists of two key elements: *kenosis* (the humanization of God in the incarnation) and *theosis* (the deification of man). The "humanity of God," as Valliere translates *bogochelovechestvo* in his major study *Modern Russian Theology*,[14] captures very nicely the kenotic and incarnational aspect. It concisely expresses the Christology of the Council of Chalcedon (451): In Christ two distinct natures, the divine and human, are united without "division or confusion" in one person. The human retains its distinct identity even alongside the divine, a clear vindication of its intrinsic worth. But the "humanity of God" does not work as well for the theotic aspect of Athanasius's formula, which was, I believe, the more important one for Solov'ëv. For him, *bogochelovechestvo* meant the divinity of humanity as much as the humanity of God.[15] "Godmanhood" more readily suggests Solov'ëv's conception of God and man as ultimately one absolute, divine-human being: divinity that is also human (intrinsically and not only in the incarnation) and humanity that is also divine (by origin and vocation). Crucially, it also conveys the idea of a state that is to be achieved, in a way that neither the "humanity of God" nor "divine humanity" does.

Godmanhood was not an initial dogmatic premise for Solov'ëv, but rather the logical conclusion of sound philosophical method. His point of departure was not God but man,[16] specifically human consciousness and morality. He believed that morality—our consciousness of absolute ideals and the capacity to act on them—is not only the most distinctive property of human beings but also our primary testimony to the ultimate nature of reality. Solov'ëv's method, proceeding up to the divine from analysis of the human, is brilliantly deployed from the very beginning of his famous *Lectures on Godmanhood.* In the first two lectures, he introduces important aspects of his philosophical anthropology by looking at the decline of religion and rise of secular humanism in modern European intellectual history. He contends, in particular, that contemporary European consciousness lacks a clear idea of the absolute and that this is reflected in its understanding of human nature. His remarks, though somewhat cursory, are highly revealing of his own approach to the problem of the absolute and the ground of human value.

First, Solov'ëv makes clear that religion is, or should be, about the absolute: "Religion is the connection of humanity and the world with the absolute principle and focus of all that exists. Clearly, if we admit the reality of such an absolute principle, it must determine all the interests and the whole content of human life and consciousness."[17] These words were spoken by a mystic, someone whose whole life experience was permeated with absolute divine content, but the "pitiful thing" that was contemporary religion left Solov'ëv with little doubt that the absolute was far from the concerns of most educated Europeans.

At the same time he held that the absolute could not be eradicated altogether from human consciousness; we inevitably think in terms of absolutes and ideals. The issue is whether the absolute is consciously recognized, clearly represented, and concretely related to all aspects of human life, or rather disguised, distorted, and disfigured. Contemporary Western civilization, having abandoned the task of dealing with the absolute on its own terms, "is striving to substitute something for the rejected gods" (LDH, 2). This unconscious religious striving has given rise to two powerful ideologies: socialism and positivism. As forms of modern humanism, both proclaim human dignity. In this Solov'ëv recognizes their truth: they are right in thinking that human beings are absolute. But they are wrong in supposing that human beings can be absolute without the absolute, that we can be absolute in value while also being only facts among a multitude of other facts (LDH, 18-19). Thus Solov'ëv's main criticism of modern humanism is that, in Valliere's formulation, it does not appreciate the implications of its basic assumption.[18] Solov'ëv draws out these implications and concludes that the very capacity to conceive of ourselves as absolute entails the reality of the absolute, i.e., a theistic metaphysics.

His underlying argument is that there is something radically "unnatural" about our self-conception and human consciousness in general. The idea of "absolute," present in our thought at all levels whether we consciously recognize it or not, is a striking anomaly in an empirical world of relative facts. Even evaluations such as the world as "empirical" and facts as "relative" demonstrate the inevitability of the absolute perspective of consciousness. It is the nature of the mind to evaluate, and in doing so we rely on absolute, ideal norms (LDH, 30). The data of empirical experience convey nothing of these ideals and norms. The upshot is that our capacity to evaluate—and to value ourselves as absolute—when experience confronts us with only facts, seems to indicate that the natural world is not the only one. In other words, the very idea of "absolute," as in our own self-conception, implies its reality. From this logic (more implicit than explicit in his text) Solov'ëv draws a stark conclusion: "belief in oneself, belief in the human person, is at the same time belief in God" (LDH, 23).

There is another aspect to Solov'ëv's understanding of absolute human value, one that goes to the heart of his concept of Godmanhood. The Russian philosopher takes "absolute" quite literally. Absolute means that which cannot be surpassed or excelled. To say this of human beings is necessarily to equate our value with God's, which is precisely what Solov'ëv does. He uses both "absolute" and "divine" to describe the value of human beings: "The human person . . . has absolute, divine significance" (LDH, 17). Since there can be no gradation at the level of absolute, human beings and God are equal in value. We are equally persons, or, in other words, all persons are divine, beginning with God. This divine-human equality has momentous implications. It alone makes possible genuine, free union between man and God.

> Such a union would be impossible if the divine principle were purely external to humanity, if it were not rooted in human personhood itself. If it were not so rooted, our relationship to the divine principle could be only one of involuntary, fateful subordination. The free inner union between the absolute, divine principle and the human person is possible only because the latter also has absolute significance. The human person can unite with the divine principle freely, from within, only because the person is in a certain sense divine, or more precisely, participates in Divinity (LDH, 17).[19]

Human freedom relative to God is so important because it is the essential condition of the fuller realization of human divinity. Thus the human person "is in a certain sense divine" because our divinity is an intrinsic potential that must be freely, *humanly* realized, and this is impossible without divine-human equality. The realization of our divine potential rests on human autonomy, self-determination, and freedom of conscience. This is a highly distinctive aspect of Solov'ëv's thought: the realization of our divinity depends on the proper exercise of our humanity.

THE THREE PRINCIPLES OF HUMAN NATURE

Solov'ëv calls human consciousness of the absolute the divine, religious, or mystical principle in man. It is one of three principles in his overall conception of human nature. The other two are the material principle, by which human beings are part of the natural world, and rational freedom or autonomy (reason and morality), which is the distinctively human principle, the middle principle between the divine and material (LDH, 158). The human principle is the capacity for self-determination in the direction of either the material or the divine, the capacity to "become" more (or less) than we presently are, to infinitely perfect (or degrade) ourselves (LDH, 142). Solov'ëv sees the capability to "become" as distinctively human. Non-rational beings do not "become," they can only "be" what they are by nature; their natural capacities are realized over the course of their life by instinct, not self-determination. God, too, according to Solov'ëv, can only "be," in that he is already perfect. Only human beings (and in principle other free rational beings) are capable of "becoming," which, if directed toward the divine, takes the form of infinite self-perfection.[20] The autonomous human element, as noted above, is an indispensable component of Godmanhood.

Solov'ëv introduces his tripartite conception of human nature in the last two *Lectures on Godmanhood*, as part of his Christology. His philosophical anthropology in effect extends the Chalcedon dogma of the two natures of Jesus Christ to all human persons and even to all existence,[21] with the divine nature thus becoming more an intrinsic potential that must be freely realized by the human. The possibility of such a free, human realization of the divine was vitiated by the Fall (in the first Adam), which enslaved human will to nature, but was restored by the incarnation (in the second Adam). In Jesus Christ,

> the human principle, having placed itself in the proper relationship of voluntary subordination to, or harmony with, the divine principle as inner good, thereby once more receives the significance of the intermediary, uniting principle between God and nature. And nature, purified by the death on the cross, loses its material separateness and weight and becomes a direct expression and instrument of the Divine Spirit, a true *spiritual*

body (LDH, 163).

But the human realization of the divine—our deification (theosis) and through us the spiritualization or divinization of the cosmos—while restored by Christ as a possibility, remains a task that we must actively work to accomplish. Otherwise the Kingdom of God, understood as deified humanity or Godmanhood, would have come with him. It is something we must take responsibility for and work toward as the goal of human progress, not something to be awaited from the external action of divine grace.[22] Thus Solov'ëv's Christology revises mainstream Christian ideas of salvation since Augustine if not earlier: with Solov'ëv Christ does not so much save us as make it possible for us to save ourselves. For Russia's greatest religious philosopher, "salvation" largely meant the self-realization of our own intrinsic divinity.[23]

The conception of human nature (divine-human-natural) that Solov'ëv introduced in *Lectures on Godmanhood* forms the basic philosophical framework of his subsequent works. In them he stresses that human autonomy, the middle principle and the condition of Godmanhood, is the ground of human dignity. In *Critique of Abstract Principles* he embraced Kant's conception of human autonomy and dignity, calling it the "essence of morality."[24] For Solov'ëv the divine principle is not, by itself, the source of human dignity. The source is self-determination and perfectibility according to our consciousness of the absolute or divine. In *Lectures on Godmanhood*, he affirms absolute human value, human divinity, and divine-human equality, but it is really autonomy, the self-realization of our intrinsic divine potential, the capacity to *become* divine (theosis), that is the core of human dignity.[25] Were this realization externally rather than internally determined (heteronomously rather than autonomously), human dignity would be deprived of its basis. "Salvation" apart from human free will would violate human dignity or at any rate be accomplished past it. For this reason, the source of human dignity is not God but Godmanhood. This is the humanist thread that runs through Solov'ëv's philosophy.[26]

Solov'ëv was very concerned that human autonomy not be overwhelmed by the divine principle. This led him to downplay or reconceptualize the role of miracle, revelation, and dogma in religion, all of which, he feared, risked undermining true faith, autonomy, and self-determination by purporting to manifest the divine as if it were something external and knowable as a positive fact.[27] He understood, with Dostoevsky, that miracles can enslave, impairing the free, human realization of the divine. This understanding shaped his Christology, which, as we have seen, is philosophical and universalistic. He maintained that "strictly speaking, the incarnation of Divinity is not miraculous, that is, it is not alien to the general order of being" (LDH, 157). In his 1891 speech "The Collapse of the Medieval Worldview," he commented on Luke 9: 49-56 as follows: "James and John did not know the spirit of Christ, and they did not know it just because they believed above all in His external miraculous power. Such power there was, but it was not the essential thing."[28] The Russian philosopher closest to Solov'ëv, Evgenii Trubetskoi, expressed the spirit of his Christology in writing, remarkably, that "Christ's complete sacrifice saves man not as sorcery from outside, but as spiritual influence *liberating him from inside* and transforming his nature only on the condition of the *autonomous* self-determination of his will."[29]

"FREE THEOCRACY" AND CHURCH UNION

For Solov'ëv Godmanhood was necessarily a social and cultural project, since human perfectibility, the ever fuller realization and development of human potential, is inconceivable apart from society and history. This takes us to Solov'ëv's social philosophy, which he treats as a branch of moral philosophy (applied or "objective" ethics in contrast to pure or "subjective" ethics). He presented his moral philosophy (pure and applied) in *Critique of Abstract Principles* (his doctoral thesis) and then, in a revised and definitive version, *Justification of the Good*.

Critique of Abstract Principles, written concurrently with *Lectures on Godmanhood*, is an indispensable exposition of Solov'ëv's whole system. An "abstract principle" is one that is abstracted from and mistaken for the whole, whether the whole is person, society, or, ultimately, the "unity of all." Solov'ëv shows how the material, human, and divine principles can each be abstracted or put in place of the whole. Even so, he is much less concerned with the dangers of rational autonomy (the human principle) being an abstract principle than of it not being firmly included in the whole, between the material and divine principles. The vision of the social whole that he lays out in his doctoral dissertation is "free theocracy," "free" precisely because it purports to respect human autonomy.

In Solov'ëv's social philosophy, the principle of rational autonomy takes the form of law, based on recognition that human beings are persons, ends-in-themselves, and bearers of rights.[30] In Valliere's felicitous expression, "law is grounded in metaphysical personhood (freedom and reason), the inalienable glory of the human being."[31] The virtue of law, according to Solov'ëv, is that it makes possible the realization of all higher potentials of human nature, for it is the very condition of civilized life and peaceful society. Law makes people equal in a way that they are not in the state of nature or in unlawful societies, where the strong brutalize the weak and themselves in the process. By equalizing human relations, law enables people to develop as persons. It is an essential spiritualizing force. This was Solov'ëv's ultimate justification of law and, more generally, of "objective ethics."

Law is an essential but not the highest principle of Solov'ëv's social philosophy. It deals with the means by which people pursue their ends, but not the ends themselves. Solov'ëv was not satisfied with the liberal individualist response that people determine their own ends and pursue them within the limits of the law. He believed that society ought to have a positive content, a morally normative end that would unite its members. Meanwhile law divides them. In *Critique of Abstract Principles*, he wrote that the equality of all before the law actually means that "all are equally *limited* by law, or all equally limit each other; this means there is no inner or positive unity among them, only their correct division and demarcation."[32] Only the divine or mystical principle in human nature, not law, can provide inner, positive unity among people. The philosopher provides a succinct formulation of his social ideal in the preface to his book. The ultimate moral significance of society, he writes,

> is determined by the religious or mystical principle in man, by virtue of which all members of society are not limits for each other, but rather internally fulfill each other in the free unity of spiritual love, which must be immediately realized in a spiritual society or the church. Thus the normative society has as its foundation a spiritual union or the church, which defines its absolute ends.[33]

But the realization of the divine principle in society must be approached freely and consciously, it cannot be based on external clerical authority or blind faith, it must fully respect the human principle of rational autonomy, both in morality—where it takes the form of freedom of conscience—and law. "Thus the true, normative society must be defined as free theocracy."[34] It was the way to the realization of humanity's divine potential (Godmanhood).

Solov'ëv insists that free theocracy must respect the material and rational principles in human nature at both the individual and societal levels, our natural being and the economy as well as reason, self-determination, and law. Abstract clericalism or false theocracy (Islam and the medieval Catholic church are his main historical examples) suppresses all of them. It rejects the physical and natural element as sinful, preaching asceticism and mortification of the flesh. "In personal, inner life it suppresses the purely human or rational principle, the principle of reason and inner freedom or freedom of conscience," Solov'ëv writes. Church power reigns over all spheres of reason. "Since God is understood only as an external being, alien to man and nature, it is clear that the revelation of such a God happens only in an external fact—in lightning and thunder, completely drowning out the quiet voice of reason and conscience." At the societal level abstract clericalism externally rules over civil society and the economy, subordinating them and violently distorting their development.[35]

In view of the historical record of theocracy, Solov'ëv was at pains to stress that his vision of "free theocracy" preserved human autonomy, the very condition of Godmanhood. At the individual level the concept of autonomy means self-determination according to absolute ideals that are freely recognized by reason. It is the essence of the principle of freedom of conscience, which Solov'ëv championed both in his philosophical and publicistic works. At the societal level autonomy means that the relative independence of each component part is necessary for the integrity of the whole. In his formulation:

> In normative society (free theocracy) all the various elements of society, all the aspects and spheres of social relations, are preserved and exist not as isolated spheres closed-off in themselves and irrelevant to each other, or as spheres striving for exclusive predominance, but as necessary component parts of one complex whole. . . . It is impossible here to have contradiction and exclusivity among these elements, for if they are all necessary for each other, then they also are all autonomous and yet dependent on each other.[36]

At the metaphysical level, the very concept of the "unity of all" assumes the relative autonomy of constituent parts. Authentic diversity and free development are conditions of genuine unity. Any oppressive or monistic unity, like any exclusive self-affirmation or anarchic particularism, is evil, false, and ugly.

The meaning of Solov'ëv's theocratic ideal has long vexed scholars. A society freely united in love of God, all of whose members seek to fulfill each other in that love, is one that has attained a vastly higher level of moral development than anything in Solov'ëv's day or ours. The Russian philosopher may have wanted to suggest that the Kingdom of God would not be possible until, at least, "free theocracy" was. Kostalevsky proposes, helpfully, that theocracy was both means and end: "For Soloviev, the aim (the abiding foundation) was theocracy in the sense of the Kingdom of God, while the means (the practical action) was theocracy in the sense of a form of society that is capable, due to its attained perfection, of entering into the Kingdom of God."[37]

Solov'ëv believed that free theocracy, both as means—the Chris-

tianization of life—and end—the final triumph of the Kingdom of God—
rested on the reunification of the church. He devoted himself to this
task—ecumenism, as it would come to be called—in the 1880s. His first
and most important work laying out his conception of the church and
ideal of church unity is "The Great Schism and Christian Politics"
(1883).[38] In it he applies his tripartite, Christological model of human
nature to the church. Eastern Christianity represents the divine element,
and Western Christianity the human, but the historical development of
each element has been one-sided or "abstract," to use the terminology of
Critique of Abstract Principles. Orthodoxy took the divine without the
human and approached it as an object of passive devotion rather than a
matter of active practice and free human assimilation. Catholicism asserted the human in place of the divine and falsely represented it as the
divine. The result was not the genuine autonomy of the human element
but its despotism, the "false theocracy" of the medieval Roman church.
The ideal of the church, in contrast to these historical distortions, is the
free inner union of both the divine and human elements. "In Christ,"
Solov'ëv explains,

> divinity was not a passive object of worship and contemplation for His
> human consciousness, but was inwardly united with His human will and
> acted through it, regenerating His physical nature. Likewise in the Church
> the divine essence or holiness must not be merely revered and worshipped
> but, united with the practical powers of man, must actively penetrate
> through them into all the elements of the world so as to sanctify and spiri-
> tualize them. The divine principle of the Church must not merely abide and
> be preserved in the world but *rule* the world,

which requires free human agency and cooperation, but not domination
(77).

Rome was not wrong in exercising its human will and power in trying
to create a worldwide theocracy; it was wrong in replacing these means
for the end. Rome's ultimate purpose, perfectly correct, was the Kingdom
of God on earth; the means, also correct, were the church's spiritual
power. But, Solov'ëv writes,

> it was easy to lose sight of the fact that spiritual power only serves to pre-
> pare and lead mankind to God's kingdom in which there no longer is any
> power or domination. The contemplative East sinned by not thinking at all
> of the practical means and conditions of carrying out God's work on earth;
> the practical West erred in thinking of those means first and foremost and
> making them the end of its activity (82).

These contrasting approaches, and even more so the underlying cultural differences between East and West, not the *filioque* or unleavened bread, caused the great schism between Rome and Byzantium, traditionally dated at 1054. After that Byzantium eventually fell to Islam (1453) while Rome increasingly gave in to its "jealous love of power" (84).

It is interesting that Solov'ëv does not condemn the Church of Rome's supreme central authority, hierarchical order, and discipline. He says they were necessary practical means for its purpose of building the Kingdom of God on earth and even endorses the formula of the "Church militant" (86). But Rome forgot that papal power, governing only the human side of the church and its temporal militant organization, was a means, "conditioned by a mystical reality, for carrying on God's work on earth" (89). The result of mistaking the means for the end was the peculiarly pernicious form of absolutism called papism. It perverted the idea of theocracy by giving it the character of compulsory domination. Papism betrayed the true idea of theocracy, that supreme authority belongs to spiritual, not secular power, and that it must be exercised by spiritual, moral means. Instead it tried to rule the world by worldly means, "reducing the Church to the level of the state, and the spiritual power to the level of the temporal" (91). From this Solov'ëv draws a striking conclusion: "The fault of papism was not that it exalted, but that it humiliated papal power" (92). Furthermore, the papist church, by reducing itself to the level of the state, deprived the secular world of its ideal and so of the possibility of assimilating the image of the true church. It thus deprived secular state and society of their model for inner Christianization, the true meaning of theocracy (91-92).

Papism's sin against individual freedom was even greater. Solov'ëv is referring here to the church's efforts to force people, through in some cases the most heinous forms of torture, to submit to itself as a condition of salvation. This was an attempt to coerce human conscience and will, a fruitless attempt by its very nature, "and thus all the more revolting." "In exacting submission by external means," Solov'ëv continues, "ecclesiastical authority sought to deprive man of the power of moral self-determination," that is, of the very condition of "salvation" (Godmanhood). "By addressing itself not to man's moral powers but to his physical weakness the Church lost its moral superiority over individual minds and at the same time roused their just opposition," which took the form of Protestantism (93). This was a deeply moral protest, from the depths of human personhood, in defense of the inviolability of personal conscience and against "the tyranny of the spiritual power that had forgotten its spiritual character" (94). Protestantism affirmed that *"man cannot be saved by compulsion,"* one of Solov'ëv's own deepest convictions (95).

Despite the "relative justification" of the main historical movements against Rome, the end result, Solov'ëv laments, is that the Christian world is divided and finds itself in its present "deplorable state." "True Christian life," he says, "will begin only when all free forces of humanity . . . voluntarily and conscientiously set to work upon all that medieval papism tried to achieve by violence and compulsion. That will be the end of the great schism and the beginning of Christian politics" (96). Thus the immediate aim of Christian politics or policy should be the re-establishment of church unity. Solov'ëv believed that the papacy, having abandoned its former papism, would naturally head the reunited Christian church. As he made clear in works published over the next several years,[39] he accepted not only the supremacy of the Roman see but also the Catholic dogmatic innovations of the *filioque*, immaculate conception, and papal infallibility, all of which he justified by the principle of "dogmatic development."[40] But recognition of the supreme authority of the Roman pontiff would not mean "Romanization," for the reunited church will be truly universal, embracing and reconciling (without effacing) the distinctiveness of both its halves, Eastern and Western, and the divine and human principles corresponding to them (97). The universal church will then better conform to the truth of Godmanhood, bringing the divine and human principles, historically "abstracted" from each other in the Eastern and Western churches, into closer approximation to their complete unity in Christ.[41]

The universal Christian church, understood as perfect divine-human union, already exists, of course, but as a transcendent, mystical unity. "The one holy, catholic and apostolic Church," Solov'ëv writes, "essentially abides both in the East and in the West, and shall abide forever, in spite of the temporal hostility and division between the two halves of the Christian world" (98). Our task is to bring the earthly reality of the church into ever closer conformity with its mystical essence. In his words, "The essential unity of the universal Church, hidden from our eyes, must become manifest through the visible reunion of the two ecclesiastical communities divided in history, though indivisible in Christ" (100). The reunion and completion of the church will achieve "free theocracy." "Then the truth of Godmanhood, *given* to us in its inner essence, will also prove to be our own *work* and find embodiment in actual human life" (101).

Solov'ëv had an operational plan to make his ecumenical vision a reality: Christendom was to be reunited by an alliance between the Russian emperor, Alexander III, and Pope Leo XIII. He championed this plan in his works and among Roman Catholic leaders whom he visited in central and western Europe. Nowhere, perhaps, is it more clear that Solov'ëv the mystic had difficulty distinguishing between this world and the higher one. Pope Leo XIII had a clearer sense of the difference: when he learned of Solov'ëv's plan he said it was a beautiful idea but impossible without a miracle. Surely it operates on a very different level than free theocracy as a philosophical ideal stipulating a moral transformation so radical that it would bring humanity to the threshold of theosis.

JUSTIFICATION OF THE GOOD: HUMAN PERFECTIBILITY IN THE IMAGE AND LIKENESS OF GOD

In the 1890s Solov'ëv came to agree, it seems, with Leo's verdict. He grew disillusioned with his practical (or so he had imagined) plans for theocracy, though never with the ideal itself. The great Russian famine of 1891-1892 was a turning point, convincing him of the huge gap between Russian reality and his theocratic ideal.[42] He returned to the type of philosophical work that had engaged him a decade earlier. *Justification of the Good*, his magnum opus, appeared in 1897. By common consensus it is the most important Russian work of moral philosophy. Arguably it is one of the great modern works of ethics and religious philosophy more generally. It is Solov'ëv's most powerful and systematic defense of human dignity—the book's overall theme.

Justification of the Good is divided into three parts, "The Good in Human Nature," "The Good from God," and "The Good through Human History." In the first part Solov'ëv applies the three principles of human nature to an analysis of moral experience, identifying three "primary data of morality": shame, compassion, and reverence. Shame corresponds to the material principle in human nature, compassion to the purely human, and reverence to the divine. He regarded religious experience (reverence) as a very important component of moral experience, so much so that his overall conception is really moral-religious experience. Part II of *Justification of the Good*, "The Good from God," develops this aspect of his moral philosophy. Throughout he emphasizes the immediacy and authenticity of our religious experience. "The reality of the Deity is not a *deduction* from religious experience but the *content* of it. . . . *God is in us, therefore He is*."[43] This conviction in the veracity of moral-religious experience as testimony to the ultimate nature of reality is the foundation of his whole philosophy.

Solov'ëv delineates the content of religious experience into three constituent elements: consciousness of God as absolute perfection, consciousness of our own imperfection, and conscious striving toward divine perfection. Our consciousness of divine perfection is the "image of God" in us and our striving to perfect ourselves according to that image is our "likeness" to God (145). This is a creative and powerful interpretation of the "image and likeness" verses (Genesis 1:26, 9:6); Solov'ëv will often invoke it. He also refers here (and on a number of occasions) to Matthew 5:48—"Be perfect even as your Father in heaven is perfect"—but explains that the imperative can only be accomplished by the *process of becoming perfect* (perfectibility), so that "be perfect" actually means "become perfect" (147).

Russia's greatest religious philosopher now explicitly defines human dignity as consisting in our consciousness of absolute perfection (the image of God) and in our striving to perfect ourselves (the likeness of God) (152). He calls the image of God the power of representation (of absolute perfection) and the likeness of God the power of striving (to achieve it). This "double infinity" belongs to every person. "It is in this that the absolute significance, dignity, and worth of human personhood consist, and this is the basis of its inalienable rights" (176). Further, the human person contains an element of intrinsic value, "which can never be merely a means—namely, the possibility, inherent in it, of infinite perfection through contemplation of and union with the absolute fullness of being" (196). And in perhaps the most capacious lines from *Justification of the Good*, Solov'ëv writes, "The absolute value of man is based, as we know, upon the *possibility* inherent in his reason and his will of infinitely approaching perfection or, according to the patristic expression, the possibility of becoming divine (*theosis*)" (296).

Human autonomy, dignity and perfectibility are the conditions, we know, of Godmanhood or the Kingdom of God, which Solov'ëv defines here, in a pivotal chapter of *Justification of the Good*, as the "unconditional principle of morality": "*participate, as fully as in thee lies, in the work of making thyself and everyone more perfect, so that the Kingdom of God may be finally revealed in the world*" (152). The Kingdom of God, he says, cannot be expected by the immediate action of God. Indeed "God has never acted immediately"—a striking comment meant to reinforce the necessity of free human participation in God's work. Why, he asks, wasn't the Kingdom of God established long ago or from all eternity? "What was the need for all these centuries and millenniums of human history," which will no doubt long continue (149)? The answer, clearly, is that the Kingdom of God must be humanly realized, through our self-determination toward the divine and the self-realization of our divine potential. His premise throughout is that an achieved perfection is greater than one that is bestowed.[44]

In Part III of *Justification of the Good*, "The Good through Human History," Solov'ëv turns from "subjective ethics" to "objective ethics" (social philosophy), but without the emphasis on "free theocracy" of

Critique of Abstract Principles. Again the fundamental principle is human dignity. It is the "moral norm of social life," as he calls one of his chapters. The just society ought to recognize that each of its members has the right to a dignified or worthy existence, and it ought to materially provide, where necessary, for this right (296-298, 306). In this belief that the state ought to provide a certain minimum welfare for its members, in his protest against dehumanizing social conditions and concern for the poor and urban working class, Solov'ëv was a modern "new" liberal.[45] His views on criminal justice, including his devastating critique of the death penalty, are also quite modern and entirely consistent with the "moral norm" of human dignity.

The gradual realization of human potential in history, the process of human perfectibility and striving toward Godmanhood, is called progress. This seems to be the very concept of the "justification of the good" and to explain why humanity was not created perfect and why the Kingdom of God is our task rather than God's gift.[46] (Were it merely a gift, it ought to have been given from the moment of creation, in order to prevent human evil.) That Godmanhood is an ideal to be achieved can only mean that perfectibility is itself the highest good, and so justifies the "absolute" good (God) for permitting (or enabling) the whole process.[47] In other words, the justification of the good is a type of theodicy: perfectibility as the highest possible good justifies the costs (moral evil), although how must remain unfathomable to human minds (151-152).

Solov'ëv remained reluctant, even in *Justification of the Good*, to part with his ideal of "free theocracy," although he scrupulously avoids the term itself. He calls not for separation of church and state but rather for their distinction, fearing that complete separation would lead to the conflation and usurpation of the functions of one by the other. He still spoke of a Christian state that recognizes *"the supreme spiritual authority of the universal Church"* (394), and even of the harmonious cooperation of prophet, priest, and king in working to bring about the Kingdom of God (401-403). These are good reasons to conclude, with Valliere, that, "for all its modernism and moderation, *The Justification of the Good* remains the work of a mystic, a prophet, and a Christian theocrat."[48]

CONCLUDING REMARKS

There is no doubt that Solov'ëv himself continued to recognize *"the supreme spiritual authority of the universal Church,"* in the mystical sense in which he understood it in his 1883 essay "The Great Schism and Christian Politics." In 1896 he received communion from a priest of the Uniate (Greek Catholic) Church in Moscow. The meaning of this act is controversial, with some of his Catholic admirers interpreting it as his conversion to Roman Catholicism, especially since the philosopher first read aloud the Trent confession of faith. It seems reasonably clear, however, that for Solov'ëv it was only an affirmation that he saw himself as belonging to the one universal Church that transcended historical divisions.[49] In other words, he did not feel himself bound by confessional requirements. A letter he wrote in 1892 effectively sums up the matter: "I am as far from the narrowness of Rome as from that of Byzantium, or Augsburg, or Geneva; the religion of the Holy Spirit which I profess is wider and at the same time fuller in content than all particular religions."[50]

Yet Solov'ëv was steadfast in his conviction in the supremacy of the Holy see. In an 1896 letter he wrote that all Christians should unite around the "traditional center of unity—the see of Rome," explaining that, "this is all the more practicable because that center no longer possesses external compulsory power, and therefore everyone may unite with it *to the extent indicated by conscience*."[51] While little remained of his messianic hope in Russia (and he had long deplored the sorry state of the Russian church), there is no indication that he suffered similar disappointment in the contemporary Church of Rome. Indeed Leo XIII's affirmation of the dignity of labor in his famous encyclical *Rerum novarum* (1891) was consonant with Solov'ëv's "social gospel" theology.[52] The Russian religious philosopher would surely have welcomed the Second Vatican Council, perhaps especially its declaration on religious liberty, *Dignitatis humanae* (1965). The election of Cardinal Karol Wojtyla as Pope John Paul II would also likely have pleased him greatly, since he (Solov'ëv) regarded the Poles as a theocratic nation, together with the Russians and Jews. John Paul returned the compliment, as it were, by expressing his admiration for Solov'ëv in his encyclical *Fides et ratio* (1998).[53] The pope's last word was reported to have been "Amen," as if to consummate a life dedicated to the work of the Lord. A century earlier Solov'ëv's last words were "hard is the work of the Lord."[54] Our work, and it continues.

NOTES

1. Quoted by Marina Kostalevsky, *Dostoevsky and Soloviev: The Art of Integral Vision* (New Haven: Yale University Press, 1997), p. 80.

2. Edward Crankshaw, *The Shadow of the Winter Palace: Russia's Drift to Revolution, 1825-1917* (New York: Viking, 1976), pp. 270-271, on the execution.

3. *Krizis zapadnoi filosofii (Protiv positivistov)*, in *Sobranie sochinenii Vladimira Sergeevicha Solov'ëva*, eds. S. M. Solov'ëv and E. L. Radlov, 2nd ed., 10 vols. (St. Petersburg, 1911-1914), vol. 1, pp. 27-170. Vladimir Solovyov, *The Crisis of Western Phi-

losophy (Against the Positivists), trans. and ed. Boris Jakim (Hudson, NY: Lindis farne Press, 1996).

4. *Filosofskie nachala tsel'nogo znaniia, Sobranie sochinenii*, vol. 1, pp. 250-406. There is no English translation.

5. *Chteniia o Bogochelovechestve, Sobranie sochinenii*, vol. 3, pp. 1-181. Vladimir Solovyov, *Lectures on Divine Humanity*, revised and ed. Boris Jakim (Hudson, NY: Lindisfarne Press, 1995), based on *Lectures on Godmanhood*, trans. Peter P. Zouboff (London, 1948).

6. *Kritika otvlechënnykh nachal, Sobranie sochinenii*, vol. 2, pp. v-xvi, 1-397. There is no English translation.

7. Paul Valliere, "Vladimir Soloviev (1853-1900)," *The Teachings of Modern Christianity on Law, Politics, and Human Nature*, ed. John Witte Jr. and Frank S. Alexander, vol. 1 (New York: Columbia University Press, 2006), p. 535.

8. Solov'ëv distinguishes between two poles of the absolute. The first is self-subsitent (God), the second is in the process of becoming (man), "and the full truth can be expressed by the word 'Godmanhood.'" *Kritika otvlechënnykh nachal*, pp. 315-324 (quotation at p. 323).

9. It is the first of the "central teachings" identified by Jonathan Sutton in his *The Religious Philosophy of Vladimir Solovyov: Towards a Reassessment* (New York: St. Martin's Press, 1988).

10. His works of the period include *Dukhovnye osnovy zhizni* (1882-1884), translated as *God, Man and the Church: The Spiritual Foundations of Life* by Donald Attwater (London: James Clarke, 1938); "Velikii spor i khristianskaia politika" ("The Great Schism and Christian Politics") (1883); "Evreistvo i khristianskii vopros" ("The Jews and the Christian Problem") (1884); *Istoriia i budushchnost' teokratii* (*The History and Future of Theocracy*) (1887); *L'Idée russe* (1888); *La Russie et l'Église universelle* (1889), translated as *Russia and the Universal Church* by Herbert Rees (London: Geoffrey Bles, 1948); and *Natsional'nyi vopros v Rossii* (*The National Question in Russia*), two vols. (1888, 1891).

11. *Opravdanie dobra: nravstvennaia filosofiia, Sobranie sochinenii*, vol. 8, pp. 3-516. Vladimir Solovyov, *The Justification of the Good: An Essay on Moral Philosophy*, trans. Natalie A. Duddington, ed. and annotated Boris Jakim (Grand Rapids, Mich.: William B. Eerdmans Publishing Company, 2005).

12. *Tri razgovora o voine, progresse i kontse vsemirnoi istorii, so vkliucheniem kratkoi povesti ob antikhriste i s prilozheniiami, Sobranie sochinenii*, vol. 10, pp. 81-221. Vladimir Solovyov, *War, Progress, and the End of History: Three Conversations. Including a Short Story of the Anti-Christ*, trans. Alexander Bakshy, revised by Thomas R. Beyer, Jr. (Hudson, New York: Lindisfarne Press, 1990).

13. Solov'ëv quotes Athanasius and knew well the work of other eastern church fathers, especially Maximus the Confessor. See Richard Gustafson's seminal essay, "Soloviev's Doctrine of Salvation," in *Russian Religious Thought*, ed. Judith Deutsch Kornblatt and Richard F. Gustafson (Madison: University of Wisconsin Press, 1996), pp. 31-48.

14. Paul Valliere, *Modern Russian Theology. Bukharev, Soloviev, Bulgakov. Orthodox Theology in a New Key* (Grand Rapids, Mich.: William B. Eerdmans Publishing Company, 2000).

15. Konstantin Mochul'skii, *Vladimir Solov'ëv. Zhizn' i uchenie* (Paris, 1951), p. 10, uses these two phrases together to gloss "bogochelovechestvo."

16. At times I will translate the Russian *chelovek* as man, because it captures the

notion of both individual human beings and humanity as a whole, while "human being" generally means one person and "humanity" means the whole. "Human beings" works for "man" in many cases, but it would be awkward here.

17. Solovyov, *Lectures on Divine Humanity*, revised and ed. Boris Jakim, p. 1. Subsequent references to this work will be cited parenthetically as "LDH."

18. *Modern Russian Theology*, p. 147.

19. In another formulation Solov'ëv writes, ". . . Divinity belongs to human beings and to God, but with one difference: God possesses Divinity in eternal actuality, whereas human beings can only attain it" (LDH, 23).

20. He stresses this human capacity to "become" in many of his works. In *Justification of the Good* he calls it the "essentially human attribute" (Jakim edition, p. lv). In *The Meaning of Love* (1892-94) he writes that human consciousness is formed by "universal ideal norms" and a "sense of truth" by which we evaluate the phenomena and facts of life. "Considering his actions with this higher consciousness, man can infinitely perfect his life and nature *without leaving the boundaries of human form.* And therefore, he is indeed the supreme being of the natural world and the effective end of the world-creative process." This essay is included in *The Heart of Reality: Essays on Beauty, Love, and Ethics by V. S. Soloviev*, ed. and trans. Vladimir Wozniuk (Notre Dame: University of Notre Dame Press, 2003), pp. 83-133 (quotation at p. 92). Also see "The Idea of a Superman," in *Politics, Law, and Morality. Essays by V. S. Soloviev*, ed. and trans. Vladimir Wozniuk (New Haven: Yale University Press, 2000), pp. 255-263.

21. As the Russian philosopher Semën Frank observes in his introduction to *A Solovyov Anthology*, ed. S. L. Frank, trans. Natalie Duddington (London: SCM Press, 1950), pp. 15-16. This classic volume was reissued in 2001 (London: The Saint Austin Press) with a lengthy new introduction by Cardinal Hans Urs von Balthasar, who compares Solov'ëv to Aquinas's importance in the history of thought (*A Solovyov Anthology*, p. xvii).

22. Orthodox theology in general has not drawn the sharp opposition between nature and grace that has characterized much of western Christian thought. See Valliere, "Introduction to the Modern Orthodox Tradition" and "Vladimir Soloviev," *The Teachings of Modern Christianity on Law, Politics, and Human Nature*, vol. 1, pp. 508, 554. For Solov'ëv, "grace" comes as human beings freely perfect themselves and is a result of that process. See, for example, *Istoriia i budushchnost' teokratii, Sobranie sochinenii*, vol. 4, pp. 337-342.

23. I would argue that Solov'ëv's philosophical anthropology does not rest on the Christian dogmas of a human nature corrupted by the Fall and redeemed by Christ. One can simply take the three principles as a description of human nature and proceed from there. However, the triumph over and spiritualization of the flesh in the Passion and Resurrection of Christ is more distinctively Christian. Solov'ëv himself calls it "the final and distinctive truth of Christianity." *Dukhovnye osnovy zhizni, Sobranie sochinenii*, vol. 3, p. 375. Gustafson, "Soloviev's Doctrine of Salvation," pp. 36-38, provides a good, concise reading of this section of *Lectures on Godmanhood*, which Solov'ëv largely repeats in *The Spiritual Foundations of Life.*

24. *Kritika otvlechënnykh nachal, Sobranie sochinenii*, vol. 2, p. 44. He closely para phrases Kant's *Groundwork of the Metaphysic of Morals* at some length. In fact much of what he presents as a paraphrase is a direct translation of key passages from the *Groundwork. Kritika otvlechënnykh nachal*, pp. 44-62.

25. This connection between human dignity and theosis is most explicit in *Justification of the Good* (see below).

26. Both Berdiaev and Frank stress the essential humanism of Solov'ëv. See Nicolas Berdyaev, *The Russian Idea*, trans R. M. French (London: Geoffrey Bles, 1947), p. 91, and *A Solovyov Anthology*, ed. S. L. Frank, p. 30.

27. One of the many places Solov'ëv specifies his view that true faith cannot be coerced but rests on "the evidence of things not seen" (Hebrews 11:1) is his essay "The Jews and the Christian Problem" (1884), which is translated in part in *A Solovyov Anthology*, ed. S. L. Frank (here, p. 112).

28. The speech is translated in *A Solovyov Anthology* (quotation at p. 62).

29. E. N. Trubetskoi, *Smysl zhizni* (Berlin, 1922), p. 204 (italics his).

30. *Kritika otvlechënnykh nachal*, pp. 139-140.

31. "Vladimir Soloviev," *The Teachings of Modern Christianity on Law, Politics, and Human Nature*, vol. 1, p. 546. A comprehensive account of Solov'ëv's legal philosophy can be found in Andrzej Walicki, *Legal Philosophies of Russian Liberalism* (Oxford: Oxford University Press, 1987), pp. 165-212. Solov'ëv's essay *Law and Morality: Essays in Applied Ethics* (1897) serves as a good overall statement of his philosophy of law. It is translated in *Politics, Law, and Morality*, ed. Wozniuk, pp. 131-212.

32. *Kritika otvlechënnykh nachal*, p. 167.

33. *Kritika otvlechënnykh nachal*, pp. viii-ix.

34. *Kritika otvlechënnykh nachal*, p. ix.

35. *Kritika otvlechënnykh nachal*, pp. 161-162.

36. *Kritika otvlechënnykh nachal*, p. 185.

37. Kostalevsky, *Dostoevsky and Soloviev*, p. 115. "Theocracy" is a poor term for the Kingdom of God. Although it literally means "the rule of God," by firm historical association it connotes an earthly state in which power is exercised by the church. Thus one of E. N. Trubetskoi's main criticisms of Solov'ëv is that he introduced state power into the Kingdom of God, where it surely can have no place. Trubetskoi, *Mirosozertsanie Vl. S. Solov'ëva*, vol. 1 (Moscow, 1913), pp. 178, 567, 578. Solov'ëv himself, however, stated that the Kingdom of God "is obviously incompatible with the state." *Justification of the Good*, ed. Boris Jakim, p. 386. In his earlier essay "The Great Schism and Christian Politics" (1883) he said the same (see below). Valliere proposes that "theonomy" may be a better name than "theocracy" for Solov'ëv's ideal ("Vladimir Soloviev," pp. 550-551).

38. The essay is translated in part in *A Solovyov Anthology*, ed. S. L. Frank, pp. 75-101. Subsequent references cited parenthetically in the text. In places I have modified the translation.

39. See especially *La Russie et l'Église universelle* (1889).

40. He wrote an essay on this principle, "The Development of Dogma in the Church in Connection with the Question of Church Union" (1886). It is analyzed in Valliere, *Modern Russian Theology*, pp. 178-192.

41. It is not clear whether Solov'ëv thought the re-establishment of church unity would actually be the Kingdom of God on earth (theosis and spiritualization) or the next step toward it. The position I have formulated in this sentence is the more conservative one.

42. Solov'ëv was involved in organizing famine relief. E. N. Trubetskoi argued that Solov'ëv's disappointment with Russian state and society in the wake of the famine spurred the collapse, or at any rate marked de-utopianization, of his theocratic idea. *Mirosozertsanie Vl. S. Solov'ëva*, vol. 2, pp. 3-38.

43. *The Justification of the Good*, ed. Boris Jakim, p. 144. Subsequent page references cited parenthetically in the text.

44. Sutton, *The Religious Philosophy of Vladimir Solovyov*, pp. 74-75, demonstrates

that Solov'ёv was indebted to Schelling on this central point.

45. Walicki, *Legal Philosophies of Russian Liberalism*, pp. 195-196, 203-205. The subtitle of Walicki's chapter on Solov'ёv is "Religious Philosophy and the Emergence of the 'New Liberalism.'" Also see Valliere, "Vladimir Soloviev," pp. 560-562.

46. "Perfection is not a thing which one person can make a gift of to another; it is an inner condition attainable through one's own experience alone" (150-151).

47. Solov'ёv writes that in God there can be no process of becoming perfect, only "eter- nal and unchangeable" perfection (150). This seems inconsistent with his overall philosophical approach. If an infinite perfection, one that transcends itself and increases in perfection, is greater than one that is "eternal and unchangeable," then that must be God (as the greatest possible perfection). Many of Solov'ёv's uses of the term "absolute" imply "infinite absolute," and the very concept of Godmanhood surely suggests that God is enriched in the process of our perfection. This whole problem may explain Solov'ёv's introduction of two poles into the absolute.

48. "Vladimir Soloviev," p. 564.

49. For details see the first appendix to *A Solovyov Anthology*, ed. S. L. Frank, "Was Solovyov a Convert to Roman Catholicism?" pp. 249-252, and Andrzej Walicki, "Catholicism and the Eastern Church in Russian Religious and Philosophical Thought," *Soviet Union/Union Soviétique* 15: 1 (1988), pp. 52-59.

50. *A Solovyov Anthology*, p. 24.

51. Ibid., pp. 26, 251 (italics in original).

52. See Greg Gaut, "Christian Politics: Vladimir Solovyov's Social Gospel Theol-ogy," *Modern Greek Studies Yearbook* 10/11 (1994/95), pp. 653-74. The main title of Rev. William C. Graham's study *Half Finished Heaven: The Social Gospel in American Literature* (Lanham, Maryland: University Press of America, 1995) captures perfectly, if unwittingly, the essence of Solov'ёv's idea of Godmanhood.

53. The pope names Solov'ёv first among the "eminent scholars" of theology and phi-losophy in the Russian context (chapter 6, section 74).

54. Quoted by Frank, *A Solovyov Anthology*, p. 27.

THEOLOGICAL CHALLENGES
TO COMMUNITY ORGANIZING

Lee Stuart

I stand before you this afternoon having recently entered my 20th year of community organizing in one form or another in the South Bronx. As most of you know, the South Bronx was notorious as the spectacle of the nation's poverty from the mid-70's through the early 90's, and still conjures up images of urban destruction, mayhem and dysfunction in the collective imagination. The truth is, however, that the South Bronx of today, while still not a paradise, is largely transformed from the days when the spread of fires was tracked using mathematical models of epidemiology, from the days when crack ruled, where fewer than one-third of high school students graduated and less than 3 percent went on to college.[1] You won't find elementary school principals forcing children to eat their lunch while sitting on the floor at the request of custodial staff who find it too difficult to clean the cafeteria if tables are set up. You may still find schools, however, where the water fountains are turned off because of the lead in the pipes. You won't find acres of abandoned land and burnt-out buildings, but you will still find families, largely immigrants from current hells on earth, living eight to ten or even twenty to a room. You won't find a "borough beyond the law" as we used to say only a few years ago, but you will still find a too-thriving trade in heroin, as well as prostitution, though the latter is now behind closed doors rather than behind blankets strung on ropes between trees on vacant lots.

In fact, from the mid-80's until today, over 65,000 units of housing have been rehabilitated or newly constructed in the Bronx,[2] crime is down about 73 percent,[3] most schools have been repaired and children no longer have to sit on radiators or in closets or dodge leaks in order to study. A great victory has been won in the South Bronx, and it is the result of an unprecedented and largely unheralded combination of public, private and non-profit effort. It wasn't without contention, and it is not complete. It was, by and large, a "faith-based effort" but long before the language of "faith based" became federal jargon.

It has been my great privilege over the past nineteen going on twenty years, to have worked side by side with the lay and clergy leaders of South Bronx Churches, who as much as any group, primed the pump for the transformation of the South Bronx. South Bronx Churches broke the mold of business as usual by being interfaith, not just Protestant and Catholic, which would have been a significant advance in and of itself, but also Muslim. South Bronx Churches broke the mold of business as usual by uniting African-American and Latino interests when ethnic based political separation was axiomatic.

South Bronx Churches broke the mold of business as usual by enlisting the collective wealth of the Evangelical Lutheran Church in America, two endowed Episcopalian parishes in New York City (Trinity Wall Street and St. James Madison Avenue) and four Roman Catholic religious orders which had worked in the South Bronx for over a century to provide the investment capital for housing development. Financed by $3.2 million in these no interest loans, over nine years the South Bronx Churches Nehemiah program built 268 single-family homes, 288 condominiums and 209 two-family homes, for a total of 974 residential units with a current assessed value in excess of $128 million. We paid the bishops back, and with a modest profit slightly in excess of $1,000 per unit, the organization now has a million dollar endowment.[4]

South Bronx Churches broke the mold of business as usual in education by forcing the NYC Board of Education to co-sponsor an academic high school in the South Bronx in 1992—the Bronx Leadership Academy High School.[5] BLA as we call it, is not an exam school, but was created with the vision that all children could succeed in school and go on to college provided the educational environment and the school staff were committed to that goal. Getting there meant overturning some union practices, overturning some Board of Education raw prejudices, and standing down corrupt influences in the community and within the Board of Education. After eight years of incredible success, with over 90 percent of the students graduating within four years and going on to college, the Board of Education began to pay attention. While BLA only has 150 open seats a year, 5,000 students apply annually. How could they not pay attention? The school became a model for the current revolution in the New York City school system in the creation of small schools with high standards and closely knit educational leadership. The brilliant first principal of BLA, Katherine Kelly, is now a key mentor for principals throughout the New York City school system. And so, it does me good today to be able to lift up the work of South Bronx Churches as a testimony to the effectiveness of broad-based community organizing.

SBC is an affiliate of the Chicago-based Industrial Areas Foundation, since the 1940's a leader in bringing the art of organizing into the common faith practices of thousands and thousands of congregations of all denominations and faiths in communities throughout the United States, Germany, Great Britain and South Africa. Created from the vision of Saul Alinsky in the 1940's and led by Ed Chambers since 1972, the IAF has pioneered and led a technology that brings together lay and clergy leaders across religious, economic, racial, ethnic, language and geographical lines to identify common interests and build the collective power to meet those interests. Both Mr. Chambers and other members of the national staff of the IAF have written extensively on the work of the IAF. I recommend their books and essays to you.[6]

Tonight, I'm taking a somewhat different view, the view of someone who takes more of a systematic approach, rather than a partisan one of what organizing is and might be. Over the past twenty years, from creating the SHARE food assistance program, then working as the lead organizer of South Bronx Churches as a whole and then specifically on the educational and housing initiatives of South Bronx Churches, I have seen trends, both within organizing and within society, that raise serious questions about organizing's continuing efficacy in the coming years.

The principles remain universal: power tends to corrupt; absolute power corrupts absolutely. Similarly, powerlessness tends to corrupt, and absolute powerlessness corrupts absolutely. Diversity is more powerful than unity. Standing for the whole is a primary virtue especially when faced with overwhelming power differentials. Power and effectiveness in using that power flow from relationships with one another, rather than issues. Power for social change can be more easily organized by organizing institutions of institutions, rather than individuals. Power is a theological virtue, perhaps the most under-taught and ambiguous theological virtue, but a virtue nonetheless. Holy anger is likewise a theological virtue. Thucydides was right: the standard of justice depends on the ability of power to compel.[7] In other words, the amount of justice you get depends on how much you can organize to get it.

So, what do I really mean, theologically speaking, when I say organizing? I am talking about the full range of Moses' action, except for his first two public actions, the taking of a human life out of unbridled anger and then running away and trying to forget the whole thing. I'm talking about what happened to Moses from the burning bush until his death. The burning bush called Moses back, and for those of us who listen and see, God puts burning bushes in our path that call us back to the great works of liberation, community building, and creating the Promised Land through our thoughts, words and deeds. Moses went through many phases as an organizer—he organized a liberation movement to free the Hebrews from Pharaoh, he outmaneuvered a nasty internal counter-organizing effort by those who preferred the fleshpots of Egypt over the uncertainty of freedom. He organized a massive social service delivery program, a super soup kitchen, if you will, that kept the Children of Israel in manna, quail and water through forty years of desert wandering. He wore himself out and neglected his own family trying to do it all by himself. He created a bureaucracy. He was at the point of giving up in despair time and time again. He was bitter, angry, and resentful and took it out on God and his fellow travelers. Ultimately, just short of asking God to take his life and spare him the continued frustration of leading 625,000 recalcitrants, he followed God's instructions to organize the "Tent of the Presence," that wonderful place where the leaders of all the tribes would assemble (as well as a few of those who didn't quite make it to the Tent on time) so that the spirit of God could fall on them as it had on Moses. Then he died before reaching the Promised Land. The succeeding 5,000 or so years of salvation history have been a continuous tale throughout the earth of attempting to recreate the promise of the Tent of the Presence, in many different traditions, in many different historical contexts, through rivers of blood and glimpses of glory.

Those of us who are motivated by faith are still at it. In fact, it is *the* call of the three monotheistic religious that were cradled in what is now known as the Middle East, and which in my lifetime has been most known for incessant conflict in the name of God. The Christian tradition teaches that the reign of God is at hand, and that we are to live our lives in such a way that the presence of God is among us, as it was when Jesus walked. Until he returns, we are his hands and eyes, and it is our job as Christians to spread his Good News of redemption and liberation until he comes in glory. Easier said than done. The Jewish tradition in which Jesus grew up is the basis of the teachings to love God above all else and to love our neighbor as ourselves. The mystical tradition of *tikkun olam*, "heal the broken world," is based on a story that when God was looking over his creation, he saw that it was whole and complete, but missing only one thing—humankind. But since creation was whole and complete, God had to break it a little to make room for us folks. So the brokenness of the world is in a way our fault, and thus it is a deep human responsibility, a moral imperative, to do whatever we can to heal that broken world.

Similarly, easier said than done. Islam has a tradition which at its essence calls on all people to live rightly with one another and rightly with God. Again, easier said than done.

Now there are many ways to organize for God's reign on earth, many ways to heal the broken world, and many ways to live rightly with one another and with God. We organize internally through worship and liturgy. We organize at the walls of the church, temple or mosque through programs of social services and charity. More rarely, we organize in the public square—well outside our walls, in the domain more commonly dominated by values of the market or values of the state rather than the values of covenant and creed and family which are the basis of our call to worship and to charity.

I am not going to discuss the theological challenges to internal organizing, that is the theological challenges facing liturgy and worship today. As a Catholic in the pew, I can assure you, there are indeed such challenges, but I haven't the training or the wisdom to know how to address them. I am however, based on the last twenty years, competent to discuss the theological challenges of organizing at or beyond the walls.

I am going to touch briefly on the theological challenge at the walls, but my primary focus is the theological challenges to organizing beyond the walls. As I see it, the primary theological challenge of organizing for charity is what it has always been: how can you take an entire system that is based on a separation between the haves and have-nots, with the second providing the service to the first, and not violate the theological principle of Imago Dei, treating people as if they were the image and likeness of God? And second, the mere existence of a charitable program points to a fundamental injustice in society, an injustice which is not only not challenged, but is allowed to persist or even facilitated through the administration of the charity. It is a rather vicious circle. If you decide to use advocacy to get out of the circle, then you are on the theologically dangerous ground of what the IAF calls "breaking the Iron rule"—doing for others what they can do for themselves, and in so doing, you again violate the principle of Imago Dei and teach dependence rather than liberation. If you fall back on empowerment as a way out of the vicious circle, you are on another slippery slope because when has power ever voluntarily been transferred to the powerless?

Power must be claimed, it can not be given. Every human being already has it if we are made in the likeness of God the All Loving and the All Powerful. Who are we to pretend that we can give more than that through our empowerment programs? I'd like to rid the social service world of the concept of empowerment. I'd rather use the word "power" instead. Try it out—who could not be for Black Empowerment? The empowerment of women? The empowerment of immigrants? But what about Black Power? Power to the Women! Immigrant Power! That type of terminology certainly makes people nervous! We are ever so much more comfortable if we limit that to empowerment. And this is another theological trap—our social structures tend to limit power as a zero-sum concept rather than see it as it is, a limitless capacity to act.

In a brilliant essay written a quarter of a century ago, Bernard Loomer made the critical distinction between dominant power, power over or against another, and relational power, or power with another.[8] Dominant power is certainly a zero-sum game; if I've got it, you can't have it. Dominant power is like original sin—we are born into it and can't escape it. We so live in a world that is shaped by dominant power that we are usually completely unconscious, or at best barely conscious, of the ways in which our charitable programs perpetuate "power over" and do little to build "power with." We shrug, and although we know that somehow in our service to the poor we are getting something from it, that they are giving us a gift through their participation in our service, most of the time, at the end of the day, we are still up and they are still down when it comes to the social hierarchy. We go home to home, they go to a shelter. We buy clothes and are usually the first to wear them! Our meals are the first fruits of the harvest, not the gleanings.

So the ultimate theological challenge to charity is the theology of dominant versus relational power. Jesus preached and taught relational power. He taught against the dominant power of his day, both in the civil and in the religious structures. Importantly, Jesus could perform no miracles without a relationship to the individual being healed. No power could flow without relationship.

The theological challenges to organizing beyond the walls, to community organizing to create social change in the market and public sectors are even thornier. First, let me explain the paradigm I am using to define organizing. I have no idea who first came up with this paradigm, but the person I first heard use it attributed it to Peter Drucker. The basic concept is that society is divided into three sectors: the market sector which focuses on production and trade of goods and services; the public sector which focuses on issues of governance; and the "third sector" or "voluntary sector" where the citizenry self-organizes (hence voluntary) into institutions such as the family, worshipping communities, labor unions, political and social clubs, interest groups, neighborhood associations, and the like.[9] First in time in the course of human evolution was this "third" sector. As society grew more complex, various governance and trade structures were created. Two million years of social evolution, ten thousand years since the agricultural revolution, and several hundred years of the capitalist experiment have tilted the distribution of power away from the third sector and toward the public and market sectors.

The apparent primary value today within the market sector is the creation of wealth and profit. The apparent primary value within the public sector is the maintenance of the status quo. The apparent primary value within the third sector is more variable, but ultimately revolves around the mutual assistance and well-being of those with whom we voluntarily associate. It is in the third sector where altruism, sacrifice and covenant surface. The analysis goes on to state that the greater power, that is the ability to get things done, while theoretically residing in the third sector in liberal democracies, actually resides in the public and market sectors. Organizing is seen as a way to build power in the third sector, through the knitting of relationships between and among groups and interests, to compel the greater power in the market and public sectors to a higher standard of justice (distributive power from the ground up if you will).

The stories I told you earlier of the work of South Bronx Churches illustrate how this form of organizing works. By organizing parents and students into a united front, SBC was able to create enough of a force to bring the Board of Education to the table to discuss what was badly needed in the South Bronx—a high school, just one, that was not restricted by exams but that would provide a college preparatory education as its normal standard. The push and pull to actually accomplish this was incredible, but at the end of the day, Bronx Leadership Academy was born, and the entire experience met the absolute acid test of relational power. Both sides, that is the New York City Board of Education and South Bronx Churches, grew as a result of the exchange. When dominant power is exercised, only one side grows; the other is diminished. When relational power is exercised, both sides grow. In any transaction, if both sides are not growing—don't fool yourself—dominant power is at work.

The same mechanism worked with SBC's Nehemiah housing. The money we borrowed from the bishops, orders and churches created one form of power: organized money. It took some pretty serious negotiations with three mayors and a Cardinal, not to mention a 5,000-person rally, to engage the public sector and have the City of New York understand that "city-owned land" actually belonged to "we the people." In contrast, it was comparatively easy to organize the private sector in support of housing because housing development is a tried and true economic engine in the private sector. SBC provided free land and free money, not to mention political cover against the evil things that crawl out from under the rocks in a construction project, so that free of risk, builders could create housing at a fraction of the normal cost. Again, everyone grew through the experience—New York City's Department of Housing Preservation and

Development, South Bronx Churches, the builders and of course the 974 families who live in the new homes. The presence of nearly a thousand new families, building equity and investing in their neighborhood, had spin-off economic effects that multiply by many times the actual value of the initial investment. In addition to the multiplication of the $3.2 million loans from the churches to the $128 million current value of the homes, the monthly mortgage payments of the Nehemiah homeowners are roughly *half* of the market-rate rents in the area, meaning nearly $5.25 *million a year* in additional cash that is available to the homeowners for education, investment, or whatever. Staggering.

So what are the theological challenges to organizing? What are the challenges to something that works so well and so recently? I am going to focus on five: 1) a shift in relative power from the state to the market; 2) the lessening impact of traditional organizing methods; 3) the confusion of Meribah for Canaan; 4) the wholesale takeover of theological language by the government accompanied by the silencing of theological support for loyal opposition and 5) the lack of theological imagination when it comes to positive social action.

First, most community organizing in the past 60 years has been focused on the public sector, that is, organizing so that public resources such as land, tax revenues, bond issues, etc. are directed at meeting the needs of the organized neighborhood. Labor organizing, on the other hand, has been focused on the private sector, working to even out the benefits of capitalism to both workers and owners. Political forces, both local and global, are now threatening the efficacy of both community organizing and labor organizing. In short, we need a new theology for globalization. Catholic social teaching about the right to self-determination and the right of workers to organize was more applicable to the early industrial era and to the period when relative power still resided more in the structures of the state and when industrial control was still local rather than in the structures of the global market. We need to develop new social teaching for the new global economy, and then we have to make sure that the new social teaching does not remain the Church's best kept secret as the current social teaching has been!

In my lifetime, the balance of power has shifted from the state to the market. Common methods to get the attention of government, e.g. petitions, public hearings, demonstrations, voter turn-out, aren't effective when the government is less powerful than the market, or worse, when the government is more and more a servant of the market. Recent prosecution of criminal CEO's notwithstanding, it does not take much insight to notice that big bucks buy influence. It's Halliburton, Brown and Root, and Northrup Grummond who are benefiting most from recent political events. The huge "soft money" that now swamps political parties is another example. The selection of issues and candidates is less and less a political process and more and more an economic one. A power analysis of today's situation would place the power squarely behind Eisenhower's quaint-sounding "military industrial complex" and how vastly more complex it is today than when Dwight Eisenhower coined the phrase! As for organized labor, it is but a shadow of its former self. The increasing scarcity of jobs, the willingness of people to cross picket lines, the willingness of people to work for less than the union rates, and the willingness of government to break or outlaw its own unions and to support the breaking of industrial unions, all weaken the power of organized labor. Organized labor helps its own demise through continued corruption and work rules which benefit neither the worker nor the owner.

In organizing terms, what is happening is that the power of organized money is more and more trumping the power of organized people. In New York City, as recently as fifteen years ago, we could organize enough people to counteract organized money. Now, that is increasingly difficult to do. Methods of organizing that were developed to deal with a dominant public sector are not tuned to dealing with a dominant market sector, and much less a non-localized market sector. All politics is local, but increasingly, economic decisions are made on a global scale, and local politics can do little but sit and watch as a century-old sugar warehouse closes on the Brooklyn waterfront to make way for luxury condos, as a seventy-year old plant manufacturing pots and pans in the South Bronx moves to Mexico and when tax breaks to an automobile manufacturing plant bankrupt the Tarrytown school system and the plant closes anyway. Traditional community organizing, relatively powerless even in the old days of government strength, is even more powerless when the stage is global. Effective organizing is based on relationships and the types of relationships that organizing has depended on so far are undeniably local. In global economics, local doesn't matter much. It feels as if we're on the edges— good edges, to be sure, and certainly important in the day to day lives of people, but edges nonetheless.

Another challenge to organizing is that the methods that drove everything from Indian independence to the passage of the Civil Rights Act to the withdrawal of American troops from Vietnam are now so common as to be virtually ineffective. This is a harsh judgment which many will reject. A cardinal rule of organizing is to act within your experience, but outside the experience of your opponent, and from the mobilization and escalation tactics that Moses used against Pharaoh through the anti-war movements in the mid-70s, the tactics of movements were outside the mainstream and could cause serious challenge. Now the media, and dominant power however constructed, can be fairly certain that the million men on the Mall today will be gone tomorrow, or at the latest, the day after tomorrow. The mayor of New York was recently quoted as saying that nobody pays attention any more to demonstrations and press conferences on the steps of city hall. In short, protest politics has become commonplace. Dominant power is so used to dealing with it, that event managers now create special spaces for "legitimate" protests, and various dissenting groups have to sign up for their turn, as the recent World Trade Organization summits (not to mention the most recent Republican and Democratic National Conventions) have taught us. The once cherished right of assembly has been turned into a mockery.

The internet based organizing of MoveOn.Org and the global mobilization prior to the US invasion of Iraq last year, as impressive as it was, did not work. Oh, for a few very precious days, the global conversation for the first time in the history of humanity turned to what it meant to wage peace, but ultimately, global opinion and the mobilization of millions and millions of people, and the approbation of virtually the entire world, were insufficient to arrest the US military industrial complex, an extreme example of both organized people and organized money.[10]

Even at the local level, globalization has introduced a significant new factor in organizing in the United States. Throughout the early days of organizing in South Bronx Churches, we were able to use the theology of an exiled people pursuing the Promised Land as a powerful teaching metaphor to give people hope in the face of seemingly overwhelming odds. We could rely on Moses and Nehemiah and Ezra and Jeremiah to teach us about getting out from under the domination of Pharaoh, the Assyrians, or the Babylonians. We could count on Jesus to teach us a third way of non-violent resistance and solidarity.[11] But now, as we have had victory after victory, and as our ranks are joined increasingly by people coming from lands ravaged by war or economic collapse, the scene has shifted. We are increasingly mistaking Massah and Meribah for Canaan. No question about it, the South Bronx is a far cry from perfect, but it is the Promised Land if your context is Sierra Leone, Liberia, Haiti, the slums of Mexico City. Why organize for better schools and risk the anger of the teachers and principals when for the first time in your life your children have the right to go to school and it doesn't cost anything and there are no bribes to pay and they even serve breakfast and lunch? Why organize against the sweatshop owner who pays less than the minimum wage if there are eighteen or eighty other people behind you who will gladly work for even less? Why risk losing a job that is allowing you to double the monthly income of your family in Haiti by a mere $25 a month you send down? But the confusion of the desert for the Promised Land is not only among new immigrants. It is deeply embedded in an American middle class that is rapidly losing economic ground by any conceivable measure. We need to develop the stories and the ritual that will unite us in our confusion, to help us keep our eye on the prize, and not be distracted by faith-based language coming from the state, or covenant language coming from the market.

A particularly insidious theological challenge is the near wholesale takeover of the language of faith by the past two presidential administrations. The White House Faith-Based Initiative is but one scary example. Christ's actions and the early days of Christianity were marked by being in opposition to the dominant political and religious structures of the day. From the days of Constantine to the Reformation some of the most basic tenets of Christianity were severely compromised as Christianity became an arm of the state. The disestablishment of religion and the rise of secular democracy in the late eighteenth century provided a new arena for the religious community to again be a critic, sometimes friendly, sometimes not, to the power of the state. The social movements of the 60's in the United States were led and inspired by an independent religious sector. The fall of Communism and in particular the fall of the Berlin Wall were rooted in non-state-supported religious action. On the other hand, the rise of sectarian states, where faith is again an arm of government, has seriously and repeatedly threatened and destabilized whole regions of the world. The current fundamentalism and triumphalism not only in Christianity but also in Judaism and Islam are antithetical to the higher vision of all three faiths. To the extent that the historic faith communities in the United States are silenced by becoming economic partners with the government and dependent on "faith-based initiatives" for their survival, the United States will lose a historical counter-force and critic against dominant action by both the state and the market apparatus.

Organizing has had difficulty in many communities getting beyond the "main line churches," most of which are losing members. It doesn't bode well that our organizing relies on shrinking institutions. We need to do something about that. The growing fundamentalist and evangelical communities often do not have a tradition of engagement with "the world" and often have a theologically based prejudice against ecumenical, to say nothing of interfaith, cooperation. (I can't really get clear on my own experience of trying to organize evangelical and Pentecostal congregations as part of South Bronx Churches, when at the local level they say they "stay out of politics" and yet we see the wholesale conversion of evangelical political interests into a PAC for the Republican party, so I am unclear about how or when the evangelical engagement with "the world" takes place.) Complicating the issue, at least in the United States today, is the undercurrent that *any* criticism of the government, particularly a government which is so loudly religious sounding, is somehow unpatriotic and for Christians, dissent is seemingly un-Christian. This of course is not a theological challenge merely to organizing, but to civil society writ large. Theologians and preachers would do well to put their heads together and start shouting us instructions from the roof tops. We are confused as were the troops in II Kings—those whom we know as enemies, or at least those whom we know have not acted in our interests in the past are sounding now as if they are us.[12] Yet they do things which are clearly against our interests, but they are using our language. What do we do?

Of all the challenges to effective organizing I have mentioned above— the shift in power from the state to the market, the lessening impact of organizing methods as dominant power becomes thoroughly familiar with them, the confusion between where we find ourselves and the Promised Land, and the confusion that stems from misappropriation of faith-based language and values by the state (and to a lesser extent) the market—the biggest challenge of all is the lack of a theological vision for positive social change. Our bag of tricks is worn out. We have sung "We Shall Overcome" ten million times. We have marched, fasted, demonstrated, gone to jail for civil disobedience, put our bodies in front of tanks, and reminisced about the "movement." We've gotten pretty good, even amazingly good, at creating social programs and local power experiments that have significantly altered the social landscape of cities throughout the country. We haven't figured out how to do it in smaller cities or rural areas. We haven't figured out how to stem the sucking sound of jobs. We have had various degrees of success when the organizing objective has been economic as compared to political. We have tried every form of protest known to humankind and have used also used tremendous creativity to organize for major social reforms (as opposed to organizing against injustice). And, twenty years later, although we have won significant battles in the South Bronx and elsewhere, and have made unbelievable advances, we are not keeping up with the now global forces that are filling our cities with new immigrants and weakening the middle class.

We're getting older and the political crucible forging young activists today is of a much different tone than in the 50's and 60's. I was inspired to do the work I do from my mother's knee! I was highly conditioned from the time I was a young child to fight for the rights of others, to defend the weak, to stand in solidarity with the poor and to put my talents to use for the world. I was inspired by political leaders of vision, a shocking number of whom were felled by assassins' bullets. When I was growing up it was considered not only desirable but inevitable, and in fact the national conversation was that we could eliminate poverty, hunger, and disease (and go to the Moon). Now, the edge has worn off. Even though compared to thirty years ago, we are in an infinitely better position to eliminate poverty, hunger and disease, it's as if we no longer want to. We gave it a good fight for forty, fifty, sixty years and now the forces of the global marketplace are washing it away. Rationally we know that in India, Bangladesh, Africa, China and other nations, the positive impacts of globalization are raising living standards and easing suffering. But we are not in the vanguard and we are not sure that economics is all there is. And we particularly don't like it that it is we who are losing ground.

This is where we need a new or renewed theological imagination. We need something that will do for us today what Bruggemann's "Prophetic Imagination" opened to the clergy of the South Bronx as they came together twenty years ago for the first time to imagine a future so radically different from their past.[13] I first thought about the paucity of our Christian theological imagination immediately after 9/11, which ultimately was a theological act, no matter how horrible. As I contemplated the damage that could be done by one hundred, or at most two hundred people with a theological vision of martyrdom and destruction, and as the wake of terror has spread through other countries, most recently in Spain, I wonder why a theology of love, reconciliation, redemption and liberation is so silent and so weak. What many people don't realize in the vengeance mood that swept the country after 9/11 was that most of us in New York City did not share it. At the center of the destruction we wanted nothing more than *no more destruction*.

So the greatest theological challenge to organizing today is the challenge to organize an action or actions that will transcend the murder, the war, the destruction, the slaughter, that terrorism and our reaction to it has caused. We are clearly not on the right path. We know that violence begets violence, yet we persist. We know that injustice in one generation can and does pass to the seventh generation. Maybe we have to re-imagine ourselves in a radically different way. We've been imagining ourselves as the righteous, the enowim, the exiles. Maybe, just maybe, we're on the wrong theological side. Maybe we are not wandering in the desert. Maybe we've crossed over, not the Jordan, but the Nile. Maybe we are Pharaoh. We are not struggling against an imperial consciousness, we *are* the imperial consciousness. And so perhaps the greatest theological challenge of today is not to try to figure out how to organize against a dominant market culture, or for a more equitable impact of globalization, or for an independent faith-based critique of both the market and the state. Maybe the greatest theological challenge today is to organize repentance and reconciliation. Individually, corporately, nationally. Our country is the greatest supplier of weapons in the world. We have the largest stockpile of weapons of mass destruction and chemical and germ warfare capability in the world. Our armies are deployed in Iraq, Afghanistan, Haiti, Korea, Europe, and Kosovo. We consume more of the world's resources than anyplace else. Our agricultural overproduction threatens our own health and survival through obesity, but also the agricultural survival of the world's farmers, particularly the women food farmers of Africa. Our genetically modified crops threaten the biodiversity that is a product of 3.5 billion years of plant evolution. Our pharmaceutical industry protects its profits while millions suffer with AIDS in Africa.

When I was meditating after 9/11 trying to come up with an equivalent action that 100 of us might do that would do as much good as the action against the World Trade Center towers did bad, I drew a profound, frustrating and painful blank. If 100 people could do so much damage, why was it so hard to think up something as comparatively good as that was bad? Where were the symbols for good, for justice, for freedom that we could manipulate to send as powerful a message of love as those airplanes did of hate? It brought to mind another universal of organizing—it is always easier to organize against rather than for.

I soon came up with the answer—the only thing we had that had the power to counteract the destruction of the World Trade Centers was the death and resurrection of Jesus. Nothing more and nothing less. I am embarrassed to say it, but the very next thought after my fleeting insight that the counteraction to the World Trade Centers was Jesus' death and resurrection, was something like, "Right. Been there, done that. Now what?" But who is being crucified now? Certainly some people and some interests in the United States. But we would be disingenuous if we thought that was all there was to it. We're more often the Pontius Pilate, the occupying forces, the crucifier, not the crucified. It is comparatively easy to organize for a national vision, or even a local vision, when you're on the short end of the stick. From a position of relative powerlessness, it is really easy to organize a vision that leads to shared power at a minimum and unfortunately, dominant power too often as a goal. It is even easier to organize for greater dominance when you are already the biggest force in the world. It is damnably difficult, however, to organize oneself *out* of a position of dominant power into relational power. Bernard Loomer would say it is impossible, as would Paolo Freire. They would say that dominant power can not reform itself. Power does not cede; it must be taken.

The best counter example we have today, however, is South Africa. Perhaps in its transformation from apartheid to democracy, through the reconciliation and truth-telling process, there is something we can learn. Not in the spirit of denial or self flagellation, but in the sure and certain knowledge that our repentance is required for our own survival, just as it was for South Africa. The standard of justice depends on the power to compel, and while we still are the dominant compelling force on the planet it behooves us to evaluate our own exercise of power and to repent of its misuse. It will take enormous humility to redirect our national vision from God's chosen to one among God's equally chosen people. Imago Dei is not a local concept but a universal one shared with every human being on the planet. We need to organize strenuously for the enlightened self-interest that recognizes that we cannot persist if our persistence impoverishes two-thirds of the world.

When I was growing up, grasping for light as an adolescent does, I bought into all those wonderful sayings of Gandhi, Martin Luther King and Robert Kennedy. I thought and still think that we can win the War on Poverty, though having dealt with the aftermath of Model Cities for twenty years, we can certainly come up with a better plan! I am completely convinced that we can eradicate hunger from the planet and that every person in the world can have clean drinking water, a basic primary education, and freedom from infectious diseases. I know without a doubt that the world's resources are more than sufficient to meet these needs sustainably *and* go to Mars if we like. It's simply a question of organizing. So far the organizers of death and destruction are better at it than we organizers of life and light. They seem to have mastered scale better than we have, which rather than being discouraging should inspire us because they have demonstrated that a relatively small group of people can indeed have a global impact. As Robert Kennedy said, "Each time a man (and I might add woman) stands up for an ideal, or acts to improve the lot of others, or strikes out against injustice, he (she) sends forth a tiny ripple of hope, and crossing each other from a million different centers of energy and daring, these ripples build a current which can sweep down the mightiest walls of oppression and resistance."[14] It's time to start organizing the ripples. We've got the wrong current running now in our country. We've go the current of oppression. We've got the current of fear. We've got the current of dominant power. We've got the current of vengeance. We've got the current of might makes right.

There is a movement afoot in the country which is based on might, on money, on fear, on war, on dominance. Well meaning people can point to evidence of why this is so necessary. But it's not the only path, not the only option, no matter how firmly we're on it. Unfortunately, the counter-movement spawned by the current environment is only to the point of protest, not to the point of generation and creativity of an alternative vision and an alternative way. It does not do any good to organize an effective protest if you don't have any idea what to do if you win. The situation in Iraq is an example of this on one side, and the loss of the faith-community leadership in transforming Europe after it provided the critical mass for Communism's downfall is another. Victory without governance is hollow. The vacuum will be filled by power structures which might have been momentarily toppled, but are organized to regain dominance, or at minimum to create chaos until people long again for the fleshpots of the past, no matter how coupled to oppression.

So this is the theological challenge before the country: to develop the theological language and vision which will touch our souls and lead from fear and aggression to repentance and hope. We don't need a new Moses now. We need a new Isaiah. In this Easter season when the world is new again, we still need to look back to Ash Wednesday's instruction: Repent and live the Gospel. Can we follow the example of South Africa but extend our reconciliation and truth-telling to the whole world, not just internally to our own country? What kind of world would be possible if we crucified our lust for dominant power and acted again as one of the elders in the Tent of the Presence, intent on getting *all* of the tribes into the Promised Land, not as if we ourselves were God? And this gets us back to organizing—getting *all* of the tribes into the Promised Land is not in the primary interest of either the public or private sector (and doesn't even get on the radar until those sectors are challenged in some way, and in today's world they most certainly are not challenged). Getting *all* of the tribes into the Promised Land is in the domain of the "Third Sector." The impetus can only come from us. The government and market can't do it. Will we?

NOTES

1. NYC Board of Education, Division of Assessment and Accountability, Office of Systemwide Evaluation and Accountability: "The Class of 1997—Final Longitudinal Report"; see also http://www.nycenet.edu/daa.

2. Shill, M., Ellen, I. G., Schwartz, A. E., Voicu, I. (2002): *Revitalizing Inner-City Neighborhoods: New York City's Ten Year Plan*. In: *Housing Policy Debate* 13(3), 529-566.

3. New York City Police Department CompStat Unit (2006): Patrol Borough Bronx: Report Covering the Week of 12/04/2006 through 12/10/06. CompStat 13(49).

4. Stuart, L., Heinemeier, J. (2006): *The Nehemiah Strategy: Housing as an Interfaith Organizing Strategy*. In: Shook, J. (ed.): *Making Housing Happen: Faith-Based Affordable Housing Models*. St. Louis, MO: Chalice Press, 196-213.

5. Stuart, L. (2000): *The Bronx Leadership Academy High School: The Challenges of Innovation*. In: Ravitch, D., Viteritti, J. P. (eds.): *City Schools: Lessons from New York*. Baltimore, MD: The Johns Hopkins University Press, 117-137.

6. Chambers, E. T. (2003): *Roots for Radicals: Organizing for Power, Action, and Justice*. London: Continuum International Publishing Group; and Gecan, M. (2002):

Going Public: An Insider's Story of Disrupting Power as Usual. Boston, MA: Beacon Press.

7. Thucydides. *History of the Peloponnesian War.* Book V:LXXXIX. London: Penguin Books, 1972, p 402.

8. Loomer, Bernard (1976). *Two Kinds of Power. Criterion,* 15:1, 11-29.

9. Cohen, Jean and Andrew Arato. *Civil Society and Political Theory,* MIT Press, Cambridge, MA, 1992.

10. The war in Iraq has now continued for over four years.

11. Wink, Walter. *Engaging the Powers.* Augsburg Fortress, Minneapolis, MN, 1992.

12. Brueggemann, Walter. "The Importance of a Sectarian Hermeneutic," *Horizons in Biblical Theology* 7 (1985):1-42.

13. Brueggemann, Walter. *The Prophetic Imagination.* Fortress Press, 2001.

14. Kennedy, Robert F. "Day of Affirmation Address (June 7, 1966) in *Ripples of Hope: Great American Civil Rights Speeches,* Josh Gottheimer, ed. Basic Civitas Books (Perseus), New York, NY, 2003.

FAITH AND VALUES IN THE PUBLIC ARENA: AN AMERICAN CATHOLIC IN PUBLIC LIFE

James L. Oberstar, M.C.

The test of a Catholic in the public arena—by which I mean elective office—is to preserve one's moral integrity and be true to one's conscience.

Toward that end, I have been guided by my upbringing in an iron ore miner's family in Northern Minnesota, my undergraduate formation at the College of St. Thomas, the works of John Courtney Murray and the inspiration of Joseph Cardinal Bernardin.

David Hollenbach, S.J., described the Jesuit theologian John Courtney Murray as "the preeminent practitioner of public theology and public moral discourse in the whole history of American Catholicism." Fr. Murray said that we are called to base our political views on our "particular understanding of the human person and the common good." He was a compelling advocate of genuine dialogue, respectful public discourse on common issues in our pluralistic society, in order to enlighten the public on the moral rationale underlying proposed legislation. He wanted us to speak, but also to listen—qualities even more needed today.

Cardinal Bernardin, in what he elegantly called the "seamless garment of life," argued that it is not sufficient to be opposed to abortion, we must also support pre- and post-natal care of mother and child; we must advocate for education, health care, jobs with a livable wage, housing and food for the needy; oppose the death penalty; and resist unjust war.

Let me put these thoughts in some context. Jeb Magruder, a Watergate "plumber," in his book, "An American Life," wrote:

"No one forced me or the others to break the law. Instead we ignored our better judgment out of a combination of ambition, loyalty, and partisan passion.

"If we consider how many people broke the law in the Watergate Affair, men who were usually model citizens in their private lives, we must ask if our failures do not somehow reflect larger failures in the values of our society.

"I, and many members of my generation, placed far too much emphasis on our personal ambitions, on achieving success as measured in materialistic terms, and far too little emphasis on moral and humanistic values.

"We had private morality, but not a sense of public morality."

That quality of "public morality" is uniquely tested where I work in our nation's capitol. There are few environments as pressure-filled and laden with temptation as the Washington scene, whether in the public arena, the private sector, or in academia. This place seethes with the beckoning finger of ambition: beating-the-competition-at-all-costs kind of success, in Nuernberg-style amorality.

I believe we have to start each day with the question: "how will my faith influence my decision-making today?" And end the day with: "how did my faith influence my decision-making today?"

How many of my actions, day by day, does my faith inform? Do I do the right thing when I am under great pressure, or when I am in a threatening environment, regardless of the group's approval or disapproval?

When we arrive at our workplace, neither Christ nor the Holy Spirit meets us at the door to guide us through the day. We have to rely on our personal moral foundation as informed by faith and the scriptures, in order to take Sunday into the weekday; to discern the relationship between our human purpose and God's purpose—to discern the relationship between the scriptures and the life we lead, and the work we perform.

Each of us, surely, can think of some difficult moral decision we made; let me share with you one of mine:

In 1984 I was caught up in an intense campaign for the endorsement of the Democratic-Farmer-Labor party to be its candidate for the United States Senate. A vital factor in winning the party's endorsement was support from the DFL's major pro-choice group, with whom I engaged in an extensive three-hour dialogue, two thirds of which was on abortion.

Toward the end of the meeting, one of the leaders said: "You are so right on all the social and economic issues, the international issues such as human rights, nuclear war, etc.—we could support you if you would make the commitment not to speak out on this issue of abortion."

The words of Matthew's Gospel rang in my heart: "The devil took him up to a very high mountain and showed him all the kingdoms of the world, promising, 'all these will I bestow on you if you prostrate yourself in homage before me.' Jesus said: 'Away with you, Satan.' "

I didn't quite put it that way, but I did say: "That, I cannot and will not do," and effectively abandoned a career in the U.S. Senate.

The French theologian, Louis Evely, wrote that prayer "is not us speaking to God, but listening to Him talking to you." Evely's central thought is that it is God who prays, or speaks, to us and mankind who does not heed His prayers.

In that spirit, our examination of conscience should be: do I conduct my life so that the people I meet see our Father in me, or do they simply see my day-to-day face. Do I have enough faith to see God hidden in my neighbor, waiting to be loved in a special way.

Public office is essentially service to our fellow human beings. The Greeks gave us the term: politics is service to the "polis"—the people. In my view, it requires, as does prayer, emptying ourselves of ourselves so that we can be totally open to the needs and call of others who cannot do so well for themselves. Christ, in the gospels, is asking us to break into other people's lives, to busy ourselves with their needs—something my late wife, Jo, and our children and I did regularly, cooking gallons of spaghetti and sauce to be served at the Washington inner city kitchens of So Others Might Eat (S.O.M.E.).

In the gospels, the condemned are accused not so much of violating the commandments as for failing to address themselves to those in this world living in misery. They are condemned less for what they have done than for what they have failed to do.

In the mid-1980s, the Reagan White House set forth successive budgets of program cuts for the poor and tax cuts for corporations and wealthy individuals under the slogan: "Private economic initiative is the source of wealth in our country."

The Catholic bishops countered with a pastoral entitled: "Economic Justice For All." "The Christian ethic," they wrote, "is incompatible with the primary, or exclusionary focus on maximization of profit." That so many people are poor in a nation as rich as ours is a social and moral scandal that we cannot ignore. "Private charity and voluntary action are not sufficient to alleviate poverty."

The federal government, the bishops continued, should sponsor "direct job creation programs, provide more support for economic planning, and cut military spending."

"People of all faith," they counseled, "must measure their actions and be judged in the light of what they do for the poor, what they do to the poor and what they enable the poor to do for themselves." These are the same Bishops, by the way, who call for an end to abortion and are roundly criticized for it.

I served on the Budget Committee in those days when we grappled with mountainous deficits and Hobson's choices in cutting spending in order to reduce the deficit. I often reminded my committee colleagues of the words of Proverbs 22:13, "He who shuts his ear to the cry of the poor will, himself, also call and not be heard."

Read Leviticus 23:22: "When you reap the harvest of your field, you shall not be so thorough that you reap the field to its very edge, nor shall you glean the stray ears of your grain. These things you shall leave for the poor and the alien. I, the Lord, am your God."

If you are looking for a moral underpinning for public policy, you can find Food for Peace in those words, as well as the school lunch program, meals on wheels, and congregate care.

Or if you look to Leviticus 25:25: "When your countryman becomes so impoverished beside you that he sells you his services, do not make him work as a slave."

Again, I think you can discern in those words the moral underpinnings of a minimum wage law.

When Pope John Paul II appealed to the World Bank, the International Monetary Fund, and the G-8 nations to forgive a large portion of Third World debt, it was not a mere humanitarian gesture, it was a call based upon and inspired by Isaiah's decree of a Jubilee Year, an injunction to the Israelites to "let the fields lie fallow, and forgive debts"—a moral imperative from the words of eternity.

In all that I undertake in public life, I am guided by the firm belief that, at the end of life, we will be judged, not by the volume of grain in our bins, not the size of our budget surplus, nor the might of our armies.

We will be judged by:

"I was hungry and you gave me food.

I was thirsty and you gave me drink.

I was a stranger and you made me welcome.

I was naked and you clothed me."

When we nourish the human spirit, take in the dispossessed, shelter them with love, and clothe the naked with human dignity, we are surely doing the Lord's work on Earth in our daily lives, in our service of the polis.

Part III

Genesis, Conversion, and Distant Horizions: The Shape of the Journey

"THE MISFIT," THE GRANDMOTHER, AND GENESIS IN FLANNERY O'CONNOR'S "A GOOD MAN IS HARD TO FIND"

Mark McVann, F.S.C.

INTRODUCTION

Flannery O'Connor, who died in 1964 at the early age of thirty-nine, was truly remarkable for a number of reasons. The first thing that sets her apart, of course, is that she was a prodigiously talented writer. She was remarkable also because she was a deeply devout Catholic who lived in the Protestant, especially Baptist, world of the American South. These together, her phenomenal talent and the religious environment, however, offer only a partial view into the world in which the redoubtable Flannery O'Connor lived and wrote her fascinating and challenging fiction. In order to have a sharper appreciation for her talent and her art, we must try to understand them in their broader historical-cultural context.

The context is post-World War II of the American South in the late 1940s and 1950s. And that context is (like the people we meet in her stories) formal, shallow, and oppressive. This highly unflattering description is derived in part from the stories themselves and serves both the comic and tragic purposes of those stories. I want to address each of these three characteristics in turn, but they must themselves first be placed in a context of their own: the deeply conservative, even reactionary, fundamentalist Protestantism of the southern United States.

CONTEXTS

The modern world in some ways has left the American South behind. It is true that there are wealthy and sophisticated cities like Atlanta and

Nashville, where some of America's best universities and medical centers are to be found (I myself had the great good fortune to study at Emory University in Atlanta), and some brilliant writers of the English language, like William Faulkner, Tennessee Williams, and a surprisingly large number of others, came out of the American South. But it is also true that the South, in comparison to much of the United States, continues to be poor, ill educated, racist, and anti-Catholic.

During the years that I lived in Atlanta (1981-1984), there appeared a series of comic books that were viciously anti-Catholic. Published by fundamentalist Protestants in southern California (Jack Chick Publications), they claim to unmask Catholicism as a diabolical movement that seeks both the destruction of Protestantism and world domination.[1] Soon after the publication of these scurrilous cartoons, there were reports of Catholic high school students being attacked and beaten by their Protestant classmates after school in towns outside Atlanta, simply because they were Catholic.

And there was in the American and international press a scant four or five years ago, the scandal surrounding Trent Lott, a senator from the southern state of Mississippi and the then leader of the Republicans in the U.S. Senate. He attended the one-hundredth birthday party of another Senator from the South, who, forty years before, had run for the American presidency on a platform of anti-black racism and racial segregation. In a speech at that party, Trent Lott said that he had voted for the racist senator for president and that had the senator won, the United States would not have so many problems today. These comments exposed his racism and he was, justly, driven from his position of leadership in the Senate.[2]

There is also the famous case in South Carolina of the flying of the Confederate battle flag, the "Stars and Bars," the banner of the slave-holding, secessionist Confederacy, above the state capitol. After repeated and bitter debates, that symbol was removed from the capitol, but many whites there resented what they regarded a suppression of, rather than a laying to rest of, a sad chapter in the state's history.[3] Such open contempt for blacks and the rejection of contemporary society that it implies came as a shock to many who may have had small idea that some sectors of the American South continue to be resentful of modernity and suspicious of its democratic, progressive, and egalitarian ideals.

And the South, unfortunately, also too often has regarded itself with contempt and loathing. As an effective, even if too brief an example of this: in my subject story, in response to the Grandmother's cliché that "Tennessee has the mountains and Georgia has the hills," John Wesley sneeringly repeats her pairing of the states: "Tennessee is just a hillbilly dumping ground and Georgia is a lousy state, too." June Star is quick to agree: "You said it" (139).[4]

This, then, is in part the world of Flannery O'Connor and of her remarkable short story "A Good Man Is Hard to Find": it is an angry, resentful, and suspicious world, on its surface polite and proper but just underneath, seething. And it is a world at a crossroads between a falsely remembered chivalrous past and a cynical present. I said above that I wanted to take in turn the terms formality, shallowness, and oppression which I used to describe O'Connor's context and characters.

FORMALITY OF SOUTHERN CULTURE

First, then, the formal. It is very clear that the two main characters in the story, the Grandmother and The Misfit, are painfully aware of etiquette and politeness. But this formality is comically and ironically empty: the mass-murderer apologizes for not wearing a shirt in front of the ladies, one of whom he orders shot and the other of whom he himself will shoot three times. This sense of formality is seized upon by the Grandmother who hopes, in vain, that it will keep The Misfit from killing her: "You wouldn't shoot a lady, would you?" (147).

The Grandmother herself constantly harps on manners and politeness and how things aren't how they used to be. She responds to the children's sneering about Georgia and Tennesee: "In my time, children were more respectful of their native states, their parents, and everything else. People did right then" (139). This theme sounds again in the restaurant where they eat their lunch. June Star insults Red Sammy's waitress-wife after doing her tap dance routine: "Ain't she cute? . . . Would you like to come be my little girl?" But June Star "wouldn't live in a broken-down place like this for a million bucks." The Grandmother hisses her disapproval, "Aren't you ashamed!" which of course, June Star isn't (141). The Grandmother and Red Sammy lament the general decline in morals— "People are certainly not nice like they used to be," says the Grandmother (141)—and they complain, quite comically and irrelevantly, about how Europe is the problem, evidence of the South's xenophobia.

In this context, we learn that two fellows had come to the filling station and Red Sammy let them charge the gasoline they took. He tells the Grandmother that they came in an old beat-up car, but a good one, so he let them take the gas on credit. "Now why did I do that?" "Because you're a good man!" the Grandmother exclaims (142). The conversation then turns to The Misfit and later we wonder if those two young men who conned Red Sammy into giving them the gasoline are The Misfit's accomplices whom we will meet driving an ominously "big, black, battered, hearse-like automobile" (145). The young men, we can easily believe, politely and formally asked for credit. In any case, the story gives ample evidence of the culture's devotion to, and the high value it places upon, observing proper social forms of politeness and etiquette.

SHALLOWNESS OF THE FORMALITY

And it is precisely the shallowness of these forms that strikes readers hardest. The forms are carefully observed and yet they are clearly empty. Indeed, none of the characters in the story ever has a real conversation. They speak in clichés or short barks, needle one another, complain or whine, insult each other, nag or give orders, all intended to manipulate and conceal rather than communicate and reveal. Even the conversation between the grandmother and Red Sammy is a comically inane commentary on current events. And perhaps the empty forms are so carefully observed precisely because they *are* empty. This prevents any real problems from coming to the fore or the admission of troubling questions or tensions. Rather, the empty formalism functions as a sort of social lubricant, deliberately devoid of content. It almost seems like a conspiracy intended to keep things the way they are. Indeed, it is easy to understand the children's contemptuous treatment of the Grandmother and Bailey and his wife's relentlessly ignoring her: she can speak only in maddening clichés, genteel reproofs, and with a sappy nostalgia for a past that never existed.

OPPRESSIVENESS OF THE FORMALITY

And directly from this shallowness flows the claustrophobic oppressiveness that we find omnipresent in the story. Indeed, oppressive formality is what The Misfit complains about most: if they got the papers on you, they got you. The papers, which make things formal, put you in prison and keep you in there and make the punishment far worse than the crime, a crime you can't remember anyway and which in any case is irrelevant since all that matters is that you be punished. Papers (here, the law) and oppression go hand in hand, justifying one another.

However, there are different kinds of oppression in the story. That experienced by Bailey and his wife at the hands of the Grandmother is really little more than annoyance: constant and irksome, but finally not an example of immorality or evil. Indeed, it offends in its banality. The same is true of their determined ignoring of the old woman and of the insults of those bratty children. These dynamics are evidence of nettlesome irritations of domestic life rather than of genuine moral evil. As O'Connor herself wrote in a letter to a teacher about the story:

... It's interesting to me that your students naturally work their way to the idea that the Grandmother in "A Good Man" is not pure evil and may be a medium for grace. If they were Southern students I would say this was because they all had grandmothers like her at home. These old ladies exactly reflect the banalities of the society and the effect is of the comical rather than the seriously evil. But Andrew [Lytle] insists that she is a witch, even down to the cat. These children, your students, know their grandmothers aren't witches.[5]

With The Misfit, however, we encounter another category altogether: in him we find an example of strong, unreconciled evil and the result of the real oppression he has encountered in his life.

The story draws a comparison between The Misfit's unremembered crime and original sin. When the Grandmother placatingly suggests he might have been brought up on false charges, he declares: "Nome. It wasn't no mistake. They had papers on me." Papers, in this metaphorical instance, means Scriptural as well as legal proof. He also scorns the old woman's further suggestion that his crime has been theft—the apple myth literally interpreted.[6]

"Papers" is an allusion to Scripture, specifically to the Second Creation Story in Genesis, Chapters 2 and 3: the fall of humanity as narrated in the story of Adam and Eve. Thus, The Misfit seems to represent Adam after the Fall, that is, he represents humanity living under the full consequences of Original Sin: as such he is thoroughly alienated, chaotic, bent on destruction, and murderous. As he says: "'then it's nothing for you to do but enjoy the few minutes you got left the best way you can—by killing somebody or burning down his house or doing some other meanness to him.' 'No pleasure but meanness,' he said and his voice had become almost a snarl" (152). It seems, then, that the story of Adam and Original Sin might be exactly what O'Connor has in mind where we read that The Misfit recoiled from the Grandmother's touch "as if a snake had bitten him" (152). The connection between the snake and death cannot be missed in Genesis and should not be missed here either, especially recalling the snake in this, a primeval setting of a "woods tall and dark and deep" (145), a woods that "gaped like a dark open mouth" (146). This woods is not Eden, but the hostile forest just outside that garden's now closed, fiery gate.

This identification of The Misfit with Adam is strengthened in at least two places in the story: the first is where he tells us his Daddy's comments about him: "My daddy said I was a different breed of dog from my brothers and sisters. 'You know,' Daddy said, 'it's some that can live their whole life without asking about it and it's others has to know why it is, and this boy is one of the latters. He's going to be into everything!'" (148). And a bit later, immediately after Hiram and Bobby Lee kill Bailey and his son, we see that The Misfit's daddy was right: he did get into everything: "I been most everything. Been in the arm service, both land and sea, at home and abroad, been twice married, been an undertaker, been with the railroads, plowed Mother Earth, been in a tornado, seen a man burned alive oncet. . . . I even seen a woman flogged. . . ." (149). This is The Mifit as universal man, Everyman, Adam.

In the first quotation above, Adam is set apart from other creatures of creation as sharply distinct from them (cf. Gen. 2:18-20), so The Misfit, according to his Daddy, is set apart from the rest from his brothers and sisters, i.e., all other creatures of creation. In the second quotation, The Misfit represents universal humanity: found on land and sea, a settled farmer and a nomadic wanderer, a witness to both suffering and death. The Misfit, then, may indeed represent the human condition, as in Adam: a sinner, a rebel, a wretch condemned to death.[7]

THE GRANDMOTHER

If what we have said so far is fair, then we have to ask ourselves, who, then, is the Grandmother, or what might she represent, especially in this setting which seems to recall the story of Original Sin? She is doubtless a silly old woman whose life has been ruled by slavish and unthinking adherence to convention and the constant seeking of small advantage in a rigid society and an ungiving family. But this silly old woman, "a hypocritical old soul," as O'Connor calls her,[8] has a moment of grace at the end when: "her head clears for an instant. She saw the man's face twisted close to her own as if he were going to cry and she murmured 'Why you're one of my babies. You're one of my own children!' She reached out and touched him on the shoulder."[9]

O'Connor herself has written the following about this passage in the story:

I often ask myself what makes a story work, and what makes it hold up as a story, and I have decided that it is probably some action, some gesture of a character that is unlike any other in the story, one which indicates where the real heart of the story lies. This would have to be an action which was both totally right and totally unexpected; it would have to suggest both the world and eternity; [it would have to be on] the analogical

level, that is, the level which has to do with the Divine Life and our participation in it. . . . It would be a gesture which somehow made contact
with mystery.

There is a point in this story where such a gesture occurs. The
Grandmother is at last alone, facing The Misfit. Her head clears for an
instant and she realizes, even in her limited way, that she is responsible for
the man before her and joined to him by ties of kinship which have their
roots deep in the mystery she has been merely prattling about so far [Jesus
and prayer, 151-152]. And at this point, she makes the right gesture.[10]

In light of this, then, perhaps we may say that the Grandmother here represents the exact opposite of The Misfit because she grasps or recognizes
the forgiveness of Original Sin as extended through the Jesus whom she
and The Misfit have just been talking about but not understanding. She
appealed to Jesus hoping to distract The Misfit from his murder; he to justify it. But the forgiveness of Original Sin, effected by the same Jesus they
have just been talking about, allows the Grandmother to see The Misfit
for an instant as her own, her child, her flesh and blood. She recognizes
her union with him, simultaneously immanent and transcendent, despite
the great gulfs between them, despite his murder of her family. For a
moment here she incarnates the mystery of redemptive love when she
sees clearly The Misfit's twisted face, hears his cracking voice, and sees
his eyes about to cry. In his agony of utter abandonment, she touches him
in love and forgiveness. Thus, if The Misfit represents *unredeemed*
humanity after the Fall, the Grandmother represents a redeemed humanity that can forgive and love its enemies. This exact same grace at this
exact same moment is extended to The Misfit who kills the Grandmother
in his absolute refual of it, his absolute rejection of forgiveness, love, and
redemption, in his clinging to Adam's legacy, rather than embracing
Christ's.[11]

This theological interpretation of the climax of the story is, I think, the
story's meaning, not in the sense that I want to reduce it to a theological
proposition or an illustration of biblical doctrine. Indeed, O'Connor herself rejected such reductions of her fiction or any good fiction: "A story
isn't really any good unless it resists paraphrase, unless it hangs on and
expands in the mind."[12] At the same time, however, she insisted that the
principles underling her fiction are: "the central Christian mysteries.
These are assumptions to which a large part of the modern audience takes
exception. About this I can say only that there are perhaps other ways
than my own in which this story could be read, but none other by which
it could have been written."[13]

And this brings us again, then, to the question of historical and cultural context with which we opened this paper. In the same way that O'Connor's stories could not have been written apart from the central Christian mysteries, neither could they have been written in any other context than the American South, that great territory of the United States with its rich and wretched, glorious and grief-filled history. O'Connor said that:

> I don't want to equate The Misfit with the devil. I prefer to think that, however unlikely this may seem, the old lady's gesture, like the mustard seed, will grow to be a great crow-filled tree in The Misfit's heart, and will be enough of a pain to him to turn him into the prophet he was meant to be. But that is another story.[14]

OTHER STORIES

And speaking of other stories, many of Flannery O'Connor's other stories are as shocking and funny and amazing as this one. There is, for example, her other most famous short story, "Good Country People." Here we have a tale of a young woman with a wooden leg and a Ph.D. in philosophy. She despises religion and her contempt for young men knows no bounds. Readers are amazed, then, that when a young Bible salesman comes peddling Bibles at her house, she agrees to see him the next day. They end up in a barn where the Bible salesman reveals himself to be fully prepared for a fun-filled afternoon with a bottle of whiskey, a deck of pornographic playing cards, and a condom. She is amazed by this transformation of the young man she thought to be an innocent. Even more to her amazement—and the readers'!—he steals her wooden leg from her and runs off leaving her stranded in the barn loft.

There are dynamics in this story comparable with "A Good Man Is Hard to Find," the most important of which is the shocking denoument of the stealing of the leg (like the shocking murder of the Grandmother). The philosopher who insists she believes in nothing is quite startled to learn that the Bible salesman believes in nothing and has, he tells her, since the day he was born. The theft of the wooden leg—a symbol of the woman herself as both empty and false—is the woman philosopher's moment of grace: readers hope she understands that she has been a fool and lived an angry lie because she was never reconciled to the loss of her own leg. Having the false one taken away creates the possibility of a new life for her, of her finding a new and authentic self. Other stories by O'Connor are structured in a similar fashion and have similarly shocking tragic-comic denoument and moments of grace.

CONCLUSION

So much, then, for her stories, those wildly funny and deeply shocking tales. But what about us, the readers of her stories? O'Connor writes:

> When you can assume that your audience holds the same belief you do, you can relax a little and use more normal means of talking to it; when you have to assume that it does not, then you have to make your vision apparent by shock—to the hard of hearing you shout, and for the almost-blind you draw large and startling figures.[15]

And so, here we are, the hard of hearing and the almost-blind, listening to Flannery O'Connor shouting, trying to hear her; gawking at her large and startling figures, trying to make them out. Here we are, reading these amazing stories, stories of the action of grace in the world in these impossible situations among these impossible people. The Grandmother's action of touching The Misfit might not finally be a strong enough mustard seed, as O'Connor hoped, to make a great crow-filled tree grow in The Misfit's heart and turn him into the prophet he was meant to be. But for us, reading Flannery O'Connor's powerful and prophetic fiction just may plant a mustard seed strong enough to work a transformation in *us*, and turn us from the hard-of-hearing and almost-blind into a people carefully attuned to the rumors of grace and dazzled by its beauty: a people with ears to hear and eyes to see.

NOTES

1. A simple Google search will provide the home page of Jack Chick Publications along with related sites, including one which offers amusing, if sometimes pornographic, parodies of the simple-minded bigotry of the original publications.

2. Another simple Internet search will yield page after page of information on the sorry saga of Senator Trent Lott.

3. Again, the Internet is a great resource for information about such topics. Search "South Carolina State Flag Controversy" on Google, for example, and a cornucopia of reportage will be made available.

4. All quotations from the story are taken from Flannery O'Connor: *Collected Works*, *Literary Classics of the United States*, New York: 1988.

5. Quotations from criticism are all taken from Flannery O'Connor, "A Good Man Is Hard to Find," ed. Frederick Asals (New Brunswick, NJ: Rutgers University, 1993), 61. This is an invaluable resource for readers interested in a full-length treatment of this great short story.

6. W.S. Marks, "Advertisements for Grace: Flannery O'Connor's 'A Good Man is Hard to Find,'" in Asals, 89-90.

7. When this paper was presented at the College of Saint Scholastica in November of 2004, Prof. William Hodapp of the English Department there asked if the biblical allusion intended with The Misfit is Cain, the first murderer, rather than Adam, the first man. Later, a colleague of mine, Bula Maddison, wrote in the margin of a draft of this paper: "Is Adam so bad?" Perhaps, then, a word is needed about Adam. These questions are asked because we all "know," of course, that Eve is the bad character in the creation story and because in Christian thought we have an inadvertently rehabilitated Adam since Saint Paul wrote about Christ as the new Adam (Rom 5:12ff): how bad can Adam be since Christ is like him? But this misses the point precisely becauseChrist is as *good* as Adam was *bad*: Adam's rejection of God in his attempt to become like God is what starts the terrible chain of death, chaos, alienation, despair, and the rest of it that are the tragic themes of the Primeval History in Genesis 1-11: *this* is Adam's legacy, *he* is its author. As the note on the passage in Romans 5 about Adam and Christ, has it: "Sin, as used in the singular by Paul, refers to the dreadful power that has gripped humanity, which is now in revolt against the Creator and engaged in the exaltation of its own desires and interests" (note on Romans 5:12-21, *New American Bible*). It is from this "dreadful power," Adam's legacy of sin, that Christ came to save us. So, "Is Adam so bad?" Well, yes; but now through Christ redeemed.

8. Asals, 57.

9. Asals, 152.

10. Asals, 57-58.

11. O'Connor writes: "The Misfit is touched by the Grace that comes through the old lady when she recognizes him as her child, as she has been touched by the Grace that comes through him in his particular suffering. His shooting her is a recoil, a horror at her humanness, but after he has done it . . . the Grace has worked in him and he pronounces his judgment: she would have been a good woman if *he* had been there every moment of her life." Asals, 61.

12. Asals, 56.

13. Asals, 57.

14. Asals, 59.

15. O'Connor, "The Fiction Writer and His Country," *Collected Works*, 805-806.

THE SEARCH FOR FAITH AND PASCAL'S WAGER

Anthony Barrett

The oddity of my giving a Catholic Studies series presentation is probably not lost on you. The other speakers have impressive degrees from impressive institutions. They are experts in theology, philosophy and other areas of profound wisdom. While my PhD in Economics holds its own, the "Athletic Director" title is a clue that I'm probably not going to be like other speakers. I was raised a Presbyterian, although I have not regularly attended church for a generation. In college (Catholic Georgetown, by chance), I was considered religious by friends because I read the Bible. Over the years, I have tried learning from many different religious traditions: Jewish, Buddhist, Taoist, and various Christian ones. But my mind never has been able to get around what I perceived to be logical inconsistencies that required a leap of faith. I don't think I have ever been able to find that "faith," and I remain envious of all who have it.

I might note, however, that I surprised myself recently when I was in the hospital for a heart procedure. The admitting person asked my religious preference and I said "Catholic." I suppose after sixteen years of being associated with the College of St. Scholastica, the Sisters, the role model of John Paul and some other factors, I have gravitated towards that particular church.

Father Graham asked me to be a part of the "Here Comes Everybody" lecture series after he heard my CSS "Last Lecture" in April 2005. In the "Last Lecture" series, a professor selected by the students and student-life staff is asked to pretend he or she has one last lecture to give. Ironically, I was asked during my last semester of teaching before my career change to Athletic Director, so it was very appropriate timing. What surprised me was that I didn't know what to say. Reticence is not a quality usually associated with me, but when faced with what I would say at the profound level required for a "Last Lecture," I was lost. Twenty-five years of teaching economics—that's about 5,625 lectures—and I get to the last one and I don't know what to say.

I eventually came up with something and I think it went over rather well. After my presentation, Father Graham said it was a perfect example of Pascal's Wager and I had to be in his (Father Graham's) projected series of lectures. Despite hardly having heard of such a wager and since committing to things in the distant future is easy, I agreed - and here I am. I knew Pascal's name for his contributions to early economic thought but was only vaguely aware of his famous wager. However, Father Graham assured me I could find out everything I needed to know in readily available sources and I'd be fine. You'll be the judge of that.

First, I'll lay out a bare-bones explanation of Pascal's Wager and his critics' three major attacks on it. Then I'll trace my position regarding religion/faith and we'll see where the commonalities and differences are. We'll have plenty to times for questions because I am sure there will be vagueness where you will want specifics.

Pascal was a mid-1600's French thinker. In those days, before the specialization of thinking, he could be a mathematician, scientist and philosopher all at once. He died when he was only thirty-nine, and the wager we are to discuss is one of three found in notes for an unfinished paper. Pascal's Wager was not an attempt to prove the existence of God. He was applying what may be called early game theory (hence his connection to economics) to show that a prudent life style would be a Christian (in his case, Catholic) one. Essentially, he was saying it was in a person's self-interest to believe there is a God. If that turns out to be true, the payoff is eternal life. If it turns out there is no God, Pascal claims that we haven't lost anything. On the other hand, if we believe there is no God and there turns out to be one, we are faced with eternal damnation: a not insignificant cost. Given the extreme payoffs for believing and not believing if, in fact, there does turn out to be a God, Pascal argues that it's in a person's best interest to believe.

Now a lot of people, mainly atheists, have spent a tremendous amount of time shooting holes in Pascal's reasoning. The three main criticisms of Pascal's argument are as follows. First, which God do you follow? Second, there are costs (such as time spent in church going and "sinful" behavior foregone) to believing there is a God. Last, if we behave as if there is a God, but don't really believe it deep down inside, won't God know? Those are good points, certainly fun to discuss. But it's worth noting that while critics disparage Pascal's argument, the fact is that it is still being discussed over 350 years after it was found in his notes.

Essentially, that is what we are doing here today. The objective of this presentation is to expose my personal faith status and assess whether or not I am a living example of a person's placing his money (or more specifically, his soul) on Pascal's wager. Returning to the intent of the Last Lecture, I started with what I know. I mean deep down *"Know,"* with 100% certainty. There's not much. Certainly not in economics. I know seat belts and care seats save lives. Eighteen years ago next week, my children and I were hit head on by a reckless driver on a country road in Missouri. While all of us were very seriously hurt, we didn't die. Thanks to seat belts and car seats, my children have lived to become fine, interesting adults and I had a chance to marry a woman who taught me it is possible to be happy in a relationship. I have had nineteen more years of life.

And that leads easily to the second thing I know: I am going to die some day. I still remember the moment sitting on the porch of my sister's farmhouse in Perth, Ontario, when that realization sank into me at a profound level. This is essentially our only life. Even traditions that believe in reincarnation don't believe we can connect consciously with previous lives. That's a New Age concept. So, if this is our one life, the greatest tragedy would be to be on our deathbed thinking, "Man, I wasted this life," or "I have a list of regrets a mile long."

Since then, I have tried to live my life in a way that minimizes regrets. Now, that's not all that earth-shattering. No one would argue that we should maximize our regrets or waste our lives. In modern management lingo, I have, with my deathbed scenario, a strategic vision. And, like most strategic visions, it's short on day-to-day details. Finding the way to operationalize the vision has been trial and error. And now we have to get personal.

For me, it is a constantly evolving process. My key beliefs don't change much anymore; but they *do* change, as you'll see. How I translate those beliefs into actions is a day-to-day struggle. When I was younger, I thought older people got more religious because they were covering all their bets as they neared death. Now I realize it's because the kids have moved out of the house, careers have settled into a groove, and we have time to reflect on whatever we care to do. Some persons focus on religion. Additionally for me, being in a place that has a spiritual aura like CSS has helped.

Where am I now and where does Pascal's Wager fit in? Faith is defined as "unquestioning belief" and belief is defined as "acceptance that something is true." I will use those meanings of the words.

I have faith there is a God. Why? Bottom line: I have had prayers answered. I have seen things where the simplest explanation is that there is a God. Which God? Who's God? I really don't think about that. If you pin me down, I'd probably say "You know, I think they are all the same God." Very Hindu of me. But, trying to grasp the nature of God is so obviously beyond the grasp of this mind (which finds it close to impossible to remember people's names) that I don't think about the nature of God that much.

I was born, raised and live in Judeo-Christian Western Civilization. So, when I work on minimizing regrets and not wasting my life, I turn to Christianity. Instead of following the teaching of Jesus, why not Buddha? Confucius or Lao-tse? Fine. It seems to me when you get to the core message of the original teachings of the religions of which I am aware, there is not much difference in the ways in which we should to treat our fellows. So, I rely on Christian teachings and traditions.

And, here is an area where one of my key beliefs has changed in the past couple of years. Years of frustration and guilt went away. About two years ago, after trying a round of churches, searching once again for the lightening bolt of faith to come to me, I made the decision: I can aspire to be a bad-church Christian.

I have read a lot of early Christian history. It is amazing how we went from a plethora of "gospels" and traditions about Jesus to an orthodoxy in about 300 years and then have taken that relatively small collection of sayings and actions of Jesus and split again into thousands of Christian churches, variations on variations. Two millennia of learned people have piled so much "stuff" on top of the teachings of Jesus that it's perfectly acceptable to me to say to the churches: sorry, but I think you're wrong on some of these issues. And the big issue is as central and profound as the nature of Jesus, where I have learned that I am a docetist (Mark 1:10 and 15:34). The word *docetist* comes from the Greek *doceo*, meaning "appear" or "seem." The claim was that while Jesus was a flesh and blood human, Christ was separate, a divine being who as God cannot experience death. In this view, Christ descends from heaven and enters into Jesus' body. That's Mark 1:9-11, saying of Jesus' baptism, "and it came to pass in those days, that Jesus came from Nazareth of Galilee, and was baptized by John in Jordan. And straightaway coming up out of the water, he saw the heavens opened, and the Spirit like a dove descending upon him: and there came a voice from heaven saying, Thou art my beloved son, in whom I am well pleased." The docetist would claim that the Spirit, being God, stays with Jesus through his ministry, leaving Jesus at the crucifixion. This leads to the powerful passage in Mark 15:34, "My God, My God, why hast thou forsaken me?"

This is the interpretation of the nature of Jesus that I am currently most comfortable with. Yet, it is clearly totally at odds with the core of virtually all Christian thought, the Holy Trinity. Consequently, I remain a bad church Christian. But, for the day-to-day action plan to enact my strategic vision, I rely on the teachings of Jesus.

WWJD. When I first saw that on a T-shirt in a mall, I rolled my eyes. But, that is in most respects the action plan for my "minimize regrets" strategic vision. And to find out "what Jesus would do," I turn to the gospel of Mark, the earliest gospel. There's enough instructions and guidance for me in that one short gospel. Whatever one believes about the nature of Jesus, I can't see how one can disagree with his teachings about how to live life.

So, back to Pascal's Wager. Am I placing my soul on his wager? First, one difference and I'm not sure how important it is. Pascal emphasized the payoff of eternal life for behaving as if there is a God. I do not. I can honestly say I can't remember the last time I thought about what happens after death. We can't know. We'll find out when we get there. To me, the payoff for trying to do what Jesus would have me do is how I feel on my deathbed. I'm not sure of the significance of this distinction since I just thought of it as I prepared for this presentation. It does put me in the position of being the judge of my own life. I don't know if that's good or bad.

I do know that my approach escapes at least two of the three main criticisms of Pascal's Wager. First was, which God do we follow? Whatever one you want, I say. Yes, religions differ on whether or not to eat pork or beef, which day is the Sabbath and how we are to observe it. And there are major differences in ritual observances. But they are all in essential agreement on how to behave towards our fellows. Second, what about the time and money I am potentially wasting by believing there is a God? Well, unlike Pascal who was Catholic, I don't attend and tithe to a church, so that's a huge savings. As for the forgone "sinful" ways I am passing up, I will feel good about it on my deathbed.

The third criticism was: won't God know if I don't truly believe deep down inside? Or, a variation, what if God is a stickler for details and I am wrong on the nature of Jesus item? Well, all I can say is that I hope God gives me a pat on the back and credit for trying to live a good life.

I had thought I would end with that, but as I worked on this essay and lay awake in the middle of the night thinking about it, a thought kept trying to intrude. I have searched for faith for decades. Read, prayed, attended churches. And, if asked today I would say I still haven't found it. However, this exercise that Father Graham has put me through has created this nagging idea. Haven't I found faith? I believe in God. I don't believe in the Holy Trinity that is the foundation of Christian theology.

But I believe in God and try to reflect that in my day-to-day behavior through the teachings of Jesus as written in Mark. It may be that I reached my faith destination in the past couple of years and didn't realize it. Very human of me. I'll have to continue thinking about it.

AVERY DULLES: FROM CONVERT TO CARDINAL

Anne-Marie Kirmse, O.P.

INTRODUCTION

On November 26, 1940, a first-year student in Harvard Law School was baptized in St. Paul's Church in Cambridge, Massachusetts. What made this occasion especially noteworthy is that the young man was a member of a prominent family both in politics and in religion. His great-grandfather was Secretary of State under President Benjamin Harrison; his great-uncle was Secretary of State under President Woodrow Wilson, and his father would become Secretary of State under President Dwight Eisenhower. His family were devout Presbyterians, and his paternal grandfather was a noted Presbyterian theologian and pastor of the early twentieth century.

On February 21, 2001, this same man, now an octogenarian and a Jesuit priest, knelt before Pope John Paul II to receive the red hat of a Cardinal. What made this occasion especially noteworthy is that this Cardinal was the first United States-born theologian who is not a bishop to receive this honor. What happened between those two momentous events is the topic of this essay, the life and ministry of Avery Dulles, S.J.

A CIRCUITOUS ROUTE

Avery Dulles was born in Auburn, New York, on August 24, 1918, the third and youngest child of Janet Avery Dulles and John Foster Dulles. As he himself describes it, his journey to the Roman Catholic Church took a rather circuitous route. His early childhood was spent within the confines of his religious family environment, but his own personal beliefs began to wane when he was sent to Le Rosey, a preparatory school in Switzerland. Later, at the Choate Preparatory School in Connecticut, he was attracted to various materialistic philosophies, and, by his own admission, even dabbled with atheism.[1] After graduation from Choate, his family wanted him to attend Princeton University, his father's alma mater, but Avery's desire to study history and literature led him to Harvard College instead.

It was while an undergraduate student at Harvard that Dulles began the search which would eventually lead him to rediscover faith. Already in his freshman year, he became disenchanted with personal pleasure as the sole criterion for life's decisions. If philosophy had led him away from God, it was philosophy which would help to lead him back again. Through his college courses, he became acquainted with Plato, Aristotle, and the medieval philosophers. Their teachings provided an antidote to the materialistic philosophies which once claimed his allegiance. In the Spring of his junior year, he encountered God once again as a loving, personal Being, and was able to return to prayer for the first time in many years.

Avery Dulles's search for a Church in which to nurture his reclaimed belief was a serious venture. Specializing in Italian Renaissance studies at Harvard, he realized that "at every point I found myself more at home with the Catholic tradition than with its Protestant counterparts."[2] The piety of the parishioners in the local Cambridge Catholic churches also made a deep impression on the young Dulles. Finally, his careful application of the four marks of the true Church and his assiduous research led him to desire to become a Catholic, despite the fact that at the time he did not even know how to meet with a priest. His commitment to finding the true Church was so strong that forty years later he could still say: "Catholic preachers and teachers, by and large, can be counted upon to transmit not simply their own personal opinions, but the faith of the Church. If I had not perceived this to be the case, I, for one, would not be a Catholic."[3]

With the outbreak of World War II, Dulles joined the United States Naval Reserve, serving in the Caribbean Sea, and also in the Mediterranean theatre of operation. For his part in the war effort, he was decorated with the Croix de Guerre by the French Government. Shortly after his discharge in 1946, he entered the Society of Jesus (the Jesuits). He was ordained a priest in 1956, and received his doctoral degree from the Gregorian University in Rome in 1960. Since then, he has served on the faculties of Woodstock College, Fordham University, and The Catholic University of America, and has been a visiting professor in colleges and universities in the United States and Europe. He retired from Catholic University in 1988, and is currently the Laurence J. McGinley Distinguished Professor of Religion and Society at Fordham University.

At eighty-eight years of age, he continues to teach at Fordham and at the Archdiocese of New York Seminary at Dunwoodie, lectures here and abroad, and serves as a consultant to the Committee on Doctrine of the United States Conference of Catholic Bishops.

A Fundamental Theologian In Foundational Theology

Dulles is a prolific writer as can be seen in his list of publications. He has published 23 books, with one more in press scheduled for publication later this year, and over 800 articles. His writings concentrate on revelation, faith, ecclesiology, and ecumenism, but are not limited to these topics. To date his writings have been translated into Italian, French, German, Spanish, Portuguese, Dutch, Greek, Polish, Korean, and Hungarian, and are available in digital versions and on-line.

The number of lectures and articles Dulles writes each year almost staggers the imagination, and each is carefully researched and prepared. It would be an impossible task to try to present the many topics he has treated in the course of one lecture. He describes himself as a fundamental theologian, i.e., someone who works in the area of foundational theology.[4] This area has been the focus of his teaching career. But his writing and many of his lectures have dealt with ecclesiology, and therefore, this evening I will concentrate on his ecclesiology as the focal point of my presentation.

A good place to begin is to look at his methodology. Throughout his academic career, Dulles has basically employed two kinds of methodologies, viz., typology and the use of models. Typology is a means of classification, e.g., topics may be arranged according to specific themes, to authors holding similar viewpoints, or to historical periods, to cite but a few. From the beginning of his academic career, Dulles has displayed a fondness for this particular way of organizing his material. His usual procedure is to group various theologians together according to pre-chosen similarities, present their insights in a systematic fashion, and then to compare and contrast each type with the others. Looking at Dulles from the viewpoint of typological methodology, he appears to be more of a commentator on the positions of other theologians rather than an innovator in his own right. Commenting on this method, Dulles gives us an insight into his own personality: "Characteristically reflective by temperament, typologists seek to avoid the fray and reconcile the warring parties. Conscious of the partial perspectives of others, they wish to keep their options open."[5]

Dulles has popularized the use of models in theology, a methodology originally used in the fields of the physical and social sciences.[6] In his theological system, a model may be described as "a relatively simple, artificially constructed case which is found to be useful and illuminating for dealing with realities that are more complex and differentiated."[7] Models provide the opportunity of describing those things which do not readily admit of precise definitions, of comparing diverse opinions, and of critically assessing data.

To understand how Dulles uses models in his works, it is necessary to begin with his appreciation of the centrality of mystery in theology. Mystery is at the core of all Dulles' theological undertakings, and the models approach is his way of protecting and respecting this element of mystery. Since mystery cannot be captured once and for all, the experience of it must be interpreted through the use of analogies. The analogies chosen to express a particular dimension of mystery lead to their articulation in images. Images provide an important service to the concept of mystery, because not all truth can be explored in a completely literal fashion. Images then lead to the creation of models, and Dulles sees an integral connection between image and model: "When an image is employed reflectively and critically to deepen one's theoretical understanding of a reality it becomes what is today called a 'model.'" [8]

Dulles classifies models in two ways: 1) explanatory, which synthesize what is already known, and 2) exploratory, which have the capacity to lead to new theological insights.[9] His use of models may then be summarized in the following ways. The experience of mystery is interpreted through analogies which are expressed in images. These images are then constructed into models. Or, coming from another direction, experience may be classified by means of the selection of types, with ideal types becoming models.[10] While this approach is the basis of his two books which feature the word "model" in their titles (*Models of the Church and Models of Revelation*), it forms the basis of many of the articles Dulles has published as well.

A major asset of using models in theology is to maintain a healthy pluralism, which is a hallmark of his theological method. Dulles believes that the various models used to illustrate a theological concept must be kept in dialectical tension with one another, and that each should be used to critique and complement the others. To choose only one as paradigmatic would lead to distortion.[11]

For many persons, the name Avery Dulles is almost synonymous with the term, "models of the Church," as this is the title of the book in which he presented the rich insights of *Lumen Gentium* and the other ecclesiological pronouncements of Vatican II. The impact of this book in our country was nothing short of phenomenal. Avery Dulles and his models approach became, if not a household name, at least popular among the clergy, religious educators, and Catholic intelligentsia. Those who did not read *Models of the Church* themselves were introduced to its concepts through their pastors and parish personnel.

What was the reason for the immense popularity of this small book? I think that much of the credit for its widespread acceptance must be attributed to the way in which it was written. In the first place, Dulles has a tremendous sense of history, enabling him to situate the only experience of Church most of his readers would have had within the larger framework of the experience of Christianity's almost two thousand years of existence. Secondly, he was able to find good points and bad points in each of his models, thus easing the transition to the broader vision of the council's presentation of the Church. Lastly, but by no means least, the scholarly investigations and conclusions were presented in a very sensitive manner. One must remember the tenor of the times of the early 1970's. It was a period of confusion and disillusionment, as previous structures, both in Church and in society, were being questioned. This process of re-evaluation led to very painful polarizations, as many persons became enmeshed in their own viewpoints and refused to investigate any other options. I believe that Dulles' adamant opposition of any type of polarization in the Church is at the basis of the sensitivity one finds in his style.

As has previously been stated, an affirmation of mystery lies at the very heart of all Dulles' work in theology. Therefore, it comes as no surprise that his ecclesiology is based on this same premise. He presents the Church as a multi-faceted reality, one that cannot be limited to any particular frame of reference. Since the essence of the Church is rooted in mystery, it will always be greater than any attempt to describe it. For this reason, Dulles has pursued his preferred path of working simultaneously with a number of complementary images and models.

Dulles pleads for an integration of the Church as institution, communion, sacrament, herald, and servant, for it is only by looking at these five models in their mutuality and totality, that the divine/human aspect of the Church can clearly be seen. However, five must not be viewed as some sort of magical number, for Dulles has observed, "The number of models may be varied almost at will. In some presentations I have invoked as many as seven or eight. For simplicity's sake, I find it better to work with as few as possible."[12] A full explanation of each of these models is far beyond the scope of this lecture, but I would like to just present here a brief description of each of the models.

The institution model highlights the Church as a visible society, hierarchically structured, instituted by Jesus Christ which communicates salvation by authoritative doctrine, ministry of sacraments, and pastoral care. This was the predominant way the Church was experienced by most Catholics before Vatican II. The second model, community, emphasizes the Church as the People of God (or Mystical Body) bound together by fellowship in the Spirit. The third of Dulles's models presents the sacramental image, in which the Church is seen as the visible sign and embodiment of Christ's redemptive presence and work. The herald model portrays the Church as the missionary society sent to evangelize the world. And the last of Dulles's five models sees the Church as servant, an agent for social change whose task is to collaborate with God in the transformation of the world into God's Kingdom.

Although this was a very cursory sketch of the five models of the church, it nonetheless gives you a flavor for the richness contained in an encompassing vision of the Church. While none of the models should be considered the one and only way to approach the mystery of the Church, Dulles had hinted in *Models of the Church* that of the five considered, the sacramental model might be the best vehicle for the integration of the others.[13] In his next book, *The Resilient Church* published in 1977, his thinking evolved to the point where he clearly and unequivocally expressed his preference for viewing the Church as sacrament. Quoting Vatican II's description of the Church as "the universal sacrament of salvation" (LG 48), he rather boldly asserts, "after some years of work in ecclesiology, I am inclined to think that there is no better definition."[14] In *A Church to Believe In*, published in 1982, Dulles admits that "in contemporary ecclesiology the concept of sacrament is prominent."[15] However, he realizes the limitations of that model: ". . . this may not be the kind of image that can easily be popularized in our time."[16]

Therefore, in this book, Dulles now proposed a new model, viz, the Church as a community of disciples.[17] He presents the Church as a community that gathers in the presence of Jesus and imitates the first disciples. Furthermore, the Church is the place that authentic discipleship—the response to the call of God—remains possible. This image has a strong biblical foundation, for while theologians are grappling with the question of whether or not Jesus did in fact establish the Church, it is clear that he did assemble a group of disciples around himself. "'Community of disciples' is precisely what Jesus undoubtedly did found, and once we recognize this fact we can apply to our life in the Church many of the Gospel passages dealing with discipleship."[18] However valid and fruitful this contemporary application to ecclesiology may be, Dulles himself cautions against a canonization of it: "I would not go so far as to assert that the discipleship model can be used to take the place of all the others. As a mystery, the Church is irreducible to any single concept or image."[19]

Vatican II called for a renewed vision of the Church which would include a plurality of images, none of which would be taken as exhaustive. By condensing the most predominant of these images into his five models, Dulles popularized this aspect of Vatican II's ecclesiology, and literally made it accessible to "the person in the pew." However, in his reflections on the postconciliar Church, Dulles realizes that this vision has not yet been attained. In *A Church to Believe In*, Dulles notes that the Church was still commonly experienced in terms of its institutional components alone,[20] and the situation has not drastically changed since then although a quarter of a century has passed since he wrote that book.

Why haven't the beautiful images of the Church, as portrayed in *Lumen Gentium*, taken root in the self-understanding of the faithful? In evaluating the three central images—Body of Christ, People of God, and sacrament—Dulles finds an answer in the fact that none of these resonate with lived experience.[21] For this reason, he proposed the discipleship model, which, in his opinion, is true to both the teachings of Vatican II and to contemporary life. However, the potential promise Dulles saw in the discipleship model has not been realized, either. He himself has not pursued it, except in occasional references. Perhaps, despite its inherent merits, the discipleship model also does not reflect the lived situation of most Roman Catholics today.

The teachings of Vatican II have served as the focal point not only of Dulles' ecclesiology, but of his entire theological system. His book, *The Reshaping of Catholicism* published in 1988, is a collection of essays that deal specifically with the Church in light of Vatican II.[22] In that same year, he acknowledged in an interview with Peter Steinfels in *The New York Times* that, " . . . what I've been doing these last 20, 25 years really centers around interpreting Vatican II."[23] As time has progressed, it seems that he is emphasizing the conciliar documents more intensely in an attempt to challenge the Church to a greater fidelity to its mission.

There was a tendency to interpret the documents of Vatican II as calling for more secularist and political types of theology. This was especially true in the years immediately following the council. *Gaudium et Spes* called for "reading the signs of the times." Dulles is in agreement with this injunction, but he also cautions against becoming so overly identified with its surroundings that the Church loses its identity. In very simple words, he issued the challenge: "Let the Church become the Church!"[24] This sentence aptly describes his motivation through the years. While he is fully convinced of the Church's need for adaptation and renewal, he does not endorse any changes that would detract from its true mission as a sacrament of Christ's presence in the world. Not everything that would call itself Christian is worthy of the designation. Choices must be made to insure the Church's fidelity to its vocation.

He states, "we may say that the Council repeatedly and emphatically taught that the procurement of salvation is the most important task of the church."[25] The very reason for the Church's presence in the world is its existence as the "universal sacrament of salvation" (LG 1; GS 45; AG 1). According to Vatican II, the sanctification of humankind is especially present in the Church's liturgy (SC 7), forming the basis of the Church's mission to evangelize (LG 17; AG 7) and to hasten the reunification of the one true Church (UR 4).

If salvation is viewed as the most important task of the Church, it follows that service within the Church must be directed to this end. Dulles does not believe that Vatican II intended that such service be oriented primarily to the betterment of the social order. In fact, his opinions are quite the contrary. He distinguishes between what is "proper" to the Church's mission and the repercussions which flow from this mission, defining the former as "that which is specific to the church and would remain undone unless the church existed."[26] In this category, he places preaching faith in Christ and administering the sacraments. Naturally, the living of an authentic faith relationship with Christ and the deepening of this graced relationship with him sacramentally will lead his followers to strive for justice for all persons. But that is a result of the Church's salvific activity, not its cause. Dulles makes a subtle distinction in claiming that, while the erection of a just society is not proper to the Church, contributing to this society is.[27]

A VOICE OF MODERATION

While other theologians may have been constructing highly innovative systems, especially in the years immediately following Vatican II, Dulles was quietly and unassumingly pursuing his own path as the "voice of moderation." Throughout all his writings, Dulles has tried to maintain a mediating position between conservative and liberal viewpoints. He has attempted to present a balanced view of the issues at hand, describing the assets and liabilities of each side. He is grieved at the polarization which has occurred since Vatican II, and has tried to escape being labeled as either a conservative or a liberal. This is Dulles' chosen course, and one that he continues to cherish. In the interview with Peter Steinfels previously quoted, Dulles reiterated his personal goal when he stated, "I would like to be a kind of bridge person."[28] His writings have indeed served as a bridge over the troubled waters of the post-Vatican II Church.

Dulles is aware that his interpretation of the teachings of Vatican II can be viewed as ecclesiocentric; yet he maintains his position. His years of research and reflection on the conciliar documents lead him to conclude that, "the Council does not regard the world as the center and the church as peripheral, but rather the reverse."[29]

Dulles has achieved an international reputation for his lucid and prudent insights in ecclesiology. But it would be a mistake to limit his ecclesiology to the Roman Catholic Church. Dulles was involved in the ecumenical movement even before this participation was encouraged by Vatican II. During his formation period as a Jesuit, he was deeply influenced by Gustave Weigel, S.J., who was a leading figure in the pre-conciliar ecumenical movement in America. Weigel conveyed to Dulles his own passion for the unity of the church, a passion which has grasped Dulles for over six decades. This enthusiasm might seem to have an autobiographical referent, but this is not the case. Dulles himself had once suggested to Weigel that ecumenism would be a good area for him to explore, based on his own background as a convert. Weigel insisted that this fact alone would not suffice; rather, anyone wishing to pursue ecumenical theology would need to be personally convinced of its inherent worth.

In the late 1950's, Dulles was sent to Germany and then to Rome to study the thinking of Protestant theologians. In 1960, he completed his doctoral dissertation, "Protestant Church and the Prophetic Office." Thus, Dulles had a solid preparation for the teachings of Vatican II on ecumenism. His participation in ecumenical affairs is attested to by the fact that he was a member of the Archdiocese of Baltimore's Commission on Christian Unity (1962-70); was a consultor to the Papal Secretariat for Dialogue with Non-Believers (1966-73); was a member of the United States Lutheran-Roman Catholic Dialogue and of the Anglican-Roman Catholic Consultation in the United States, and is currently a member of Evangelicals and Catholics Together. He has contributed to the Lutheran-Roman Catholic Joint Statements on the "Papacy" (1974), "Teaching Authority and Infallibility in the Church" (1978), and "Justification" (1983), and "The One Mediator, the Saints and Mary"; the Anglican-Roman Catholic statement on "Doctrinal Agreement and Christian Unity" (1972); and the World Council of Churches' study paper, "Baptism, Eucharist and Ministry" (1982).

In addition to interacting with other theologians while serving on the above-named commissions, Dulles's dialogue with others primarily takes place in his writings. His style is to present the teachings of his colleagues, Catholic and non-Catholic, in the theological community, both past and present, and then to explain and evaluate their positions. This ability to synthesize, explore, and critique many divergent opinions forms a large part of Dulles' contribution to the cause of the unity of the Church.

My research indicates that the texts of Vatican II which have had the most profound influence on Dulles' thinking are *Lumen Gentium* 8 and *Unitatis Redintegratio* 11. These important conciliar pronouncements have been quoted often through the years, but here I would like to stress a sentence in each passage which is less well-known, but which I feel has nonetheless had a profound influence on Dulles' theology.

When speaking of the Church of Christ, *Lumen Gentium* states

> This Church, constituted and organized in the world as a society, subsists in the Catholic Church, which is governed by the successor of Peter and by the bishops in union with that successor, although many elements of sanctification and of truth can be found outside of her visible structure. These elements, however, as gifts properly belonging to the Church of Christ, possess an inner dynamism toward Catholic unity (a. 8).

The meaning of "subsists" in this famous passage continues to be discussed; however, it is the last sentence in this paragraph that I wish to highlight as having had an effect on Dulles' theology. How would he identify these elements which are gifts of the Church of Christ? I believe his answer would point to the heritage of the other churches. He does not ask any church to renounce its history, its distinctiveness, nor the means it offers to lead its members to God. Rather, he would advocate incorporating individual emphases with those of the other churches to provide more of a balance. This type of endeavor brings us back again to one of Dulles' favorite themes—that of catholicity. His "both/and" attitude allows for great flexibility in thought and practice, and certainly holds more ecumenical potential than the more rigid "either/or."

But this does not mean that Dulles' ecumenical thrust is based on a syncretic indifference, an "anything goes" type of mentality. He believes that the differences among the churches cannot be overcome by denying them, ignoring them, or minimizing them. Only a frank and honest appraisal of the situation holds the possibility for true ecumenism. This is the theme of the other conciliar passage, which, in my opinion, is at the core of Dulles' ecumenical theology. *Unitatis Redintegratio* contains the oft-quoted statement about the 'hierarchy' of truths, which has played an important part in Dulles' theology. However, earlier in this same article, we find the following sentence, "Nothing is so foreign to the spirit of ecumenism as a false conciliatory approach which harms the purity of Catholic doctrine and obscures its assured genuine meaning (a. 11)."

To this end, Dulles will not sanction premature reunion, or pretend that more unity exists than presently does. He calls for patient endeavor in the ecumenical movement, knowing full well that total reunion will require much time and effort. In the meantime, however, he has made suggestions which, I feel, are realistic embodiments of a true conciliatory approach.

Total communion is the goal towards which the churches are tending, but Dulles does not believe that it will be achieved in an immediate fashion. Rather, he anticipates reunion occurring in three stages. The first of these concerns the preparation and publication of a joint statement, indicating the churches' belief in Scripture and in the creeds of the early ecumenical councils. This would be followed by an acceptance of each other's doctrinal positions as not contrary to the Gospel, with an accompanying lifting of anathemas where necessary. The last step would be the acceptance of the binding doctrinal declarations of the other churches, with whatever explanatory statements are needed.[30]

Again, we see evidences of the catholicity approach. For Dulles, ecumenism is both an acceptance of the here-and-now reality of imperfect communion, and an impetus towards perfecting that communion. Therefore, he does not believe that intercommunion is an appropriate expression at this time, given the divided state of the churches. He has proposed several liturgical alternatives which are intended to sharpen our awareness of the present situation, e.g., prayerful abstention from the Eucharist celebrated in another church, and ritualizing the pain of disunity.[31] These suggestions, viewed in light of Dulles's teachings on symbol and mystery, are powerful reminders that there is much yet to be done before the Church is truly one.

Dulles used the phrase "creative fidelity"[32] to describe the connection between continuity and change in the Church. My research and analysis of various developments in his ecclesiological and ecumenical theologies indicate that this is an apt description of his writings. If he has placed more weight on one side, I feel it is in the area of continuity in the tradition. As I have stated, I find that his creativity is to be found more in the way in which he presents the tradition and reformulates it for the contemporary scene than in devising new theories.

In my opinion, Avery Dulles is the most influential of all contemporary American theologians. Through his painstaking research, his reflection and dialogue, and his clear and concise writings, he has opened our minds and our hearts to the beauty and richness of many aspects of our faith heritage. The Church, in general, and the Church in America, in particular, would be greatly impoverished without his contributions.

NOTES

1. "Coming Home," in *Where I Found Christ*, edited by John A. O'Brien (Garden City: Doubleday and Company, 1960), 66.

2. "Harvard as an Invitation to Catholicism," in *The Catholics of Harvard Square*, edited by Jeffrey Wills (Petersham, MA: St. Bede's Publications, 1993), 4.

3. "Heresy Today?" *America* 142 (March 1, 1980): 163.

4. *Models of Revelation* (Garden City: Doubleday and Company, 1983), vii-xi.

5. Ibid., 35.

6. The influence of scientists such as Ian Barbour, I. T. Ramsey, and Michael Polanyi can be seen in Dulles' exploration of models.

7. *Models of the Revelation*, 30.

8. *Models of the Church* (Garden City: Doubleday and Company, 1974), 21.

9. *Models of the Church*, 22.

10. *Models of Revelation*, 30.

11. In this, he is following in the tradition of Ernst Troeltsch and H. R. Niebuhr, and is in sharp contradistinction with David Tracy, who holds that models represent mutually incompatible options.

12. *Models of the Church*, 9.

13. Ibid., 186.

14. *The Resilient Church* (Garden City: Doubleday and Company, 1977), 26.

15. *A Church to Believe In* (New York: The Crossroad Publishing Company, 1982), 46.

16. Ibid., 5.

17. Cf. Ibid, Chapter 1, "Imaging the Church for the 1980's," 1-18, for a fuller treatment of this topic.

18. Ibid., 5.

19. Ibid., 17-18.

20. Ibid, 3.

21. Ibid., 4-6.

22. *The Reshaping of Catholicism* (San Francisco: Harper & Row, 1988), 26.

23. "Fordham's New Theologian: a Flair for Diplomacy," by Peter Steinfels, *New York Times*, 2 October 1988, Section 1, 50.

24. *The Resilient Church*, 2.

25. "Vatican II and the Church's Purpose," *Theology Digest* 32 (Winter 1985): 345.

26. Ibid., 349.

27. Ibid., 349-50.

28. Steinfels, *New York Times*, 50.

29. "Vatican II and the Church's Purpose," 351.

30. "Paths to Doctrinal Agreement," *Theological Studies* 47 (March 1986), 46-47.

31. *The Resilient Church*, 171.

32. *A Church to Believe In*, 102.

NOT SCANDALIZED, NOT SEDUCED

Matthew Lickona

"I think going to Catholic school was part of what started me down the road to losing my faith. My logical brain seized on the point—'Wait a second; you mean the first Gospel wasn't written until 70 years after Jesus died, and it wasn't written by this guy named Mark? I don't trust my own memory from last week, and I'm supposed to trust three generations of stories being handed around as fact? I can't do it.'"

> (Matt Casper, co-author of *Jim & Casper Go to Church*, in an interview [with me] for *The San Diego Reader*, a weekly newspaper)

One fewer sheep in the fold, thanks in part to that very dangerous thing: a little education.[1] It's not the greatest example of what I'm getting at: Casper was baptized Catholic, but not exactly immersed in the life of faith. And the intellectual component was only "part of what started me down the road" to atheism—the lousy behavior of his fellow students (at a Catholic university) helped as well. (On the other hand, maybe those caveats make him a perfect example. But more on that later.)

One thing is almost certain, of course: his loss of faith was not the fault of the educators. Undoubtedly, they presented Casper with the proper context for considering the question of who wrote the Gospels. Undoubtedly, they mentioned that those three generations of storytellers were staking their lives on the veracity of those stories, willingly shedding their blood to preserve and share the fledgling Christian faith. Undoubtedly, they gave him some understanding of the wealth of scholarship devoted to these questions, lest he think himself the first to question Christianity this way. Undoubtedly . . .

My brother Mark attended the University of Notre Dame in the mid-'80s. Both my parents had been the first in their family to attend college. Both had attended small Catholic colleges—Siena for my father, the College of St. Rose for my mother—situated near their homes. Part of the reason my parents were willing to put Mark on a 12-hour train to Indiana was almost certainly Notre Dame's reputation as the premiere Catholic university in the land. They were serious, intelligent Catholics; no doubt, they hoped that Notre Dame would help their son become the same.

Today, my brother is a serious, intelligent Catholic—he went on to get his Masters in Scripture and Patristics from the Catholic University of America. But for a while, it was a near thing. At the opening of his Freshman year theology class, the teacher announced that the students were going to learn that what their parents had taught them wasn't entirely true. By Easter break, my brother's Catholic faith, particularly his faith in the historical event of the Resurrection, was wobbly, even ready to collapse. *"I think going to Catholic school was part of what started me down the road to losing my faith . . . ."*

But Mark held on. However wobbly his faith, he still attended Good Friday services with us, and he remembers watching my mother pray during the service, gazing up into "the great and seemingly pregnant space" beneath our hometown church's arched and lofty roof. He remembers thinking, "My mother is no fool."

"That was the beginning of my journey back," he recalls. "The testimony of the saints took me most of the rest of the way." My brother was right—my mother is no fool. And sometimes, we have to rely on the testimony of others—hopefully, the ones we love and trust—to maintain faith. But was it a good thing that a Catholic theology class at a Catholic university drove him to that reliance?

Now it may be true that some of the things a parent teaches a child about the faith are inaccurate, or incomplete. But what would lead a teacher to make such an announcement—whence the hostility? Why set up the opposition going in? Already, "what your parents taught you" is starting to sound like Santa Claus. "Brace yourself for the real deal, kiddies—the gospels weren't written by four guys named Matthew, Mark, Luke, and John. There is no Saint Christopher. The feeding of the five thousand is really a lesson in sharing." It may not amount to an explicit attack on the faith, but it sets up a tension where tension is neither necessary nor beneficial. And more than a tension—an erosion. For the cradle Catholic, what was learned in the home was most likely the foundation of faith. If you make a point of exposing the weak points in that foundation, what do you expect to happen? What do you *want* to happen?

It puts me in mind of this bit from Walker Percy's novel *Love in the Ruins*: "Students are, if the truth be known, a bad lot. En masse, they're as fickle as a mob, manipulable by any professor who'll stoop to it. . . . People talk a lot about how great 'the kids' are, compared to kids in the past. The only difference in my opinion is that kids now don't have sense enough to know what they don't know." But my brother's teacher was starting in from day one with the manipulation, and it nearly cost him his faith. Is this a desirable outcome?

Okay, so the last three paragraphs have ended with (largely rhetorical) questions. For some glimmer of a possible answer, I'd like to turn to Anne Rice, famous author of vampire novels, and, more recently, *Christ the Lord*, a fictional account of Jesus' boyhood. I interviewed Ms. Rice for *The San Diego News Notes*, a now-defunct lay Catholic newspaper— largely because, besides writing a book about Jesus, she had recently returned to the Catholic faith of her youth.

When did she leave? When she hit college. Granted, the faith of her childhood "was a very repressive, puritanical Catholicism. It was worlds away from the kind of theology we talk about today. It seemed, on the surface, to be very anti-humanist. . . . I've always believed in the idea that wisdom comes from the physical, but that was very much against the way I was brought up." But whatever the character of her faith, it wasn't enough to stand up to her encounters with college's combination of ideas and experience.

In 1972, when her daughter Michele died of leukemia at the age of five, Rice was brought up against despair. Four years later, she published *Interview with the Vampire*, the novel that launched her career. It's usually wise to avoid reading an author's life into a novel, but Rice grants that her vampire protagonists were not chosen arbitrarily. "Louis, Lestat, Armand—they all felt as though they were damned. That they couldn't find God again; that God didn't exist for them. But they never stopped looking. They constantly searched for other ports of salvation and transcendence. That's the way I felt. The very act of writing the book was an attempt to be saved," even if the salvation was woefully incomplete. "Their being made into vampires"—victims, arbitrarily cast into a darkness from which there was no redemption—"was an accurate mirror of the way I felt about being human."

It's impossible to guess after what-might-have-been: how Rice might have responded to the death of her daughter if she hadn't left the faith. But I think it's safe to say that her equation of the vampire's plight to that of humanity is terrifying. Safe also to suppose that it might have been a good thing if she had, instead of discarding her childhood faith in response to collegiate ideas and experience, deepened it instead. Corrected it, expanded it, even complicated it—but above all, kept it.

As it happened, when she did return to Catholicism, it was scholarly effort that began the journey back. According to the essay that concludes *Christ the Lord*, it was during historical research for that novel that she "stumbled upon a mystery so immense that I gave up trying to find an explanation because the whole mystery defied belief. The mystery was the survival of the Jews. . . . It was this mystery that drew me back to God. It set into motion the idea that there may in fact be God. And when that happened there grew in me for whatever reason an immense desire to return to the banquet table."

Rice wanted the Eucharist. "I don't know why; I just know it drew me back," she told me during our interview. "The blood in the vampire novels is obviously a Eucharistic symbol, so there is clearly some obsession on my part with Eucharistic symbolism. I think it runs through everything I write—not just the vampire chronicles. The whole mystery of the Incarnation—what it means that Christ came down." Again: longing led her to embrace the mystery, but it was an idea that sparked the longing. It was education.

Further research into that era led her to conclude that "Christianity achieved what it did . . . because Jesus rose from the dead. It was the fact of the resurrection that sent the apostles out into the world with the force necessary to create Christianity." The perusal of vast quantities of research led Rice to this conclusion; it's tempting, in a sad sort of way, to wonder if Matt Casper was aware of that research's existence, let alone of its findings, when he decided he couldn't continue to believe.

Rice's investigation into biblical scholarship led her to another conclusion, one far less sanguinary: "And I had also sensed something else. Many of these scholars, scholars who apparently devoted their life to New Testament scholarship, disliked Jesus Christ. Some pitied him as a hopeless failure. Others sneered at him, and some felt an outright contempt. This came between the lines of the books. This emerged in the personality of the texts. I'd never come across this kind of emotion in any other field of research, at least not to this extent. It was puzzling . . . in general, scholars don't spend their lives in the company of historical figures whom they openly despise."

It is not my place to question whether or not anyone despises Jesus. It is not my place to suggest that anyone is deliberately trying to undermine anybody else's faith. But when I read Rice's account of the New Testament scholars, and when I hear about Matt and Mark's experiences at Catholic schools, it does tempt me to start in with the rhetorical questions. Even the sincere questions: what's going on in Catholic universities? How should they view themselves in relation to the faith? To the faith of their students?

I've been writing for the *Reader* for twelve years now. One of those years was spent profiling college students, and one of my profiles focused on three young women attending our local Catholic institution of higher learning: the University of San Diego. I'd like to take a look at that story, and offer a little editorial comment along the way, drawing on my own experience at Thomas Aquinas College, a small, Catholic Great Books school in California. I make no claims about wisdom or expertise, but I do think it makes for an interesting comparison.

First up: Lisa—a junior, brassy and upbeat. Raised Catholic, she is now a Wiccan, attracted to its devotion to nature, its belief in the law of returns and the notion that "love is the law." (I'm guessing that nobody introduced her to Augustine's exquisite "Love and do what you will," and maybe not even to the God who sees in secret, and who will repay your good works.)

"I went to church every Sunday," she tells me. "I was a youth-group leader. I even taught confirmation. I was way gung-ho Catholic, because my mom was really strict, and, you know, she's Catholic. I came here, and I broke out of my shell—I'm more of a wild child, anyway. Freshman year and sophomore year, I was still kind of hanging on to Catholicism, but then I was just, like, 'This doesn't interest me. I get bored when I go to church.'"

I don't know all the particulars of Lisa's history, but leading youth groups and teaching confirmation seems to indicate that she was more than a little involved with her religion as a teenager. It doesn't sound like the sort of thing you do just to keep Mom happy. Still, I can't judge the quality of her faith. I can, however, say that something has gone wrong when breaking out of your shell is naturally equated with shedding the faith of your youth. Catholicism is not a shell—it is quite capable of stretching as you grow.

It should go without saying that the church has a proud and profound intellectual tradition, and has been grappling bravely with the world and its ideas for centuries. It is not a religion for children, though children may be kept safe within its fold. It's sad that Lisa thought otherwise. It's sad that she got bored, and her talk about shell-breaking makes me wonder if she got bored because her faith remained the faith of a child.

A child's faith is sweet, but necessarily—even happily—lacking. Children generally lack a serious comprehension of death, and death—or rather, the defeat of it—is the whole point of the Incarnation, the Crucifixion, and the Resurrection. Further, children don't usually feel the full weight of sin, don't fully understand the depths of fallen nature, or the absolute necessity of charity and grace in rising from those depths. (Here, I speak with some measure of confidence—I've got five children of my own, and I think I know them pretty well.)

Mass, the Mass that bored young Lisa, is the re-presentation of Christ's sacrifice—the defeat of death, the supreme act of love. I'm not overly upset when my young children are bored at Mass, because at its center, it's dealing in things beyond their ken. Were those things beyond Lisa's ken as well? Why was she bored? Why didn't the drama of the cross hold her interest?

She continues: "You'd think going to a Catholic school would keep [me in the faith], but then, I got my freedom. And actually, taking these classes like 'Belief and Unbelief'—it told us all the alternatives to Catholicism and the arguments against it. The classes got me thinking and turned me kind of against it. Now I'm a pagan."

The classes she mentions were part of her theology requirements. She took "some course on Christianity"—so much for memorable—and tried to get into "Sex and Cults in America," but it was already overfull. What was formative? A course called "Belief and Unbelief." "In 'Belief and Unbelief,' we talked about a lot of different philosophers I—think that was where we did some Freud. It's a disturbing class. [The professor] tells you in the beginning, 'This is a class where, if you're Catholic, you can't get offended by the stuff you're going to learn in here.'" In other words, you're not allowed to get scandalized. What about seduced?

Lisa continues: "A lot of people are, like, 'Whoa,' because you read this stuff and it makes so much sense, too. We haven't ever really been exposed to it in depth before. When you're brought up Catholic, that's all you know, because that's all you're taught. But the older you get, the more you can make your own choices by learning stuff like that." Right. We're agreed that college ought to involve the expanding of one's world-view, the exposure to new ideas. But uncritical ("you can't get offended!") exposure to "a disturbing class" that lays out "all the arguments against" Catholicism sounds like an easy way to lead a young mind out of the faith.

In Lisa's case, that's exactly what happened, and she tells us why— "we talked about a lot of different philosophers." A bunch of 18-year-olds, running up against some of the greatest minds the world has ever produced—who ya gonna bet on? I'd guess that most freshmen don't even have the tools to enter into the debate. All they can do is sit there, not getting offended, while Friedrich Nietzsche lays waste to their beliefs. I went to a school where Catholicism permeated the air we breathed, and Nietzsche *still* nearly drove me to despair.

My mother, when she heard about classmates of mine from high school who had gone off to college and become enamored of other cultures, once remarked, "They don't know their own. They never gave it a chance." Catholic thinkers have proposed answers to the objections of unbelievers down through the centuries; they have not shied away from intelligent discourse or the truths of science. I wonder how many of them got a chance to speak in "Belief and Unbelief," to bolster the flustered student when she said, "Whoa." It's hard to read about her "hanging on to" her faith for a couple of years, as if it were a teddy bear she was hesitant to leave behind in the nursery.

Here's what Cardinal Newman said he wanted from the laity—it sounds to me like a pretty good list: "I want a laity who know their religion and who enter into it, who know just where they stand, who know what they hold, and what they do not, who know their creed so well that they can give an account of it, who know so much of history that they can defend it. I want an intelligent, well-instructed laity. I wish you to enlarge your knowledge, to cultivate your reason, to get an insight into the relation of truth, to learn to view things as they are, to understand how faith and reason stand to each other, what are the base and principles of Catholicism." Somehow, I don't think Lisa ever got a fair chance to achieve this.

College was the time when my own faith began to mature. In class, we spent Freshman year theology reading the Bible cover to cover. Sophomore year was lots and lots of Augustine, plus Anselm and Athanasius. (Augustine's treatment of nature and grace and free will was certainly well beyond—and in some respects, even contrary to—my childhood formation. But instead of dwelling on that point, we concentrated on understanding the argument. And of course it helped to know that we were reading a Doctor of the Church, though that didn't pass for an argument in the classroom.) Junior and Senior year, we read from the *Summa Theologica* of St. Thomas Aquinas.

Comprehensive? Not even close. An introduction, and an incomplete one at that. But it was a start, and it was memorable and formative. I wasn't a theology major; everyone at TAC takes the same courses all four years, and theology is one of those courses. It's not some pre-req that you get out of the way before you get on to the real business of your major; it's a constant presence, a gradually deepening conversation with some of the church's formative minds. You don't have to believe, but you're going to read the thoughts of those who do. If you leave the faith, you're going to have some idea of what you're leaving.

Outside of theology class, I got a crash course in Church history from my fellow students, plus all sorts of argument about liturgy and the life

and workings of the Church. Not all of it was beneficial to my intellectual formation, but I'm (mostly) grateful for the experience, especially
when I consider the alternative—a school's Catholicism residing largely
in its name and on the fringes.

TAC is only an introduction to the Great Conversation, but it is an
introduction aimed at producing Catholic conversationalists, grounded in
their own intellectual tradition, equipped, however basically, to engage a
world that is often hostile to their beliefs. We read plenty of people hostile to belief at the school, but it's St. Thomas who gets the longest turn
at the podium. We aren't allowed to say "but the Church teaches . . ." in
response to an offensive argument, but we are allowed to be offended, and
to respond as best we can with reasoned argument. We don't have a
Catholic studies program, but Catholic theology does serve as a kind of
ordering principle.

This is not without its difficulties. I spent two summers touting the
school's virtues to prospective students for the Admissions department,
and I don't want to lapse into cheerleading. My friend Michael, a fellow
graduate, calls it a "Catholic finishing school," where good Catholics are
made into better Catholics through exposure to great Catholics. "Iron
strengthens iron," he says, noting that while we read Augustine on
Pelagius and Athanasius combating the Arians, we don't read Pelagius or
the Arians themselves. While we spend plenty of time hashing out
Aristotle's definition of motion (a definition crucial to St. Thomas' proofs
for the existence of God), we don't spend much time critiquing that definition. When there's somewhere you need to get—say, the First Way—
you don't always have time to critique the teaching. I mention this to say
that I don't regard TAC as the final word in Catholic education. But the
approach is at least one way to answer the slippery question of how a
Catholic school ought to relate to the faith.

How exactly is USD Catholic? Lisa puts it this way: "There are
things like intervisitation hours. Guys have to be out of the girls' rooms
by midnight on weekdays and by 2:00 a.m. on weekends. And they tell
you [it's Catholic] when you come in. I think they just want you to know
that it's a Catholic denomination. But they don't make it seem like you
can only go here if you're Catholic. They say, 'Not everyone is Catholic,
and you can be whatever.'" Not everyone need be Catholic at a Catholic
university, of course, but her choice of 'whatever' for the alternative is
ominous. And here's what she comes up with for Catholic identity: an
announcement, and a bare-minimum rule seemingly designed to keep
kids from fornicating. (No, I don't suppose that she is to be taken as the
authority on this question. But that doesn't mean her answer isn't instruc-
tive.)

Still, what would I have rather had? Mandatory attendance at Mass? Compulsory Confession? No. If I don't think it's a university's place to assault the faith of its students, neither do I think it ought to mandate the practice of that faith. Here, I am again grateful to my alma mater for the way she handled the matter.

Religious devotions were not my reason for attending TAC; I chose the school because I sat in on a class discussion of Descartes' mathematics. I came for the intellectual life; the religious stuff was an added—though I think, integral—bonus. I think that was as it should be. The studies were mandatory; the religion was (constantly, splendidly) available. The Angelus—a student ringing the bell at six, noon, and six. Compline and the rosary nightly. Daily Mass three times a day. Consecration of the dorm and those within in the dorm commons every night. Benediction, Adoration . . . priests living on campus, always available for confession. It was more than a Newman society; it was a continual invitation into the liturgical life of the church. You could ignore it if you wanted to, but it was all around you, nonetheless.

It was in college that I developed a devotion to the Eucharist, both through attendance at daily Mass and through Eucharistic Adoration. There also where I became enamored of liturgical Latin, polyphony, careful attention to rubrics, and all the rest of it. Not simply because they tickled my religious sensibility—though there was certainly a measure of that. Rather, the main reason I loved these things is because they led me into the mystery being celebrated—because they disposed me to devotion.

Getting back to my trio of Catholic co-eds. My second interviewee is Kara, a sophomore. She does not come from a religious background and is here "because I wanted to learn about religion. It's easier to talk to people when you understand their beliefs and stuff. Now, I've taken a world-religions class and a scripture class, and I feel so much more knowledgeable. We went and got our nails done the other day, and we were talking to the guy about Buddhism, and I felt like I could speak to him about it."

As for the school's Catholicity, "It's not totally pushed on you, and I like that. It makes a really good, happy environment. I like just the amount of Catholicism that is on this campus. I choose to go to church when I want to, because I like it. And you can have those kinds of discussions [about faith] if you want, but I've never felt pressure to become a Catholic."

Occasionally, she does have those discussions about becoming Catholic, though little has come of them. Listening to her accounts, it's easy to see why: "My roommate is a diehard Catholic, and she gets all ticked off, because, like, I didn't know that you had to be part of the

Church to take the bread and wine, which I always did. She practically had a heart attack. Then I'm, like, 'Oh, no, now I need to go confess,' and she said, 'You can't do that either!' And I'm, like, 'I'd go into the Catholic Church if I met a Catholic guy and that was the only way that he'd marry me.' I'd be, like, 'Okay, I'll be Catholic.' And she's, like, 'How can you say that? You have to really feel it!'

Diehard she may be, but where Lisa was seduced, Kara's roommate was scandalized. I'm with her on the teaching—non-Catholics ought not to receive those sacraments, and no one should "convert" without actually believing what they profess at their baptism. But shock and horror at the behavior of non-Catholics isn't going to win souls for Christ.

It gets worse: "I dated a guy who was, like, diehard Catholic, and it really sucked because he was just, like, so not even open to my beliefs. He could count the number of days he missed church on his hands. He sort of dragged me to church, and I liked it. I went a few times, but it was sort of, like, 'I have to go, and you have to go, too.' I was just, 'All right, but can I bring my books to study?' And he's, like, 'Oh, that's horrible! Oh, my God, no!' It was sort of weird. He wanted to wait until he was married to have sex, but he would push the limit so much. It's sort of, like, isn't that a sin in itself? You know, like, 'Oh, I'm going to wait until I'm married to have sex, but let's totally get it on, but not quite.' To me, that was just as bad as if you . . . I just felt like people try to push the limits as much as they can without going overboard. But if you're Catholic and religious, you shouldn't be doing that, period. I broke up with him because I thought it was weird."

The guy is practically a cartoon-a regular Pharisee, rule-bound but devoid of charity. He's scandalized by her bringing textbooks to Mass, but willing to toss chastity out the window while clinging to the most external sort of standard. It's not even the letter of the law he's honoring—"If a man looks at a woman with lust in his heart. . . ."

I include this because it seems to me that here is where a school might to well to challenge a childish faith—not so much in freshman theology as in freshman fraternization. The ability to function alongside others unlike yourself is a basic mark of human maturation, and while I am great fan of sensitivity training, I'm happy to agree that a school can do things to restrain certain excesses. At a small school like TAC, where we had our own version of the God Squad, sometimes all that was required was a line at the end of the homily during weekday Mass.

On, then, to Kelly—in some ways, the most interesting of the three. She prefers not to give her real name, and speaks in solemn tones that sometimes melt into bald emotion—she is serious about what she says. Right away, she tells me she is "very religious. I just got confirmed here last year. I go to Church every Sunday. I pray every night. I think the Catholic life here at the school is a good one. I think there's a lot of people to help others to understand it. I think the campus ministry part of the school is awesome; the confirmation program was awesome. I think the church services at 7:00 and 9:00 o'clock [on Sunday nights] in Founders' Chapel are amazing—they are so inviting."

That inviting quality is crucial. "When I was a freshman here, I turned to alcohol—I felt I was so lost. Then I started going to church, and now, yeah, I still go out and drink, but it's not what it was for me freshman year. I don't drink to get drunk, to drown my sorrows. I just think [the church is] a place where anyone can always feel welcome. The Church has always been someplace where I feel I belong. No matter what kind of day I have, I can always walk in, and I belong. There's always smiling faces, no matter what happened the night before. Everybody always makes up in church, and it's fine after that.

"When I go home, I don't go to church with my parents. I will go to a different church. I say, 'I'm going to church at school. I don't have to go here. This isn't my church anymore.' Here, this is my community, this is my church. Church to me is my community and the people I am praying with; it's not the structure." That gets at something powerful.

"There are a lot of people who come to this school, and their parents think it's a good, upstanding school—and it is, it really is—but it's college, you know? Due to the fact that it's a Catholic school, people feel safer sending their kids to it, but once they send their kids, they're free. They have to make decisions for themselves." She and several high school classmates did "burst" upon their arrival, but they "got it all out freshman year. We're fine, and we're back in our faith."

Indeed, Kelly believes her faith to be stronger than it was when she arrived. Confirmation, a step she is proud to have taken on her own, was part of that strengthening. "One of my closest friends died here last year, and I didn't have a lot of faith. I felt like it was all taken away from me." But Mike McIntyre, who works with campus ministry and served as her confirmation counselor, came to her aid. "He would ask me questions about my life, how I think I saw God in my life. And there would be little things in which I would see God. Slowly but surely, I realized that that person died for a reason, and that was really hard for me to accept. . . . If I had anything I needed to talk to him about, I could always go and his doors were open. He really put it in perspective."

Kelly found Mike to be "an amazing individual. He knows me, and he's been there for me, and he knows how I live in my faith and that everybody does it differently. I think that's the biggest part about this school, is that it's okay and it's accepted that everybody does it differently. . . . You can't put a name on a school like this, because everybody is different."

This is where a certain sort of Catholic starts hearing warning bells ringing out, *Ut Unim Sint* . . . "it's accepted that everybody does it differently. . . ." And that certain sort of Catholic would no doubt feel justified in his suspicion, given what Kelly says next: "It's one of those things where everybody has their own belief. Granted, the Catholic teaching has one belief, but at the same time, there are others spawned off of that. Catholics aren't Nazis. There are all different types of Catholics. For example, I am completely, completely 100 percent pro-choice. I'm not saying someone should go out and have an abortion six times, but I'm saying that choice should be theirs. I am for euthanasia. The Catholic Church thinks those things are wrong."

But, I asked her, if you part ways with the Church on these matters, how are you still Catholic? It's a loaded question, I know, but I was curious to hear the answer, and she wasn't offended. "I've always been taught all my life that to be true to yourself, to be true to whoever your God is, to be true, I'd say, in your relations with your immediate family and your good friends, [is to be] true to your faith and your religion. It doesn't have anything to do with the Ten Commandments, the set of beatitudes. Granted, that goes along with it, but those things were written so long ago. And there are different ways of taking the Bible—literally or nonliterally. I think the school doesn't take it literally, which means to me that they take it seriously, but at the same time, not word-for-word. It can't be word-for-word, because it was written so long ago."

To Kelly, the essence of Catholicism is "believing in myself, believing in where I'm from, and believing that there's someone else out there who's helping me get through everything, who's watching my back."

In what almost sounds like a planned conclusion, she adds, "I think the Catholic faith is becoming more of a choice for people and less of a tradition that you have to do. I think that's the biggest part about it, and I think that's how it is at this school, and I think that's why this school does flourish in the Catholic religion."

There are a lot of strands in what Kelly says. I'd like to try to untangle a few of them. Yes, when religion becomes simply a tradition and not a personal choice, it's pretty much lost its savor. But that doesn't mean that tradition ought not to have any influence. Kelly doesn't think much of the commandments and the beatitudes because they were "written so long ago." For her, it's not an inheritance, but history. She's rootless; she has no sense that where we are now is the fruit of all that stuff written so long ago, and that getting from there to here has been the fruit of centuries of profound theological development. I think this is a poverty, and it seems to me college might be a good place to remedy that—a place where she can discover those riches.

"Being true with one's family and friends" is essential to the Christian life, as is being true to God. But the Church supposes that God is not simply "whoever your God is," and with reason: God has revealed Himself, and people have been hashing out the meaning of that for a long, long time. She might benefit from what some of those people have thought.

Yes, Scripture is open to interpretation but—Church teaching is not the same thing as Scripture. It's teaching. When the Church teaches that contraceptive sex is intrinsically evil, it's making a claim about reality. Sometimes, those claims are difficult to accept. In those cases, I try to keep in mind another quote from Cardinal Newman: "Trust the Church of God implicitly, even when your natural judgment would take a different course from hers, and would induce you to question her prudence or correctness. Recollect what a hard task she has . . . recollect how much she needs your loyal and tender devotion. Recollect, too, how long is the experience gained in eighteen hundred years, and what a right she has to claim your assent to principles which have had so extended and so triumphant a trial." I will be formed by her, regardless of my theological questions.

But here things get swampy indeed. Need my decision to be formed mean that I don't dig into those theological questions? I asked one of the priests on campus about the meaning of the term "Catholic university." This was his response: "We went through this for years and years when we were trying to unify the school. Ultimately, the Catholicity of a school has to depend on two things, more or less balanced. One is the curriculum. What are they teaching? Do the students have to take any theology courses? Well, yeah, but are they Catholic theology courses? They have to take nine units, if I remember correctly, but they can pick nine units that aren't even in the ballpark as far as Catholicism. They can take Hinduism, Buddhism, Atheism. Most of them are not taking very many Catholic courses."

"The other way it can be Catholic is by the faculty. Namely, how many of them believe in Catholicism in a practical way—don't just say they do, but they do. For example, those teaching theology can't teach just any old thing." On the point of preserving academic freedom in the face of such a mandate, he replies, "The bishops say, 'Go ahead and have academic freedom; just don't call it a Catholic school.' This is a good point."

I think Father was on to something with his question about belief in Catholicism in a practical way—I think that's what Newman is getting at when he exhorts people to "trust the Church implicitly." And I think there's something to the notion of not teaching any old thing in theology.

But theology is not the catechism; it is not meant to do the job of the catechism. It seems to me that it's when the two get confused that things get ugly, and it's easy for them to get confused in an academic environment, particularly when students haven't been properly equipped for the discussion. "I'm being taught all these arguments against Catholicism, and they seem so reasonable. . . ." We Catholics are not Gnostics. We do not hold that there is one set of teachings for the masses, and another for the enlightened few. The Church is universal. That said, neither are we all theologians. Flannery O'Connor once wrote, "It is popular to suppose that anyone who can read the telephone book can read a short story or a novel. . . . Catholic readers are constantly being offended and scandalized by novels that they don't have the fundamental equipment to read in the first place. . . ." O'Connor was writing about fiction, but it seems to me that the same might be said of theology. Meanwhile, Father is worried about seduction-people leaving the faith because of what they encounter in Catholic college theology courses.

But here's my suspicion—if the school had more of a Catholic character, if students weren't ditching their faith because Wicca (and not Catholicism) has "the law of love," if kids had both Newman's implicit trust and sufficient intellectual formation to really engage the questions—I don't think Father would be so incensed about what gets taught in theology. It's the business of theology to inquire, and yes, it has its limits. Hans Küng, after many years of dialogue that was frustrating for both sides, was denied the permission to teach as a Catholic theologian. But it is significant, I think, that Benedict met with Kung soon after becoming Pope. Significant, too, that he met with the Society of St. Pius X. For those who have "the fundamental equipment," there is a Great Conversation to be had, and it seems to me that giving students that fundamental equipment is a good start for defining what makes a college Catholic in its character, and for sending them into a world that will neither scandalize nor seduce them.

1.   Author's note: trying to take this text from a moderately interesting speech into something resembling a cogent essay has been an exercise in humility. There is so much to be said regarding the subject of "Catholic education"—a term probably as slippery as "Catholic fiction"—and I took the occasion of my first (and so far, only) talk on a college

campus as an opportunity to add to that conversation. Does it mean training students to better love the familiar (their childhood faith) and attack the unfamiliar (everything that opposes that faith)? Does it mean a simple pursuit of truth, without any particular reference to religion (a la Flannery O'Connor's definition of Catholic fiction as "a Catholic mind looking at anything")? Ought the education be ordered to religious understanding, as with my alma mater's treatment of theology as the Queen of the Sciences? I started in on trying to hash out some answers, and quickly found myself contemplating something much more like a book than a chapter. And a rather swampy book at that, full of treacherous soft spots that threatened to suck the argument down into the muck. What follows, then, is, I hope, something much more modest, something rooted in my own experience as a student and as a journalist of sorts.

THEOLOGY OF THE LAITY:
NEW HORIZONS AND RECENT ROADBLOCKS

Aurelie A. Hagstrom

INTRODUCTION

The Second Vatican Council was unprecedented in its reflection upon, and articulation of, the identity, role, and spirituality of the laity in the life of the Church and in the world. This renewal of ecclesial thought and practice was due to an emphasis on the biblical theme of the Church as the People of God, the dignity and equality of members of the Church that is rooted in Baptism, the universal call to holiness, and the common sharing in the three-fold mission of Christ as priest, prophet, and king. Vatican II was the first ecumenical council to treat the laity from a theological, rather than exclusively canonical point of view. The Second Vatican Council has thus been hailed as the dawning of a new age of the laity. This was definitely a "new horizon" in Theology.

NEW HORIZONS

Vatican II, in emphasizing the biblical model of the Church as People of God, attempted to replace the pre-conciliar "power pyramid model" of the Church. The "power pyramid" has the pope at the top, with the hierarchy, clergy, and religious on descending scales of power, and finally the laity at the bottom of the pyramid, which is the most expansive part. In this model, the power trickles down from the top. And by the time the bottom of the pyramid is reached, the laity are the ones who simply pay, pray, and obey. The renewed biblical understanding of the Church as the People of God from Vatican II emphasizes the fundamental dignity and equality of all the members of the Church, based on our common Baptism. There are no second or third class citizens in the People of God.

The conciliar theology of *Lumen Gentium* and *Apostolicam Actuositatem* envisioned the Church and its life with Baptism at the center, rather than Holy Orders. The hub of the wheel, if you will, used to be Holy Orders, and all other sacraments were the spokes emanating from this hub. Now, Baptism is put back into the center, the hub of the wheel, and everything else flows from it. The priority of Baptism and the biblical model of the Church as the People of God, helped to shape the universal call to holiness that is also found in the conciliar teaching.

The laity, along with every other member of the Church, are called to holiness of life. No longer is it the case that the lay life is seen as inferior to the monastic life. Before the Council, it was a common perception that the clergy and religious are given over to holy things, whereas the laity lives among earthly things. There was the sense that to choose the lay state was a concession to human weakness. This perception, happily, came to an end with Chapter Five of *Lumen Gentium* on the universal call to holiness. The vocation of the laity had its own non-derivative spirituality.

In terms of the mission of the laity, Vatican II presented a renewed understanding of the role that laity play. Previously, the theology of mission was centered on the hierarchy. The thinking was that since Jesus gave a commission to the Apostles to continue his mission until the *Parousia*, then it was the successors to the Apostles who carried this charge throughout Church history. This was known as the apostolate of the hierarchy. They were the ones responsible for the mission. At best, laity could share in this apostolate of the hierarchy—but only by deputation. Laity had to have a specific mandate from the hierarchy to share in their apostolate. This was the old "Catholic Action" model, for example. "Catholic Action" before the Council was a way of mobilizing the laity for an apostolate in the world, but only at the approval of the hierarchy. The laity were considered the "right arm of the hierarchy" in the world. Since laity did not have their own mission, they could only share in the hierarchy's apostolate by a mandate of deputation.

Vatican II shifted this theology of mission by stating that it is through Baptism and Confirmation, and not Holy Orders, that one is deputed for the mission of the Church. There is only one mission of the Church, and Baptism and Confirmation depute everyone to participate in this mission in the Church and in the world. This conciliar theology of mission is another result of stressing the centrality of Baptism as the heart of our sacramental identity, rather than Holy Orders.

Thus an invigorated and challenging understanding of the vocation and mission of the laity in the Church and in the world became a crucial element in the dynamic of Church renewal that followed the Council. The "wind and fire" of the "new Pentecost" of the Church were experienced perhaps most strongly by the laity, who were called to a deepened spiritual maturity and a serious ecclesial responsibility. After the Council, the revised 1983 Code of Canon Law also articulated the vocation and mission of the laity in very positive terms, giving the laity rights and responsibilities in the Church's mission *ad intra* and *ad extra*. And following the 1987 Synod of Bishops on the laity, Pope John Paul II issued his apostolic exhortation *Christifideles Laici*. This document reflected the great strides that had been made in the theology and spirituality of the laity in the twenty-plus years since the Council. The "new horizon" of the laity was expanding rapidly.

UNRESOLVED ISSUES FROM VATICAN II

For all of its beauty and dynamism, however, the conciliar teaching on the laity still left some unresolved issues. I will mention only four of them. First, the theological description of the lay state is unresolved. The Council Fathers said that they were not trying to define the lay person *per se* in *Lumen Gentium*. That is, they did not provide a normative definition of the lay state. Instead, they gave a description of the actual situation of the lay state. *Lumen Gentium* #31 provided a phenomenological description rather than an ontological definition. That is, it ended up with a positive definition "simply of the state of being a Christian itself"—and this, of course, is something that applies to *all* the members of the Church, including clergy and religious. Vatican II did not define the *particularity* of the lay state. This left some ambiguity, then, in understanding the roles of the laity.

The second unresolved issue is how the laity might fit into the theology of ministry found in the documents of Vatican II. Ministry is described as the responsibility of the clergy. And yet, *Lumen Gentium* and *Apostolicam Actuositatem* state that in the absence of clergy, there are certain ministerial roles that the laity can fulfill. These roles are in the areas of teaching, liturgy, and pastoral care. Other offices might be that of a chancellor of a diocese or an official in a diocesan marriage tribunal. The question arises: if these kinds of ministries can be *delegated* to the laity, are they *strictly* ministries of the priesthood or the deaconate? If laity can be delegated to bring Eucharist to the sick, conduct Baptisms, and lead worship, then are these ministries proper to the *essence* of ordained ministry? If these roles do not pertain to the essence of ordained ministry, then why do the laity have to be delegated to perform them? Are they not instead properly ministries of the Baptized?

The third unresolved issue from the conciliar teaching on the laity is the whole notion of the spirituality of the laity. The Council, in light of its teaching on the universal call to holiness, tried to map out a lay spirituality. First, the charisms of the laity are affirmed. The laity, as all believers, receive gifts of the Holy Spirit through Baptism and Confirmation. And these charisms cannot be exercised without being grounded in an authentic lay spirituality. According to *Apostolicam Actuositatem*, any lay spirituality must be nourished by the liturgical life, grounded in the Word of God, energized by faith, hope, and charity, and supported by community life. It is to follow Jesus' example of poverty, humility, and endurance. The problem is that none of this is *specific* to lay spirituality. The discussion of the spirituality of the laity becomes problematic since every member of the Church is called to these things. So, what makes a spirituality distinctively a lay spirituality? This remains unclear.

The fourth and final unresolved issue I will mention is a more general one, and that is, the overall interpretation of the conciliar theology of the laity. As is well known, most of the documents of Vatican II can be called "compromise documents". There were forces both liberal and conservative at the Council among the bishops and peritii. This meant that in order to get documents approved by the strict voting procedures, they had to be accommodating to both sides of the aisle, so to speak. This meant that the theological insights that grounded the pastoral vision were not always as developed as they might have been. This becomes clear in the interpretations of Vatican II in the last 40 or so years. When it comes to the conciliar theology of the laity, there have been two basic approaches. One interpretation, based on conciliar texts, stresses the distinctions between the laity and the clergy and their respective roles. That is, the clergy have the roles in the Church, and the lay role is restricted to the transformation of the world. The second interpretation of conciliar texts, by contrast, stresses the co-responsibility of the laity and clergy for the life and mission of the Church without such a strict separation of roles. Thus, depending on which interpretation is employed, two very different theologies of the laity could result.

Two Competing Ecclesiologies

It is my contention that the basis for these unresolved issues can be found in the fact that the ecclesiology of Vatican II is not uniform. Since the conciliar documents are, for the most part, compromise documents, wherein there is an attempt to harmonize the liberal and conservative views, it is not surprising that at least two competing ecclesiologies can be discerned. These two theologies of the Church have been called the juridic and the *communio* ecclesiologies. The juridic ecclesiology stresses the human and visible dimensions of the Church. In contrast, the *communio* ecclesiology stresses the divine and invisible dimensions of the Church. The Council documents, as well as the 1983 Code of Canon Law attempt to harmonize these two approaches to the reality of the Church and its mission.

How do the laity fare in each of these ecclesiologies? In the communion approach to the reality of the Church, what is stressed is the unity amidst diversity of the vocations, roles, charisms, and ministries of all the Baptized. The profound unity of believers with one another and with the Trinity is brought about by the power of the Holy Spirit. *Communio* ecclesiology emphasizes the equality and dignity of all and the common responsibility for the mission of the Church. The focus is on the divine and invisible aspects to the Church, the grace of the sacraments, and the eschatological dimension of the Church's life, ministry, and worship. In this approach, the laity are seen as equal in dignity and holiness with clergy and co-responsible with them for the Church's mission.

On the other hand, the juridic ecclesiology focuses more on the human and visible aspects of the Church. In this approach, the hierarchical and legal dimensions of the Church's mission, worship, and sacramental life are emphasized. Here the distinction of roles and the separation of pastoral responsibilities are stressed, based on the sacramental character of Holy Orders. The juridic ecclesiology portrays the Church predominantly as an institution rather than as a mystery. In this approach, the power of governance and jurisdiction are highlighted with the hierarchy as the mediating principle. Laity are seen as passive recipients of the sacramental ministry of the hierarchy and juridically unable to exercise the power of governance without a deputation. The juridic ecclesiology underlines an inherent inequality among laity and clergy, when speaking of the Church's inner life and mission.

It seems to me that the unresolved issues concerning the laity in the conciliar documents are the result of these two competing ecclesiologies that are present in the conciliar teaching. The communion and juridic ecclesiologies each offer different understandings of the vocation and mission of the laity in the Church. So, depending on which one is highlighted, a different interpretation of the lay identity and function will be offered.

TWO REALM APPROACH

Besides the two competing ecclesiologies of the conciliar documents, another challenge in developing a theology of the laity is the underlying so-called "two realm" approach to mission that can be found in these magisterial texts. By "two realm" approach, I mean that there are two distinct spheres of action in which the temporal sphere belongs to the laity and the sacred to the clergy. The focus of the mission of the laity, according to the "two realm" approach to mission, should be the consecration of the world, as opposed to intra-ecclesial ministry, which is the responsibility and mission of the clergy. This approach, which can be found in Vatican II, the 1983 Code of Canon Law, and even *Christifideles Laici*, makes a dichotomy between the spiritual order of the Church's mission, which is to be typically restricted to the clergy, and the temporal realm of the Church's mission, which is to be the responsibility of the laity.

The manner in which this kind of theology of mission is presented is by making the secular character of the lay vocation and mission an *ontological* entity, and thereby creating a hard and fast distinction between the clergy who have a sacred ministry and the laity whose call is secular. The two realm approach defines the laity as the leaven for the world rather than as participants in the inner life and mission of the Church, that is, the Church's mission *ad intra*. This distinction, based on an ontological interpretation of the secular character of the laity, is the basis for exclusion of the laity from service within the Church. A theological or ontological approach to secular character can restrict the mission of the laity simply to activity in the world, without a corresponding mission *ad intra*, or within the inner life of the Church. A two realm approach can restrict the mission of the laity to only "worldly obligations" and prevent them from taking on important intra-ecclesial roles.

RECENT ROADBLOCKS

This two realm approach can be seen in the 1997 document, "Instruction on Cooperation of Non-Ordained Persons in the Sacred Ministry of the Clergy," published by eight dicasteries of the Roman Curia. In this Instruction, a more restrictive and more circumspect approach was taken to the roles of the laity. The Roman Instruction made it clear that laity can only assist the clergy in certain *ad intra* ministries and that their "true calling" was to transform the world. The Instruction seemed to ignore the nearly thirty years of experience of the phenomenon of ecclesial lay ministry in the Church. The roadblock to the developing theology of the laity is the Instruction's "two realm" approach to the mission of the Church which restricts the laity to transforming the temporal order and restricts any ministry *ad intra* to the clergy.

The focus of the mission of the laity, according to the Instruction, should be the consecration of the world, as opposed to intra-ecclesial ministry, which is the responsibility and mission of the clergy. "The laity, by virtue of the holiness of their baptism, have an urgent duty toward the material and spiritual world, but what is purely lay—that is, the consecration of the world—is different from what is concerned by ministeriality." ("The Instruction: An Explanatory Note," *Origins* 27 (1997), p. 409.)

In fact, the "two realm" approach was criticized by theologians before and after the Council. The 1997 Vatican Instruction was written precisely to draw the line between the laity and the clergy more clearly, and therefore it adopted this "two realm" approach to ministry. In response to what the Instruction describes as a misunderstanding of true ecclesial communion, the secular character of the laity is hardened into a normative definition whereby the Church becomes the realm of the ordained and the world the realm of the laity even though Vatican II makes no such hard and fast distinction. The Instruction makes a dichotomy between the spiritual order of the Church's mission, which is to be typically restricted to the clergy, and the temporal realm of the Church's mission, which is to be the responsibility of the laity.

This two realm approach is based on a two-tiered doctrine of nature and grace which effects that laity and clergy distinction. It also divides the social and evangelical missions of the Church. Sadly, it gives the impression that the differentiation between the laity and the clergy is not a matter of different and complimentary kinds of vocations, but rather a distinction in terms of a superior or inferior rank.

CLERGY SEXUAL ABUSE CRISIS

The two realm approach to the laity, emphasizing their secular role, is also operative in the Canon Law of the Church in the area of governance and jurisdiction, as seen in the recent clergy sexual abuse crisis. It has been said that the crisis in the Church today is not a crisis of faith, but rather a crisis of governance. The question can be raised as to whether or not this crisis would have happened if lay people were part of personnel board decisions of a diocese or even privy to the past records of the priests assigned to their parishes. If laity had both a voice and a vote in the governance of the Church, rather than simply a consultative role, would the crisis have happened?

This issue of the laity's share in the power of governance in the Church is a matter of both theology and canon law. During the revisions of the Code of Canon Law after the Council, this question of the decision-making power of the laity became a matter of debate. Basically the theological question is whether or not the power to rule the Church flows from the sacramental identity of Baptism or of Holy Orders. Traditionally, governance has been linked to the character of the priesthood. However, there is a wide body of informed theological and canonical opinion that insists that it should be based instead on Baptismal character, thereby assuring that all the faithful share in the governance of the Church. Practically speaking, the point of debate today is whether the laity, by their sacramental identity, can have only a consultative vote in Church matters (e.g., parish councils, financial matters, personnel decisions or policies) or whether they can have a deliberative vote in such cases. Are the laity restricted to simply being "consultants" to the clergy in the governance of the Church, or can they exercise real decision-making power?

This issue of the governance of the laity is further complicated by the traditional description of the vocation of the laity in magisterial documents, mentioned above, which highlights the *secular character* of their Baptismal calling. As seen, the laity are typically defined as having the responsibility of a secular mission to the world, seeking to transform the temporal order with the values of the Gospel. The biblical language of the laity being witnesses to Christ as light, salt, and leaven, for the world is no doubt inspiring, challenging and energizing. However, it restricts the lay mission to the world and the mission of the clergy to the inner workings of the Church. Thus a "two realm" approach to the mission of the Church, wherein the affairs of the Church itself, including all governance issues, are left to the clergy, and the secular affairs of the world are left to the domain of the laity, has had disastrous consequences in the recent clergy sexual abuse crisis. The need for the laity to have a voice and a vote in these governance issues has been made painfully clear.

CONCLUDING SUGGESTIONS

Finally, I would like to make three suggestions for the continuing development of a theology of the laity. First, the laity should not be defined ontologically by their secular character. The whole Church has a secular mission to transform the world for the sake of the Gospel. Within this overall mission, the laity do have a unique role to play. But it is not only the laity who are called to consecrate the world to God; it is also the responsibility of clergy and religious.

Second, I would advocate for re-opening the canonical debate on lay participation in the governance of the Church. This would mean claiming the centrality of Baptism as the sacramental configuration, which enables one to exercise governance and jurisdiction in the Church. Meanwhile, the laity ought to be exercising roles of governance that the present Code of Canon Law allows, such as judge, promoter of justice, notary, and advocate in diocesan tribunals. (Interestingly, according to Pope John Paul II, in a 2001 apostolic letter, these roles are not allowed to be filled by lay people in trials of clergy accused of the sexual abuse of minors—under pain of nullity!)

Thirdly, I would suggest that there a few areas of Church governance in dire need of change. These areas are: transparency in financial matters, accountability for personnel policies and decisions, and lay participation in the selection of bishops. Basically, the laity need to move from the old "pay, pray, and obey" model of Church participation. Instead, the hierarchy should be prepared to welcome the laity as full partners in important positions of authority and in key policy and decision-making bodies. In this way, clerical culture that was to blame for the scandal could be transformed. And, in terms of the hierarchy, the authority wielded from the top that was at the root of the sexual abuse scandal could be reformed into a more collegial pastoral model.

These three suggestions, I think, would bear fruit for the Church and its mission in terms of credibility and effectiveness. As Jesus says in *Revelation*, let those who have ears listen to what the Spirit is saying to the churches!

BIBLIOGRAPHY

Beal, John, "The Exercise of Power and Governance by Lay People: State of the Question," *Jurist* 55, no.1, (1995), pp.1-92.

Congar, Yves, *Lay People in the Church*. London: Geoffrey Chapman, 1957.

_____, "My Path-findings in the Theology of Laity and Ministries," *Jurist* 2, (1972), pp.169-188

_____ "The Role of the Church in the Modern World," *Commentary on the Documents of Vatican II*, Herbert Vorgrimler, ed., Vol. 5. New York: Herder & Herder, 1969, pp. 202-223.

Gibson, David, *The Coming Catholic Church: How the Faithful are Shaping a New American Catholicism*. San Francisco: Harper Collins, 2003.

Gaillardetz, Richard, "Shifting Meanings in the Lay-Clergy Distinction," *Irish Theological Quarterly* 64, (1999), pp.115-139.

Hagstrom, Aurelie, "Can the Laity Govern the Church?" *America*, February 17, 1996.

_____, *The Concepts of the Vocation and Mission of the Laity*. San Francisco: Catholic Scholars Press, 1994.

_____,"Laity, Theology of," in the *New Catholic Encyclopedia*, Revised Edition, Volume 8, pp. 290-293, Berard Marthaler, editor. Washington, D.C.: Catholic University of America Press, 2002.

_____, "The Secular Character of the Vocation and Mission of the Laity: Towards A Theology of Ecclesial Lay Ministry," in *Ordering the Baptismal Priesthood: Theologies of Lay and Ordained Ministry*, Susan Wood, SCL, ed. Collegeville: Liturgical Press, 2003.

Herranz, Julian, "The Juridical Status of the Laity: The Contribution of the Conciliar Documents and the 1983 Code of Canon Law," *Communicationes* 17 (1985), pp. 287-315.

Huels, John, and Richard Gaillardetz, "The Selection of Bishops: Recovering the Traditions," *Jurist* 59 (1999), pp. 348-376.

Kilmartin, Edward, "Lay Participation in the Apostolate of the Hierarchy," *Jurist* 41, no.2 (1981), pp. 352-360.

Komonchak, Joseph, "Clergy, Laity, and the Church's Mission to the World," *Jurist* 42, no.2 (1981), pp. 424-431.

Lakeland, Paul, *The Liberation of the Laity: In Search of an Accountable Church.* New York: Continuum, 2003.

Oakley, Francis, Bruce Russert, eds., *Governance, Accountability, and the Future of the Catholic Church.* New York: Continuum, 2004.

Pope, Stephen, ed., Common Calling: *The Laity and Governance of the Catholic Church.* Washington, D.C.: Georgetown University Press, 2004.

Rahner, Karl, "Notes on the Lay Apostolate," *Theological Investigations*, Vol. 2. London: Darton, Longmann, & Todd, 1963.

Schillebeeckx, Edward, *The Layman in the Church and Other Essays.* New York: Alba House, 1963.

_____, *The Mission of the Church.* New York: Seabury Press, 1973.

Walsh, Kathleen, "The Apostolate of the Laity," *Modern Catholicism*, Adrian Hastings, ed. Oxford: Oxford Press, 1991.

About the Contributors

CONTRIBUTORS

WILLIAM C. GRAHAM, a priest of the diocese of Duluth in Minnesota, is Professor of Theology and Religious Studies at the College of St. Scholastica, where he is also Director of the Braegelman Program in Catholic Studies. Previously, he chaired the Theology Department at Lewis University in suburban Chicago, and founded the Master of Arts program in pastoral ministry at Caldwell College in New Jersey. His most recent book, *Clothed in Christ: Toward a Spirituality for Lay Ministers*, was published by Twenty-Third Publications in 2007. The second edition of his *Sacred Adventure: Beginning Theological Study* was released in 2006 by the University Press of America. His *Half Finished Heaven: The Social Gospel in American Literature* was published by University Press of America in 1995. He holds the Ph.D. in historical theology from Fordham, the Jesuit University of New York City.

ANTHONY BARRETT is Professor of Economics at the College of St. Scholastica where he has taught for twenty-five years and recently served as athletic director. He has a Ph.D. in economics from George Washington University where his dissertation was on international debt rescheduling. He has several publications in the field of economics but this is the first one in Catholic Studies.

DIANNE BERGANT, C.S.A., is Professor of Old Testament Studies at Catholic Theological Union in Chicago. She is concerned with how critical tools of modern scholarship can serve a theological goal. Her research interests include biblical theology and interpretation, the integrity of creation, feminism and liberationist perspectives, and world mission. She holds the Ph.D. from St. Louis University and is author of *People of the Covenant and Preaching the New Lectionary: Cycles A, B, & C*.

ELIZABETH MICHAEL BOYLE, O.P., Professor of English at Caldwell College in New Jersey, earned her M.A. at the Catholic University of America, Washington, D.C., and her Ph.D. at Drew University, Madison, New Jersey. She is a member of the Academy of American Poets and is on the Executive Board of the Dominican Institute for the Arts. Her first book, *Preaching the Poetry of the Gospels: A Lyric Companion to the Lectionary*, was honored with a First Place Award by the Catholic Press Association. Her latest work, *Science as Sacred Metaphor: An Evolving Revelation*, combines poetry and prose to reflect on Christian spirituality in the light of contemporary science.

JAMES T. FISHER is Professor of Theology and Co-Director of the Francis and Ann Curran Center for American Catholic Studies at Fordham University. He is the author of *The Catholic Counterculture in America, 1933-1962; Dr. America: The Lives of Thomas A. Dooley, 1927-1961;* and *Communion of Immigrants: A History of Catholics in America.* His most recent book, a study of Jesuit labor priests and the Port of New York and New Jersey, is scheduled to appear soon.

DAVID GENTRY-AKIN is Associate Professor in the Departments of Religious Studies and Graduate Liberal Studies at Saint Mary's College of California. He is a founding member of the Cummins Institute in Catholic Thought, Culture, and Action at Saint Mary's, and coordinator of the annual Cummins Lectures on the Catholic Intellectual Tradition. He is also on the faculty of the School of Applied Theology at the Graduate Theological Union in Berkeley, California, where he teaches courses in Contemporary Theology and Christology. He has given numerous papers at the American Academy of Religion and at the College Theology Society and has published in *Horizons, Louvain Studies, De Bazuin, Creation Spirituality* and elsewhere. He holds the M. Div. from the University of Notre Dame and the S.T.D. and S.T.L. from the Katholieke Universiteit Leuven in Leuven, Belgium.

AURELIE A. HAGSTROM is Associate Professor of Theology at Providence College in Providence, Rhode Island. Her S.T.D. in dogmatic theology is from the Pontifical University of St. Thomas Aquinas (Angelicum) in Rome, Italy. She taught theology for eleven years at the University of St. Francis in Joliet, Illinois, where she served as chair of the Theology Department. Her publications include *The Vocation and Mission of the Laity* (1994) and the article on the "theology of the laity" in the *New Catholic Encyclopedia.* Dr. Hagstrom serves as a theological consultant for the United States Catholic Bishops' Committee on the Laity and has lectured in the U.S. and Europe on the theology of the laity. Currently her work is focused on the reality of ecclesial lay ministry in the Church.

Anne-Marie Kirmse, O.P., a member of the Sisters of Saint Dominic of Amityville, New York, holds the Ph.D. from Fordham University. She has been the Executive Assistant to Avery Cardinal Dulles, S.J., at Fordham for twenty years, where she is also Adjunct Associate Professor of Theology. During her long career in education, Sister Anne-Marie has taught in elementary schools, college, and graduate programs, and has been active in teacher training and innovative educational programs. She also serves the Dioceses of Brooklyn and Rockville Centre in adult religious education programs. She was appointed to the Pastoral Institute Advisory Committee of the Diocese of Brooklyn by Bishop Nicholas DiMarzio, and was awarded the Kerygma Medal by the late Bishop John R. McGann of Rockville Centre for her work in religious education on Long Island. Her areas of interest are ecclesiology and social justice issues.

Matthew Lickona is a staff writer for the *San Diego Reader*, a weekly newspaper, where he writes on wine, religious worship, and various other topics. He is a graduate of Thomas Aquinas College in California, and is the author of the award-winning memoir *Swimming with Scapulars: True Confessions of a Young Catholic*.

Richard M. Liddy is the University Professor of Catholic Thought and Culture, Director of the Center for Catholic Studies, and a faculty member of the Religious Studies Department at Seton Hall University. Previously he was rector of Immaculate Conception Seminary/School of Theology and spiritual director of the North American College in Rome. His doctoral dissertation was on the work of the American philosopher of art Susanne K. Langer. In 1978 he published a book of poetry entitled *In God's Gentle Arms*. In 1993 he published a work on the Jesuit philosopher-theologian, Bernard Lonergan, *Transforming Light: Intellectual Conversion in the Early Lonergan*. His book, *Startling Strangeness: Reading Lonergan's Insight,* has just been published. It deals with his own encounter with Lonergan as his student in Rome in the 1960s. He has also written articles on the thought of Cardinal Newman as well as on art, education, formation and church leadership.

MARK MCVANN, F.S.C., is Professor of Religious Studies at Saint Mary's College of California in suburban San Francisco. He earned the Ph.D. at Emory University where he wrote his dissertation on the Gospel of Mark. Editor of *Listening: Journal of Religion and Culture*, he has also authored more than eighty book chapters, journal articles, critical essays, and reviews. Br. Mark has presented research at learned societies both in the U.S. and abroad, and has lectured on biblical and religious topics to academic and church audiences in Europe and Asia. He lectures annually on biblical criticism at universities in Lima, Peru and in Rio de Janeiro, Brazil.

JAMES L. OBERSTAR began representing Minnesota's Eighth Congressional District in Congress in 1975. In his 17th term, he is the longest-serving member of the U.S. House of Representatives from the state of Minnesota. He is Chairman of the Committee on Transportation and Infrastructure.

RANDALL A. POOLE (Ph.D., University of Notre Dame) is Associate Professor of History and Chair of the Department of History, Politics and Culture at the College of St. Scholastica. He has held research fellowships at the Institute for Advanced Study in Princeton, New York University, Stanford University, Columbia University, and elsewhere. He has translated and edited *Problems of Idealism: Essays in Russian Social Philosophy* (Yale University Press, 2003), written numerous articles and book chapters in Russian intellectual history and philosophy, and is currently co-editing *A History of Russian Philosophy, 1830-1930* (under contract at Cambridge University Press).

LEE STUART holds the Ph.D. in ecology from the University of California at Davis and San Diego State University. She helped develop the SHARE food program in the South Bronx to provide low cost, high quality food to about 10,000 families a month through a network of 250 churches, unions and community organizations. She served as Director of Development for Augustine Fine Arts, was the lead organizer of South Bronx Churches, and was responsible for organizing Nehemiah Homes and the Bronx Leadership Academy High School. Dr. Stuart now works as the Director of Development for The Hunger Project, a global organization committed to the sustainable end of hunger, with programs in Africa, South Asia and Latin America.

PAUL J. WOJDA is Associate Professor of Theology and Director of the M.A. Program in Catholic Studies at the University of St. Thomas. He teaches in the area of Christian morality, with a special interest in bio-medical ethics. He holds a Master's degree (*cum laude*) in religious stud-ies from Yale University Divinity School (1987) and a doctorate in moral theology from the University of Notre Dame (1993). Dr. Wojda has served as Chair of Archbishop Harry Flynn's Biomedical Ethics Commission and is a member of the board of directors of the Institute for Basic and Applied Research in Surgery, a non-profit foundation affiliated with the University of Minnesota Medical School. He has also been an ethics consultant to Catholic Health Initiatives, the country's largest Catholic healthcare provider. His scholarly articles and reviews have appeared in the *Encyclopedia of Catholicism, Pro Ecclesia, Word and World, The Annual for the Society of Christian Ethics, Theology Today, The Thomis*, and elsewhere.